THE EVERYTHING®
PARENT'S GUIDE TO
CHILDREN WITH OCD

Dear Reader,

We assembled in this book everything we thought might help you bring your child through the fight of his life—against a mighty opponent called obsessive-compulsive disorder, OCD.

For Stephen Martin . . . this means my own personal experience as someone who has dealt with OCD all my life. I've also shared what I've learned in my thirty years in private psychotherapy practice, working with parents and children to keep families together through every challenge imaginable. I have no doubt the presence of mental illness in the family is one of the hardest and most heartbreaking crises for parents to face. I hope the tools in this book help you make it through and ultimately thrive in this time of stress.

For Victoria Costello . . . writing this book has been an opportunity to share what I've gained as a science writer and from dealing with mental illness in three generations of my own family. My greatest source of strength through it all has been the support I've felt from other parents who've survived the same ordeal—with grace and love to spare.

We hope that you, too, will find the strength that comes from family and community.

Stephen Martin, M.F.T.
Victoria Costello

D1005315

Welcome to

THE

EVERYTHING®

PARENT'S GUIDES

Everything® Parent's Guides are a part of the bestselling *Everything*® series and cover common parenting issues like childhood illnesses and tantrums, as well as medical conditions like asthma and juvenile diabetes. These family-friendly books are designed to be a one-stop guide for parents. If you want authoritative information on specific topics not fully covered in other books, *Everything*® Parent's Guides are your perfect solution.

 Alerts: Urgent warnings

 Essentials: Quick handy tips

 Facts: Important snippets of information

 Questions: Answers to common questions

PUBLISHER Karen Cooper

DIRECTOR OF ACQUISITIONS AND INNOVATION Paula Munier

MANAGING EDITOR, EVERYTHING SERIES Lisa Laing

COPY CHIEF Casey Ebert

ACQUISITIONS EDITOR Lisa Laing

DEVELOPMENT EDITOR Brett Palana-Shanahan

EDITORIAL ASSISTANT Hillary Thompson

Visit the entire Everything® series at *www.everything.com*

THE

EVERYTHING®

PARENT'S GUIDE TO

CHILDREN WITH OCD

Professional, reassuring advice for
raising a happy, well-adjusted child

Stephen Martin, M.F.T., and Victoria Costello
with Linda L. Simmons, Psy.D.

WITHDRAWN

CONTRA COSTA COUNTY LIBRARY

3 1901 04411 3985

Avon, Massachusetts

The authors dedicate this book to the brave parents who are standing behind their children as they do battle with OCD. As a parent, know that through this experience your child will gain strength of character well beyond her years.

• • •

Copyright © 2008 by F+W Publications, Inc.
All rights reserved. This book, or parts thereof, may not be reproduced in any form without permission from the publisher; exceptions are made for brief excerpts used in published reviews.

An Everything® Series Book.
Everything® and everything.com® are registered trademarks of F+W Publications, Inc.

Published by Adams Media, an F+W Publications Company
57 Littlefield Street, Avon, MA 02322 U.S.A.
www.adamsmedia.com

ISBN 10: 1-59869-685-8
ISBN 13: 978-1-59869-685-1

Printed in Canada.

J I H G F E D C B A

**Library of Congress Cataloging-in-Publication Data
is available from the publisher.**

This publication is designed to provide accurate and authoritative information with regard to the subject matter covered. It is sold with the understanding that the publisher is not engaged in rendering legal, accounting, or other professional advice. If legal advice or other expert assistance is required, the services of a competent professional person should be sought.

—From a *Declaration of Principles* jointly adopted by a Committee of the American Bar Association and a Committee of Publishers and Associations

Many of the designations used by manufacturers and sellers to distinguish their products are claimed as trademarks. Where those designations appear in this book and Adams Media was aware of a trademark claim, the designations have been printed with initial capital letters.

The Everything® Parent's Guide to Children with OCD is intended as a reference volume only, not as a medical manual. In light of the complex, individual, and specific nature of health problems, this book is not intended to replace professional medical advice. The ideas, procedures, and suggestions in this book are intended to supplement, not replace, the advice of a trained medical professional. Consult your physician before adopting the suggestions in this book, as well as about any condition that may require diagnosis or medical attention. The author and publisher disclaim any liability arising directly or indirectly from the use of this book.

This book is available at quantity discounts for bulk purchases. For information, please call 1-800-289-0963.

All the examples and dialogues used in this book are fictional, and have been created by the author to illustrate disciplinary situations.

▶ Obsessive-Compulsive Disorder

(ob-sĕś-ĭv kem-pŭĺsĭv dĭs-ôŕ-der) n. Anxiety disorder characterized by obsessive, distressing, intrusive thoughts and related compulsions that attempt (unsuccessfully) to neutralize the obsessions. OCD is a neurobiological disorder affecting children and adults, which can be managed using medications and/or psychotherapy.

Acknowledgments

. . .

The authors would like to acknowledge their children. For all the dark nights and the bright mornings that followed, the lessons on how to be a better parent, and those ineffable insights that came later, and always quieter, about how to be a better human being.

Contents

Introduction

The mother of an eight-year-old girl with OCD told the story of her daughter's nightly ritual before she went to bed: The prayers she had to say for everyone she cared about, lest they meet harm before morning. The fears and tears at the thought she'd forgotten someone. The way the curtains on her bedroom window had to meet exactly equal distances from each side of the windowsill. How the bedspread had to lie without a single wrinkle. And then, once she finally got under the covers, the counting to whatever number was her magic number that day.

The girl's mother remembered one especially painful night, when her frustrated and exhausted daughter turned to look at her younger sister sleeping soundly in the bed next to hers, and asked, "Mommy, why can't I be normal?" That was the night this mother realized she had to get help, for her daughter and the entire family.

This book is for mothers and fathers who have faced a bedtime or mealtime or workday morning like this mother did. As you already know all too well, OCD is not just a problem for one child, one preteen, or one adolescent. If OCD is present in your family, you are all suffering. The good news is that treatment for OCD is possible, and a normal life is within your reach. This book is a starting place for those of you who are beginning the journey toward recovery from OCD. It's also for the parent who isn't sure whether the symptoms he sees in his child rise to OCD. If that is you, in the first chapters of this book you'll learn about the telltale signs of OCD and how to interpret them.

The authors make no assumptions that readers come to this book with any previous education in psychology, or have knowledge of the neurobiological science behind mental health disorders. OCD is a complex, constantly shape-shifting disorder. At its root is *anxiety*, the feeling of unease or fear that each human being feels when something inside him or in his environment in not right. As long as humans have walked the earth, they've relied on their perception of things being right or not right as a signal for real and present danger. For the child with OCD, these signals have run amuck, causing him to see threats where there are none. In response to these invisible threats, a child responds the only way he can: by experiencing unwanted recurring thoughts, which then prompt him to perform compulsive actions or rituals. One young man described his involuntary compulsions by saying, "Whenever I feel anxious, I wash my hands, just in case."

With treatment, up to 75 percent of children with OCD are substantially in remission by older adolescence. That is what makes early intervention so critically important. With treatment, your child will acquire the skills to do what once seemed impossible, to fight back against the OCD until life—his and yours—is once again manageable.

In the first half of this book, you'll be guided through the process of finding the right mental healthcare provider in order to obtain a definitive diagnosis of OCD and get your child started in treatment. In addition to giving you the information you need to navigate the medical world, you'll also be given the tools you need to support your child's treatment at home and school. If more help is needed to repair the wear and tear OCD has already wrought on your family, a guide to family therapy is also provided. There is also an explanation of how parents manage the financial challenges of raising a child with OCD.

Don't miss the last pages of *The Everything® Parent's Guide to Children with OCD,* where you'll find valuable resources to take you on the next steps of your journey to recovery. Check out and use the contact information for the essential national service organizations, government agencies, and online communities, and learn about more books for your immediate use and lifelong learning.

CHAPTER 1

What Is Childhood Obsessive-Compulsive Disorder?

Obsessive-compulsive disorder (OCD) is an anxiety disorder affecting one in every one hundred young people in the United States. While OCD is less often recognized and diagnosed than other childhood disorders such as attention deficit hyperactivity disorder (ADHD) and autism, that is changing as the medical community and parents learn to recognize its telltale signs. As treatment rates for OCD continue to increase, many more young people are being spared the disorder's debilitating effects, which can rob them of the joys of childhood. If your child has OCD, your involvement as a loving parent and informed advocate is critically important.

Defining OCD

The condition known as obsessive-compulsive disorder is characterized by unwelcome, unstoppable thoughts called obsessions. With these obsessions assaulting his mind, your child feels compelled to perform repetitive or ritualistic actions. The actions he performs may include repetitive washing, counting, or checking, as well as a number of other seemingly illogical, downright strange behaviors. Without treatment, his mind and body are virtually enslaved to these distressing thoughts and actions. The good news is that OCD is highly treatable, especially if detected and addressed in childhood.

Alert!

Most children engage in rituals. One signal that OCD may be behind your child's repetitive behavior is if his rituals bring him little or no relief, and he remains highly anxious after performing them.

OCD is a neurobiological condition. "Neuro" refers to the brain. "Biological," as used here, locates the problem in one or more of the brain's chemical neurotransmitters. These are the proteins whose job it is to carry messages to and from different parts of the brain's network of circuits or neurons. In OCD, the brain circuit charged with filtering information doesn't work properly. The brain is a highly complex, finely calibrated system similar to a computer. The brain of a child with OCD is comparable to a computer in need of a reboot or recalibration in order to function properly. For more on the neurobiology of OCD, see Chapter 3.

A Wide Range of Symptoms

From a behavioral perspective, OCD is an anxiety disorder with a wide range of possible expressions. In terms of severity, the expressions or symptoms of OCD are like points on a compass. This range represents symptom severity, from mild to moderate to severe. At the lowest or mildest point on the OCD range are behaviors that may reflect perfectionism or a tendency to self-doubt or worry, but these traits do not overly interfere with a child's peace of mind or daily routines. These traits are considered below the point that would indicate a need for treatment. This condition is sometimes called "sub-threshold OCD."

For example, your child may have developed a keen sense of order and cleanliness from a very early age. She may have already earned the nickname Little Miss Perfectionist to reflect her fastidious nature and early attention to self-care and housekeeping. This intense need for order or cleanliness, though it may seem odd in a young child, can still be considered within the normal range of childhood behavior.

It is only when and if your child's concerns about order or contamination result in a compulsive behavior such as excessive hand washing, or when her fears about an imagined or irrational threat cause her to perform prayers or rituals in order to stave off dire consequences (real only in her mind)—only then would she be viewed as having a mild or moderate form of the neurobiological problem known as obsessive-compulsive disorder. When a child first exhibits these behaviors, the correct parental response is to monitor her for behavioral changes, especially any additional expressions of the disorder.

Here is how Cynthia* described her son Jason's behavior, which worried her enough to ask her pediatrician if Jason might have OCD.

> Jason is three and he's already very picky about everything! When he puts his toys away, he has to do it in a very particular way. Like holding one round toy and one square edged one in each hand, always the same, and it has to be done in a very specific order. If I help him and it's "out of order," he'll throw a tantrum, dump everything out, and start all over again. Another thing he does is ask me the same question all day long. If I don't repeat the "right" answer he'll cry or throw a fit. I don't know if he's got OCD but I'm getting concerned.

*Names and personal details of this and other parent accounts have been changed for privacy and patient confidentiality.

A Basic OCD Self-Test

To help you begin the process of determining whether your child may be displaying symptoms of OCD, here are some questions used in a self-test for the disorder. With younger children, parents can ask the questions aloud and record the child's answers.

- Do unwanted, silly, or nasty ideas or images come into your mind often? (Do they stay when you want them to go away?)
- Are you washing your hands more than once after using the toilet or before a meal? (How often? Can you stop?)
- Do you keep many useless things because you feel you can't throw them away?
- Do you feel you have to check things over and over because you worry you've not done something?
- Are you frequently worried you will lose something?
- Are you often afraid of coming into contact with dirt or germs on other people or things?
- Do you worry that your thoughts about someone might cause harm to him?
- Do you have an intense need for things to be lined up a certain way?
- Do you feel the need to count things often? (Cracks on the sidewalk, tiles on the floor, for example)

Asking questions such as these aloud of your child may or may not be appropriate at this time. If, for example, doing so causes your child to become defensive, then an alternate approach would be to use the questions as a basic set of guidelines for the purpose of monitoring his behavior. The important thing is to become aware of the symptoms associated with OCD (covered in depth in Chapter 2), and then be ready to take the necessary steps if you believe your child's behavior has crossed the line from normal to abnormal.

Essential

> You must remember that this disorder is something that is happening to your child. *Your child has not become the OCD.* With your help, he can manage his condition so that both of you, and the entire family, can live a normal, productive life.

As you begin this dialogue with your child, and with mental health professionals about your concerns, know that you are at the beginning of a long journey. More than getting the right answers, it is far more important to establish relationships of trust so that you are well equipped to weather the storms to come.

OCD in Children: Three Mini-Portraits

Each of the following children demonstrates symptoms of OCD. Notice how the same obsessions, for example, a contamination fear or extreme worry about harm coming to a loved one, are expressed differently at each developmental stage.

- Josh, age six, performs an elaborate ritual every night, saying the words "Mommy, one, two, three, four, five" as he touches each truck, game, and stuffed animal lined up on his toy shelves. By taking these steps, Josh believes he can prevent his mother's death while he sleeps. If for any reason he forgets or is prevented from carrying out this nightly ritual, his anxiety will spike along with his overall distress, and bedtime becomes a disaster for all.
- Stacy, at ten, counts every word on each page as she reads her book. This elaborate process makes her reading assignments take two or three times longer, preventing her from

finishing homework on time. Still, she feels she must count, or something far worse will happen to her.

- Sixteen-year-old Sandra has developed a fear that germs in public restrooms, including the girls' bathroom in her high school, will give her AIDS. Because she can't leave the school building to go home midday, she washes up so often and harshly in the morning and afternoon that her hands and arms routinely are red and chafed.

Not all children have contamination fears. Some children limit their obsessions to a need for order. Others get bogged down in a need for certainty where there can be none. Children with OCD often change symptoms over time, or substitute one compulsive ritual for another. Another aspect of OCD is that it comes and goes, often for long periods at a time.

When Should Parents Be Concerned?

The parents of Josh, Stacy, and Sandra, whose stories are excerpted above, have cause for concern. Not only because of the specific behaviors performed (the content), but also because of their negative impact on the child's ability to cope with daily routines (the process).

There are three telltale signs of OCD in a child:

- High anxiety level surrounding child's repetitive behaviors
- Child's behaviors consume more than an hour per day
- High degree of disruption caused in child's life

If you've seen behaviors similar to these, and if your child's behaviors are accompanied by high levels of anxiety, continue to monitor your child closely, taking particular note of how often and for how long the behaviors and moods occur.

Essential

As soon as you begin to see a pattern of OCD behaviors in your child, begin a *symptom log*, noting behaviors, with days and times, and situations, these are also called *triggers*, that set them off. Include length of event, and your child's anxiety or fear level, also called a *fear thermometer*, at the time of her symptoms. A symptom log will help you and your mental healthcare provider better evaluate whether your child has OCD and the degree of its severity.

Subsequent chapters of this book will spell out in more detail what to look for, the steps to take before visiting a doctor or therapist, and some coping strategies while you come to terms with having OCD in the family.

How Common Is Early-Onset OCD?

In a recent survey of some of the five to six million U.S. adults living with OCD, 50 percent said their symptoms began in childhood. The average length of time between the onset of the illness and getting treatment for these adults was seventeen years. Many of those surveyed admitted to hiding their symptoms while they were children out of shame or embarrassment.

This type of data supports the now generally accepted view in the medical profession that the higher number of OCD cases being reported today (as compared to decades past) reflects a greater recognition and diagnosis of the disorder, and not an increased prevalence of OCD in the general population.

 **Fact**

OCD in children is not rare, just rarely diagnosed. Experts say 1 to 1.9 million young people will develop the disorder, with a typical age of onset of OCD of 10.2 years. Many mental healthcare providers also say OCD remains an underdiagnosed and under-treated chronic disorder in the United States today.

Age of Onset and Gender

OCD symptoms typically develop at two different developmental stages in young people, with onset often, but not always, linked to gender. For early school age children, OCD arrives most commonly around seven years of age, and most often in boys. The second common age for OCD to develop is adolescence, when girls are more likely to develop symptoms. Parents should be aware that some girls will develop the disorder at the younger age of onset, and some boys will not develop OCD until adolescence. There are also children of both genders who show OCD symptoms as young as three or four years of age.

In young children, boys with OCD outnumber girls by 3:2, since girls are more likely to develop the disorder in adolescence. At all ages, boys with OCD typically engage in counting, touching, and sorting compulsions. Girls, who more often get caught up in a fear of contamination, manifest a greater number of compulsive cleaning behaviors.

Rate of Onset

OCD comes on slowly or quickly, or at a rate somewhere in between, meaning the initial symptoms can become apparent in your child over the course of days, weeks, months, or even years. Many times, a parent looking back at her child's infancy and toddler years remembers behaviors that she only later realizes match the symptoms of OCD. Of course, hindsight is always easier!

When OCD Is a Family Affair

Numerous studies have established that OCD runs in families. If any of his first-tier relatives (parents, siblings) have OCD, your child's risk of developing the disorder increases 12 percent, more than four times the risk in the U.S. population as a whole. And there is evidence that this percentage may be even higher.

A 1990 study of relatives of children with OCD by Marge Lenane at the National Institute of Mental Health (NIMH) showed that 17 percent of parents and 5 percent of siblings met diagnostic criteria for the disorder. The authors of this study speculate that by loosening criteria to a wider spectrum of symptom severity, a full 30 percent of the children would have a close family member who also manifests the illness.

Michele, a mother of four, described her day-to-day life in a family where she and three of her children had varying degrees of OCD.

> My kids and I often point out to each other our OCD weirdness; it helps sometimes to make fun of it. With me and my daughter, who's fourteen, it's cleaning and arranging things so they're "just right." That usually means symmetrical or in groups of a certain number. My youngest son freaks out if anyone touches anything of his. He claims he can always tell if someone has touched his things while he was out. We try to support each other, but sometimes it's hard.

In a family in which several members show symptoms of OCD, the disorder often goes unnoticed until the child with the most severe symptoms is diagnosed, shedding light on undiagnosed issues affecting others.

Parent's Age of Onset as a Factor

Studies demonstrate that if a parent developed OCD at a young age, there is a greater likelihood that her OCD-affected child will also develop the disorder in early childhood, whether boy or girl. This, in tandem with other quickly accumulating data, overwhelmingly supports the conclusion that OCD is a highly heritable, genetically based disorder in the same way that a vulnerability to other diseases—for example, certain types of cancers, heart disease, and Alzheimer's disease—is handed down from one generation to the next. It ties a child's vulnerability to OCD to the nature component of the nature-versus-nurture debate on how a disease may be transmitted between a parent and a child.

The fact that OCD is in large part genetically determined means that if you have OCD and your child has developed the disorder you did not "give" it to him by modeling certain types of behavior in your home. Even if scientists cannot yet say with any certainty which genetic mutation "causes" the intergenerational transmission of OCD, after decades of family and twin studies now augmented by genetic research, they can say without question that genes trump environmental influences in the transmission of OCD.

It has also been noted that in cases where both a parent and child have OCD, the expressions or symptoms of the disorder appear to differ widely for each. And so for reasons not understood, it is rare for a parent with OCD to have the same symptoms as her child. For example, a mother with a fear of contamination would be more likely to have a child whose OCD manifests as an ordering compulsion as opposed to a contamination fear.

If You Discover Your Own OCD

Because OCD and other another anxiety disorders (such as panic disorder or social anxiety disorder) run in families, you may find that more than one member of your family has OCD. If OCD is present in a parent or sibling, your child has a 20 percent greater chance of developing the disorder. However, given the fact that diagnosis and treatment were less common before the mid 1990s, a parent or older sibling's OCD may not have been previously recognized.

In this scenario, the first time you see symptoms of OCD in yourself or another family member may be when you recognize its presence in your child. Perhaps you've unknowingly had symptoms since childhood. This increasingly common phenomenon was the subject of a December 2007 story in *Newsweek* titled, "Your Child's Disorder May Be Yours, Too."

It describes a mother in her fifties who identified her own attention deficit disorder after her two sons received treatment for ADHD. After learning about the disorder, she began to think about her own lifelong difficulty focusing on simple tasks such as paying bills on time and remembering appointments. When she got out her old elementary school report cards, she found descriptions of herself as "disorganized" and "has trouble paying attention." She was both relieved and prepared when she then went to her son's psychologist and received a formal diagnosis of her own ADHD. Her subsequent treatment with a stimulant medication and cognitive therapy has helped this mother manage her problem, and in her view, made her a better "coach" in her sons' treatment.

As summed up in the *Newsweek* article: "Children made miserable by a psychiatric or developmental disorder may not always want company, but they often long for evidence that they aren't the only ones putting a burden on the family . . . Having a parent with the same quirks who can talk about it eases the guilt a child may feel. The child has a fellow traveler, and in some cases, maybe more."

If you discover your own OCD at the same time the disorder is diagnosed in your child, you may be uncertain whether to seek a diagnosis or treatment right away. Perhaps you feel the best course of action is to concentrate on your child's problems, while deferring your own. However, as noted above, the opposite may be true. It can be helpful for a child to observe a parent receive a formal diagnosis and treatment at the same time or prior to his own. The parent essentially serves as a model, demonstrating what's to come for the child.

Here's how one mother of a seven-year-old daughter describes the experience.

> Two years ago my daughter began showing signs of OCD, like asking the same questions over and over. She'd ask, "Are you sure?" "Is there going to be a tornado?" "Am I going to throw up?" It's like she gets a thought stuck in her head and she can't get it out. She was so afraid of school she'd cry on the way there every day. When I took her to be diagnosed, the psychiatrist said she had classic symptoms of OCD and also some more generalized anxiety. Her medication is helping. I was first diagnosed in my twenties, after my first pregnancy, although it's milder than my daughter's OCD. I'm glad that I can help her because I think her OCD is more severe than mine. I can't imagine what her teenage years would be like if I wasn't able to get her help early.

This mother is well equipped to help her daughter face the onset of OCD because her own OCD is being treated, and because she accepts OCD as a disorder that runs in her family. If you are a parent with OCD you must dispense as soon as possible with any guilt you may feel about being the "cause" of your child's disorder. All children are the sum of their genetic and environmental inheritances. The prerequisite to healing is self-acceptance. Eventually you may even be able to see a positive side of the OCD and be able to share this perspective with your child.

Common Myths and Misconceptions

American culture is slowly catching up to the truth about OCD. Movie and television depictions of characters returning over and over again to the sink or shower to scrub invisible dirt from their bodies have given OCD its colloquial name, the "hand-washing disease." But, as parents of children with OCD know all too well, the reality of OCD is neither as funny nor as simple as these depictions suggest. The most common misconceptions about OCD and people with OCD include the following:

- They are just eccentric
- They can stop it if they want to
- It's a self-esteem problem
- They just need to relax
- Stress causes OCD
- Childhood trauma causes OCD
- They'll never get better

What most members of the general public don't realize about OCD from watching movies and TV is that real life obsessions and compulsions can be far more complex and insidious than the innocuous behaviors associated with such labels as "fussy" or "neat freak." OCD can be a debilitating disorder, especially for children and adolescents. As more affected adults and teens speak out about their disorder, the old stereotypes of the silly, hopeless hand-washer or the picky but charming perfectionist are being replaced with more accurate imagery and information about how people of all ages are challenged by this disorder.

One of the byproducts of the increase in sharing by real people of personal stories and challenges on TV and the Internet is the new openness in many different media about people living and thriving in spite of their disabilities, including OCD. For example, the Obsessive-Compulsive Foundation's teen program, Organized Chaos, hosts a national media campaign featuring an attractive, vivacious "ordinary" college freshman speaking honestly about her own journey with OCD. Children and teens greatly benefit when positive role models speak openly about their lives with OCD.

 Fact

Among the sites visited by parents and children dealing with OCD are online groups run for and by people facing the same challenges. The Obsessive-Compulsive Foundation (OCF) hosts "Organized Chaos," an OCD support site especially for teens. *MySpace.com* has an OCD public group with 2,474 members. *Yahoo.com* has a private OCD and Parenting Group with 1,554 active members. These sites offer a great way to get support without leaving the house.

Why Your Child Can't "Just Stop It"

As a parent, your first instinct when you see your child in distress is to try and remove the cause of his pain. When his OCD behaviors first appear, it's normal to feel frightened, frustrated, and even angry. You may mistake his inexplicable actions as misbehaviors aimed at getting your attention or defying authority. You may wonder if he's attempting to skip school, chores, or other responsibilities. As a disciplinarian, you're accustomed to setting rules and boundaries, and, in this role, you may try repeatedly to get your child to "just stop it." The problem is that when OCD is present, especially before a child learns strategies to manage his disorder, he really can't "just stop it."

How OCD Feels to a Child

It's important for you to know that your child feels just as much and probably more frustration than you do as a result of her OCD, especially when she can't "just stop it." Maybe, just maybe, she thinks, her rituals or prayers will work this time and she'll chase away her unwelcome thoughts. This is the result she's trying to bring about by performing whatever compulsive behavior she's acting out: counting words on a page, circling a tree, touching her head, or washing her hands—all of it an attempt to gain control over her renegade mind.

Another thing you as a parent may not understand is the degree of your child's self-awareness about her behaviors. Most children with OCD (certainly those over the age of ten and many younger) say they know very well that their obsessive thoughts and compulsive actions are "crazy" or irrational. Still, unable to quell the fear or anxiety behind these thoughts, the child opts to perform a familiar ritual in an attempt to "play it safe."

When Rituals Don't Work

When, for example, the act of counting cracks on the sidewalk doesn't quiet your child's fear about failing an upcoming math test, the child with OCD faces another frustrating choice: She can continue to perform the same ritual, or come up with a new one. If she (temporarily) gives up on these attempts to quell her fear, perhaps to please you, she may become withdrawn and depressed, or conversely filled with rage. The situation can quickly spiral downward, making treatment all the more important as soon as you recognize symptoms of OCD may be present, even if you're not sure.

When Repetitions and Rituals Are Not OCD

As you take in all of this information, it may suddenly seem as though all of your child's fearful behaviors should now be viewed with suspicion. But, this is not the case; the majority of fears and rituals seen in young children are normal and are *not* symptoms of OCD. Normal childhood rituals—for example, saying certain words, prayers, or stories at bedtime—are important; they fulfill a child's need for routine, structure, and winding down, especially at bedtime. A constructive ritual should provide peace and order to daily routines.

There is one basic rule of thumb for telling the difference between normal behavior and a possible sign of OCD. If a child does not have OCD, her rituals or routines can be interrupted, changed, or skipped without causing any undue distress. If you as a parent are concerned there might be something other than normal going on with your child's ritualistic behavior, it can be confusing until you learn how to distinguish the signs of OCD from healthy, appropriate childhood behaviors.

 Essential

Normal routines and rituals should have a calming effect on your child, but for a child with OCD, the result is often the opposite. The performance of OCD-related rituals brings a child with the disorder only fleeting relief, followed by more anxiety and distress. Any changes in this child's rituals are upsetting, causing her more worry, and provoking the need for further ritualizing.

All children experience fears at certain ages, as when a toddler fears separation from his mother or is afraid of the dark. Likewise, when elementary school age children learn about real-life dangers, they can become fearful of strangers or worry about the loss of a parent to death or divorce. As any adult can recall, normal teenagers experience phases of self-consciousness and fears of social rejection. The key to differentiating normal fears from OCD is that each of these fearful phases passes as the child matures.

Similarly, many children like to collect and count things as they grow up, often well into adolescence. Whether the objects of their affection are rocks, dolls, baseball cards, or video games, a healthy hobby or interest need not be confused with an OCD obsession. Again, if the hobby doesn't interfere with a child's ability to function, or take up too much time or space, it falls into the category of normal. As you review your child's behaviors, you can use these rules of thumb to distinguish what constitutes an age appropriate and there-fore normal fear, habit, or ritual from a possible symptom of OCD.

Review: What Makes Behavior OCD?

- It takes up more than an hour a day.
- It causes him undue distress.
- It makes him dysfunctional at home or school.

If there is one single criterion to keep in mind for distinguishing your child's normal behaviors from those that may be symptomatic of OCD, it is the degree of anxiety that is present with a particular activity. If the anxiety is chronic and pervasive, you should keep monitoring him for additional signs of OCD.

The OCD Symptom Spectrum: From Mild to Severe

Within the broad spectrum of severity of symptoms associated with obsessive-compulsive disorder, most affected young people fall somewhere in the middle. Five percent have only mild symptoms. If your child falls at the milder end of the OCD spectrum, his disorder may show up in subtle ways. For example, at an early age he may insist on ordering all his clothing by colors. Or he may become agitated if his nightly rituals are disturbed before bedtime. These lower threshold symptoms of OCD may or may not progress to moderate or severe as the child matures.

If your child has only mild symptoms of OCD, your best strategy is to monitor his behavior while you continue educating yourself about OCD. If his symptoms continue or become chronic or severe, it would be prudent to check with his teacher(s) to see if there are any similar problems showing up at school, and then raise your concerns with your family doctor either in advance of or during your child's next checkup.

At the other end of the scale, it's estimated that 15 percent of children suffering from OCD will progress to more severe and debilitating symptoms. If your child develops an intense fear of contamination or "germs," perhaps triggered by normal household objects such as doorknobs, remote controls, or even pets, this is a sign of moderate or severe OCD, and it requires immediate assessment by a mental health professional.

Symptoms Change as a Child Grows

Because OCD is an illness that changes as your child matures, you are likely to see a number of different obsessions and compulsions come and go over time. Reasons for these changes may include new stages of emotional or physical growth, a change of school or other routine, or a loss in the child's life, such as the death of a grandparent, divorce, or the loss of a beloved pet. Some changes in OCD symptoms occur for reasons completely unknown to you or your child.

 *Question?*

What happens if OCD is left untreated?
Studies show that if they receive no treatment, up to one-third or one-half of young people with symptoms of OCD will still have the disorder when they reach adulthood, and their symptoms will worsen over time. A full 75 to 80 percent of children with OCD who receive treatment will improve considerably.

What Makes a Behavior an Obsession?
There are four specific criteria that define a clinical obsession. Those criteria include:

- Recurrent and persistent thoughts, impulses, or images that are recognized as inappropriate and intrusive
- The thoughts, impulses, or images are not just concerns related to problems in life
- There are attempts to ignore or minimize the thoughts, impulses, or images
- The thoughts, impulses, or images are recognized as coming from within the person's own mind

Sometimes an obsession will seem to disappear because your child has learned to hide a particular obsessive behavior. Or, she's developed one ritual to replace another. Careful monitoring of such behavior, including keeping a log, is a good first step toward determining whether your child may have OCD.

Here is another way to think about the most common OCD symptoms, relating obsessions to compulsions.

- Fear of contamination: Washing and cleaning
- Fear of harm or danger: Checking
- Fear of loss: Hoarding
- Fear of being sinful or bad: Praying
- Body fixations: Grooming
- Need for symmetry: Arranging in order, lining up
- Need for perfection: Seeking reassurance

In most cases, a compulsive behavior is linked, either consciously or unconsciously, to an obsessive thought. That doesn't mean the child with OCD can immediately make the connection between the two. As he becomes more self-aware, connecting his obsessions and compulsions becomes easier. A parent can also help this process by learning about OCD and monitoring the child's behaviors.

Question?

> **Is there one national organization for OCD families?**
> Yes. The Obsessive-Compulsive Foundation (OCF), based in Boston, MA, is that organization. Many parents of OCD children and teens and adults with OCD join OCF for support, education, and to help advocate for greater research on the disorder. Find them online at *www.ocf.org*.

Although there are many frightening aspects of OCD for a concerned parent to take in, there is also a vibrant community of parents, therapists, researchers, educators, and doctors who have created a welcoming place for new parents to learn and support each other. This community exists both online and in cities and counties across the country, wherever parents come together to help their children cope with this formidable adversary.

CHAPTER 2

How to Recognize Childhood OCD

Recognizing that your child has OCD is a difficult and important step for any concerned parent. In order to understand how this disorder affects your child's life, you'll need to reframe your thinking so you can see her behaviors for what they really are: Attempts to cope with her own internal anxiety. Two diagnostic terms help organize this process of recognition. When a child with OCD tries to resolve anxiety through recurring thoughts, her faulty thinking is called an *obsession*. If she attempts to manage her internal emotional discomfort through repetitive actions, her behavior is a *compulsion*.

Understanding Obsessive Thoughts

Worries. Doubts. Fears. Most people have them every day, including young children, preteens, and adolescents. But when worries, doubts, and fears take over his mind and body, these thoughts are defined as obsessions.

The most likely underlying cause of your child's OCD is a chemical imbalance in his brain. Although no cure is yet known for OCD, medical knowledge and treatment of the disorder have taken great strides in the last decade. In order to help your child manage his illness, it's important to differentiate between cause and triggers, so that you can help him manage the latter.

Question?

What is the difference between an obsession and a compulsion?

An obsession is an irrational, intrusive, and involuntary thought or image that your child is unable to make "go away." A compulsion is the repetitive or ritualistic behavior that results from that thought or image. A child performs a compulsive behavior in an (always) unsuccessful attempt to vanquish his obsessive thought.

The OCD Challenge

When a child has OCD, unwelcome, intrusive thoughts do not stop despite his earnest desire to quiet or change them. This is at the heart of what makes the disorder so challenging for both children and parents. Even if his thoughts are irrational and lead to self-defeating behaviors, knowing better doesn't help him stop thinking this way. Imagine how powerless he feels!

Even people who don't have OCD can be plagued by obsessive thoughts and bouts of anxiety. Anxiety is a part of the human experience. However, the obsessions and compulsions of an adult or child with OCD are more frequent and severe than for those who don't suffer from this disorder. Their underlying anxiety is more pervasive and more easily triggered.

Picture having just finished the dinner dishes. The kitchen sink is spotless and dry. But then your husband fills a glass of water and leaves droplets of water on the stainless steel sink basin. You cannot imagine going to bed without drying it again. But it remains a constant concern for you. Even after you've dried it again, you can't sleep because the thought keeps returning, urging you to check it again and again.

Fact

Although the underlying cause for OCD is a most likely a combination of genetics and brain chemistry, a trigger is something in your child's immediate environment that provokes his compulsive reaction. It can be real or imagined; as small as a person glancing in his direction, or, simply, a belief he's being watched.

Just as logic doesn't quell the anxiety felt by an adult with OCD who worries excessively about an undone chore or an oven that may or may not be left on after she's left the house, your well-meaning efforts as a parent to point out that your child's obsessive thoughts are "silly" or "not real" are also likely to be futile. They can even be harmful; such remarks often create more frustration and tension for both of you.

Essential

As a parent, you must never lose sight of the fact that the driver behind your child's obsessions is the uncontrollable internal anxiety he feels. His OCD does not result from anything you've done or not done as a parent. It has nothing to do with a difficult toilet training or any other early childhood upsets. It is a neurobiological condition very likely with a genetic cause.

Remember, it's your child's anxiety creating his obsessive thoughts, and these thoughts are involuntary on his part. It isn't rebelliousness, or a desire for attention, even if the same behavior in another child might easily be classified as an act of defiance or a ploy for attention.

The Desire for Order

In addition to a wish for an unobtainable degree of cleanliness, an OCD obsession can also take the form of an extreme need for order in the face of perceived chaos. At an early age, your child may create rituals based on superstitions designed to protect loved ones from imagined threats. No matter what his age, his obsessive thoughts can also involve aggressions. Each of these categories of obsession requires closer examination.

Contamination Fears

One way a child attempts to manage the relentless anxiety she feels as a result of this disorder is by trying to control what is closest to her: her own body. Or, her attention can fasten on her immediate physical environment, beginning with her bedroom, the family home, and anywhere she may go outside the home. This obsessive need to be clean or make her environment cleaner comes in response to an out-of-control fear of dirt or germs, which she believes could infect and kill her. Often, no amount of cleaning or cover is adequate to ward off her fears of filth and contagion.

Margaret, mom to eight-year-old son Timmy, described how his contamination fears showed up at home.

> Timmy showers four times a day. He insists that I wash his clothes separately from his brother and sister's. When I wouldn't wash his sheets separately, too, he insisted on sleeping in his clothes.

Don't Look for Logic

The fact that perfect hygiene and a germ-free environment are impossible goals doesn't stop your young child or teenager from desiring these things or from thinking about them constantly. Once again, it's important to remember why she's driven to this extreme. She's trying to quell her own internal anxiety by putting a shield of protection around her body and everything she touches.

Alert!

Triggers for a contamination obsession can be something as simple as someone reaching out to shake your child's hand. Or her fear can be triggered by bumping into a wall or the ringing of the lunch bell at school. A contamination obsession can cause your child considerable stress and paralysis in the most basic areas of her life: bathing, dressing, eating, playing, learning, and sleeping.

At school, a fear of contamination can cause many lost learning and socializing opportunities. Among friends and on the playground, it can reap the worst social costs, including isolation, teasing, and bullying.

Question?

What's the best way to react to school teasing?
As a parent, it's painful to watch your child experience the social difficulties that result from her obsessions and yet feel powerless to help her. Remember this: Help is possible, but careful listening comes first. If she tells you about an incident of teasing, try not to overreact. Make it clear that you understand how she feels without showing strong emotions, such as anger or your own distress. It will make her feel safer the next time she wants to share hers.

Your Child's Private Fears

A child dealing with negative reactions to her OCD symptoms from peers at school can develop a great deal of self-consciousness and embarrassment. These self-doubts can result in hours spent in front of a mirror combing her hair, or "rehearsing" her expressions. It can also manifest as an avoidance of mirrors.

Be cognizant of how your child attempts to hide or disguise her obsessions and compulsions from you and others. Too much disclosure is not necessarily a good thing, but neither is an extreme avoidance of disclosure. Finding the balance takes practice and that's where group psychotherapy offers the most assistance to the child or teen with OCD.

The Need for Order

When you as an adult worry about something—perhaps a teenage son is out past curfew, or you're awaiting results on a medical test—you may choose to occupy your mind with a so-called "mindless activity," an action that in its simplicity or repetition serves to calm you. Perhaps you rearrange the spices in your kitchen cabinet or stack papers on your desk at work, anything to ease your worry about when your son will get home or what your lab results might be.

These efforts to deflect anxiety about specific issues in your life are considered healthy coping strategies. Typically, your anxious state ends when the cause of worry is gone. At that point the tasks of arranging spices or desk papers return to their previous status as occasional chores.

When Ordering Becomes Obsessive

Like you, a child with OCD attempts to gain control over his anxiety by ordering his environment. His strategy, like yours, includes arranging or rearranging objects to create order. But that is where the similarity between your strategy and his ends. That's because the anxiety he experiences is not tied to any specific, identifiable cause.

For him, the compulsion called ordering takes the form of a need to exert control over his environment to an extreme degree and on a nearly constant basis.

The Need for Certainty

The need for certainty, also called a *need to know* obsession, takes the form of a desire to erase all doubt or uncertainty from life. For a child with OCD, persistent, disproportionate self-doubt can manifest in his need to check and recheck all kinds of things in his environment. Has he locked the door (to ward off intruders)? Did he remember to line up his stuffed animals in the correct order (to prevent an accident befalling a family member)? If the answer to any of these questions is "no," his anxiety level can become unbearable.

Daniel, age eight, explained how he turned his need for certainty into a morning ritual. After he'd lined up and arranged his things just so, he would open his bedroom door, turn back around to face his furniture and belongings, and speak out loud the words, "Now everything is exactly as I want it." Only then could Daniel go to school.

Endless Questions

In another manifestation of this obsessive need for certainty, your child may ask a litany of questions that seem out of proportion to a situation or topic. His questions can be about something as straightforward as the weather forecast or the correct definition of a word. Another common behavior is a constant need to apologize, often, for things he (incorrectly) believes he's done. Did he say a swear word? Did he forget to say thank you to Aunt Mary?

This OCD behavior can be a real problem at school. Twelve-year-old Nancy's need to know caused her to constantly interrupt her seventh grade teacher during class, sometimes asking the same question over and over again. Her awareness that she asks too many questions didn't even help Nancy. It led her to frequently apologize, again interrupting class to express her relentless need for certainty.

Aggressive Thoughts

An aggression obsession in a youngster with OCD is typically a fear of acting out a violent thought. It is almost never the commission of an aggressive act. Sixteen-year-old Jason experiences a repeating image of himself pushing his younger brother into the path of a coming subway. Jason is so bothered by this obsession that he won't stand anywhere near his brother when they enter a subway station. He becomes agitated and begins perspiring and shaking in response to the violent imagery he sees over and over again in his mind. On some level he knows he would never commit this violent act, but "just to be sure," he avoids the situation. This self-knowledge, although it doesn't spare him the burden of his recurring violent thoughts, does set Jason apart from someone with a psychotic illness (such as schizophrenia or bipolar disorder) who sometimes can't tell the difference between what's real and what he sees and hears in his mind.

Still, an OCD-related aggressive thought obsession can be individually disabling and socially isolating for a young boy or girl. At its basis this fear is about a young person losing control over his impulses and injuring others. Again, a parent can recognize the youngster's wish to control what feels out of control: his own anxiety. This obsession can result in a terrified avoidance of sharp objects. It can also manifest as a more generalized fear of his own imagined tendency to create hazards for those he loves.

When you avoid the things that trigger obsessions, you make the obsessions more powerful. This basic rule for dealing with OCD is of special relevance to young people with "bad thought" obsessions. A fear of inflicting harm or violence by his thoughts alone can keep a young person stuck in an endless loop of obsession and isolation. Rather than avoid bad thoughts, cognitive behavior therapy (CBT) allows him to safely confront his worst fear—for example, by witnessing an act of violence on TV, or being in the same room with a member of the opposite sex with whom he fears he'll commit a sexual impropriety—until the things or people that trigger his bad thoughts are neutralized, and avoidance is no longer necessary.

Superstitious Thoughts

This category of obsession is often the trickiest for parents to sort out with a child. The younger she is, the more elusive her concept of reality may be. What is childhood, after all, if not magical? The problem arises when your child with OCD not only enjoys stories of superheroes and supernatural forces, but also sees herself as the embodiment of these characters and forces in her daily life.

 Fact

Children with OCD are especially prone to superstitions, defined as any belief that is inconsistent with known facts or rational thought, especially a belief in omens. Many such children believe they have supernatural powers. This is also known as *magical thinking.*

Using magical thinking, your child believes she acquires the power to control reality and, often, the fate of her family and friends. But rather than enjoying the creative fun of age-appropriate pretend games, this type of magical thinking and the catastrophic outcomes she attaches to her beliefs can become a terrible burden for your child.

This is not just an issue associated with the younger child. Here's how Connie, mother of fifteen-year-old Michael, describes her son's superstitious thinking.

> Michael can't go outside on sunny days because he's afraid that if his shadow falls on something or

someone, like a bush or a small child on the playground, the plant or child will die. He can't watch TV because he thinks if he takes his eyes off the picture or stops listening, one of us will die. Then his obsession changed into needing to count how many times the person on TV blinked. I finally took the TV out of the house.

As a child ages, he can bring his superstitions to school and into the world at large, creating another major hurdle for his ability to function normally at school and with friends.

Understanding Compulsive Behaviors

Compulsions are the excessive, repetitive behaviors of children with OCD that often mirror or manifest the obsessive thoughts just discussed: A boy who washes the walls of his bedroom after a window is left open, the girl who spends a full hour removing specks of lint from a coat, making her late for school, or the young child who gives two kisses to each of the twenty-plus stuffed animals in her room before going to bed because she fears Mommy will die before morning if she doesn't perform this nightly ritual.

All of these children are acting out compulsions. Compulsive behaviors are usually but not always linked to some form of obsession. As you read about the compulsive behaviors that follow, think back to the different obsessions at the start of this chapter to better understand how they may relate to the compulsions presented.

Common Compulsions

None of the following actions, in moderation or by themselves, are abnormal or uncommon. It is only when one or more behaviors consume an hour or more of your child's day that they are considered likely symptoms of childhood OCD. Therefore, the word "excessive" should be inserted in your thinking as you consider each of the following compulsive behaviors resulting from obsessive thinking. The most common OCD compulsions are:

- Washing
- Cleaning
- Avoiding
- Doubting and checking
- Counting
- Ordering, lining up
- Hoarding or clearing
- Ritualizing

It is important to remember that compulsive behaviors are almost always associated with a particular obsession. A fear of germs leads to an avoidance of touching doorknobs; an extreme fear of accidental death brings about superstitious rituals; a need for order causes the child to count the words on the page before she can turn to the next page and complete her homework in a reasonable time. At the bottom of all OCD behaviors is extreme anxiety not grounded in a child's reality, but powerful nonetheless.

Cleaning Compulsions

One fifth grader, late for class, waits in the hallway for another student to exit so he can catch the door with his elbow, so he does not have to touch a doorknob in order to enter his classroom. Another teenager wets her pants because she won't use a public toilet in the airport. A ten-year-old boy refuses dinner at a Chinese restaurant when his parents order several dishes family style. Why? Because it "freaks him out" that everyone takes their individual portions from common plates using the same serving utensils. These children are all exhibiting a fear of contamination in the form of a cleaning compulsion.

Samuel, age fourteen, carried his cleaning compulsion to the point where the entire family felt its effect. Before he would touch any food in the refrigerator in his family's kitchen, this young man insisted on washing his hands thoroughly and putting on surgical gloves.

Samuel feared that if he touched the food without gloves, he would transfer germs to the food and get very ill or die when he ate it. But the next problem for Samuel became the resistance of other family members, who would not follow his request that they perform the same ritual. Their refusal to do so, and Samuel's subsequent distress, were what finally brought this family to therapy.

Contamination obsessions in children and teenagers with OCD can manifest in any or all of these cleaning compulsions:

- Repetitive washing, showering of self
- Excessive cleaning of living space, clothing
- Reluctance to touch others or be touched
- Refusal to share food
- Reluctance to touch objects touched by others
- Overzealous need to clear out and throw things away
- Dressing inappropriately for the weather
- Refusal to go outdoors or enter public places

As you both acquire more knowledge about OCD, you and your child will come to recognize the common triggers for any contamination obsessions he may have. This knowledge will help your child manage his compulsive cleaning behaviors, no matter what form they may eventually take.

Ordering Compulsions

The compulsive symptoms of a child with an ordering obsession can include the excessive need to line up, sort, count, hoard, or create symmetry with any number of different objects in the home or at school. From the bottles of soda in your refrigerator to the books and pencils on his desk or the pillows on the living room sofa, your child's need to put things in order or make things symmetrical can apply to virtually anything, anywhere.

Not All Ordering Is OCD

Some ordering behavior is perfectly normal behavior; it may even be a cause for pride for a parent who maintains strict standards of perfectionism in her home. Consider Johnny, who has to line up his pencils in a prearranged order, always largest to smallest, before starting his homework. If Johnny tries to begin an assignment without ordering his pens and pencils in this manner, he becomes anxious and unable to do his work. Johnny has the same "rule" for the books on his shelves. One book can't be taller than another as they move down in size from right to left. This ordering is necessary before Johnny can feel at peace in his own room.

Johnny's ordering behaviors, although they could reflect the lower end of the spectrum of severity of OCD symptoms, should not be a cause of concern for his parents unless they impact negatively on his ability to function.

Order, Numbers, and Symmetry

A common issue for the child with OCD who has an ordering compulsion is a strong preference for even rather than odd numbers (or vice versa). Picture Irene, age seven, whose compulsion for symmetry is triggered when she comes upon an odd number of ceramic dogs arranged asymmetrically on her grandmother's coffee table, three figures instead of two or four, arranged randomly. In math class, Irene faces another ordering-related dilemma when she's called on to come up to the blackboard to write out an answer to the equation (2×4)[3] and the presence of a three on the board makes her unable to leave her seat.

Confronted with either of these triggers, Irene experiences an intense spike in her anxiety level. At her grandmother's house, she feels compelled to remove the "extra" dog on grandma's coffee table. At school, Irene wants to change the number three following the equation on the blackboard to an even number. If she's not permitted to do either of these things, Irene's anxiety grows even more intense.

But even if Irene can make these changes, her relief is likely to be short-lived. That's because the cause of her anxiety goes well beyond a simple math problem or the arrangement of ceramic figures on Grandma's table. Those are her triggers. The underlying problem is anxiety that manifests in the symptoms of OCD.

And the behavior is identical for someone with the opposite, odd-numbered manifestation of this same compulsion for order. Sixteen-year-old Harriet can only deal with odd numbers in her immediate world. She had nine different alarm clocks in her bedroom, each set fifteen minutes apart in the two hours before she had to leave for school. Everything must be divisible by three or she becomes uncomfortable. Three pencils, three of each color of clothing in her drawers, and so on.

Hoarding Compulsions

The compulsion to hoard is one of the more perplexing OCD behaviors. With hoarding, a fear of deprivation, where a child fears she will not have enough of something, is added to the OCD fear of disorder. Hoarding gives the child with OCD a false sense of control over his environment.

Typically this label is associated with an elderly person who might colloquially be called "a pack rat," a person who can't walk through his own living space because he's filled it with so much junk. But the compulsion to hoard can also affect children. The child with a hoarding compulsion is abnormally preoccupied with his possessions, including things such as toys, which are commonly viewed as belonging to him, as well as the more bizarre, for example, his own fingernails or feces. Tawny, mother to thirteen-year-old Steve, says the worst day of the week for her family is trash day.

> It's always a struggle to get him to let go of our trash!
> Last week, I got him to let go of two bags of trash, and
> that was a small victory. This week, though, it was like
> I had to pay a price for it. It's not even just the trash
> from his room; it's the kitchen trash, too. There are
> three bags waiting to go outside, but he can't let them
> go. He can't watch a car go by outside, since then
> he won't be able to keep track of it. He can't watch a
> movie on TV, because he won't be able to remember
> every bit of it and play it back in his mind.

Once again, the primary criterion to use when evaluating any behavior to determine whether it's a manifestation of OCD is its degree of severity. Collecting things is normal childhood behavior; an inability to let go of useless items around the house is not.

Hoarding can manifest as a compulsion to overeat, or, conversely, to collect food and then not eat any of it for fear of running out. It can affect things that are not even in the child's possession to begin with, such as images on a TV screen, or things (vehicles, sounds, or people) in the outside world. Logic is not the point here. In fact, the desire to find logic in these OCD compulsions will make a parent's job even harder. What's important is to be alert to early indications of any of these behaviors. If they are carried to an extreme, the behaviors should be considered as possible indications of the presence of OCD in your child.

Avoidance Compulsions

Avoidance behaviors can be difficult for the child with OCD and his parents to understand and manage. That's because your child's avoidance fears often concern "bad thoughts" about "bad things," which he may think about doing but would likely never do. Here is how Jennifer Traig explained her dilemma as a teenager dogged by "bad thoughts" that caused her avoidance compulsion in her memoir, *Devil in the Details.*

> In real life we are meek and law-abiding, but in our minds we are murderous sex fiends. Most obsessive-compulsives fear they are going to stab a loved one. [As a result] most of us can't stand to be around knives at all.

For a preteen or teenager with OCD, in addition to having fears of violent urges, his maturing body and developing sexuality will often provoke avoidance obsessions regarding inappropriate sex. These images of inappropriate sex may be both heterosexual and homosexual in nature, regardless of the teenager's sexual orientation. This obsessive fear can make him believe he'll be unable to stop himself from touching others inappropriately in public—causing him to avoid leaving his house. In some cases, any inkling of sexual arousal can scare an adolescent with this obsession to the point where he imagines the worst, seeing himself as a potential rapist. In another example of an avoidance compulsion, he may stay away from school dances and gymnasiums "just to be sure" he doesn't act out these "bad thoughts." Parents should realize that this type of OCD behavior is not uncommon.

Here is Deborah's poignant story about the special difficulty she faced when dealing with this OCD symptom in her fourteen-year-old son, Brian.

> Brian says there's a voice in his head telling him to do "bad" things to others. He told me he was trying hard to fight back against it, but that it was hard. When I noticed how anxious he seemed yesterday, I asked how he was doing with it. That's when he admitted he was having "kill" thoughts, and they were about me. I know he doesn't mean it, and he can't help it. He even knows it's not real; it's the OCD talking. But hearing him say it was like my heart was being torn out.

However upsetting and scary it is for you as a parent to hear about such hurtful things, imagine how much more difficult it would be for your child to actually experience such thoughts! The important thing to remember is that the child or teenager having these fears and going to great lengths to avoid any situations that might trigger these thoughts would no sooner commit the deeds than you would yourself. If he shares a violent or sexual fear with you, do your best not to react with alarm. Then you keep the lines of communication open between the two of you and avoid making him feel any more isolated than he already does.

Ritualizing Compulsions

The use of rituals, defined as repetitive actions or verbalizations given special meaning or power by a child to ensure her safety or to control events, is a very common OCD compulsion. Common rituals include repeatedly checking or touching things (especially in a particular sequence), and counting. A ritual can be something as simple as your child touching the top of her head five times before leaving the house.

Rituals can also be elaborate and lengthy to such a degree that they take an enormous toll on your child's ability to accomplish the simplest tasks. The National Institute for Mental Health (NIMH) offered these testimonials from young people as examples to help parents recognize OCD when it is present in a son or daughter:

> I couldn't do anything without rituals. They invaded every aspect my life. Counting really bogged me down. I would wash my hair three times as opposed to once because three was a good-luck number and one wasn't. It took me longer to read because I'd count the lines in a paragraph. When I set the alarm clock at night, I had to set it to a number that wouldn't add up to a "bad" number.

Getting dressed in the morning was tough because I had a routine, and if I didn't follow the routine, I'd get anxious and would have to get dressed all over again. I always worried that if I didn't do something, my parents were going to die. I'd have these terrible thoughts of harming my parents. That was completely irrational, but the thoughts triggered more anxiety and more senseless behavior.

The sad irony is that although the child with OCD creates rituals to bring order and control to his life, rituals often have the opposite effect of controlling him. Sometimes in an effort to stop himself from doing one ritual, he will create a whole new set of ritualistic actions and verbalizations and become similarly entrapped in a brand-new compulsive behavior.

 Essential

Although older children with OCD are aware of the irrationality of their rituals, younger children (especially those below the age of eight) often lack that awareness. This can make it more difficult to detect the specific trigger for the child's ritual. As a child develops self-awareness, knowledge of her own triggers and an awareness of the compulsive behaviors they cause will be more present, making treatment more possible.

The performance of rituals brings neither pleasure nor calm to your child with OCD. If there is any relief, it is temporary. The good news is that with greater self-awareness and treatment, and with the help of a parent, most children and adolescents can effectively manage this and other symptoms of OCD.

CHAPTER 3

Causes of OCD

It may come as a surprise to learn that 95 percent of what is known about the brain has been discovered since 1990. The bonanza of genetic and clinical knowledge acquired in this brief time has led to some reliable working suppositions about the causes of OCD. It is important for you as a concerned parent to be generally familiar with this body of knowledge so you can better assist in the diagnosis and treatment of your child. In this chapter you'll find out how to best take advantage of what today's science has discovered about OCD.

What Today's Science Says about OCD

OCD is a neurobiological condition causing persistent, intrusive thoughts and behaviors. Although OCD disrupts a child's thinking, it is classified as an "anxiety disorder," a category that also includes PTSD, panic disorder, eating disorders, social phobia, and attention deficit hyperactivity disorder (ADHD). Anxiety disorders including OCD are not classified as "thought disorders" such as schizophrenia. That's because anxiety disorders do not provoke the delusions associated with mental illnesses like schizophrenia, such as a serious, sustained impairment of contact with reality, including visual or auditory hallucinations.

Disproved "Facts" about Causes

OCD is not new or particular to the United States. It exists around the world, with cases documented as far back as 1875. The French called it *folie du doubte* or the "doubting disease," a name any parent with a child with OCD will immediately understand. Before the advent of psychiatry, religious zealots believed OCD (and most mental illness) was the work of the devil, precisely the kind of ignorance that has lead to the stigmas still dealt with today.

Up until the last half of the twentieth century, the Freudian view of OCD as a neurotic condition prevailed within the psychiatric profession. In this now out-of-date paradigm, psychoanalysts believed the disorder was caused by unresolved unconscious conflict, perhaps sexual in origin, or the result of over-controlling parents. Fortunately, there is now scientific consensus about the biological roots of OCD.

How Scientists Know What They Know

The reasons for this relative unanimity of understanding about OCD as a neurobiological condition are threefold. First is the availability of advanced imaging technologies enabling snapshots (PET scans) and "real-time" (MRI) imagery of the brains of individuals with OCD and comparisons of these images with nonaffected members of control groups. A second source of valuable information is the clinical experience of psychologists, psychiatrists, and general practitioners who collect and distribute data about the ages of onset, symptoms, OCD triggers, and therapeutic outcomes of their patients along with the relative efficacy of specific medications. This clinical experience is also shared with pharmaceutical companies, who use it in the development of new, more targeted medications.

Finally, there are the tremendous advances in genetic brain research providing pivotal clues about how OCD is passed between generations. Put together, this wealth of clinical experience and research helps connect the dots between causes, symptoms, and treatment and makes OCD the highly treatable condition it is today.

A Tour of the Brain with OCD

Using advanced brain imaging, scientists can pinpoint the most likely pathway in the brain which, when malfunctioning, prompts the symptoms of OCD. This OCD pathway involves three key locations in the brain.

- The frontal cortex, located behind the eyes, regulates proper behavior, processing stimuli from deep within the brain. It activates thought and behavioral processes in other functional parts of the brain, for example, those regulating thoughts and emotions.
- The caudate nucleus is located midbrain, in the basal ganglia, where it monitors danger signals by separating relevant from irrelevant information and by regulating "automatic" behaviors (those not requiring additional brain processing, such as walking or brushing teeth). It then sends those signals requiring action on to the thalamus.
- The thalamus, the main switchboard of this neural pathway, screens incoming signals from the caudate nucleus and sends alarm signals back to the frontal cortex, signaling when and to what degree it should react.

It is thought that in the brains of people with OCD, the caudate nucleus receives a flood of danger signals disproportionate to the external stimuli. Unable to process this overload, the caudate nucleus sends these unfiltered signals on to the thalamus, which in turn sends a deluge of alarm messages back to the frontal cortex—putting the brain of a child with OCD on overload.

The Serotonin Connection

Scientists believe the link between these three key brain locations lies in the neurotransmitter serotonin, which brain scans have shown to be at a lower level in people with OCD. In the language of brain science, there is a premature "reuptake" of serotonin in the synapses between brain neurons. This shortage of serotonin disrupts the processing of signals and turns what should be an automatic or normal response into a false alarm "high alert."

Alert!

Three antidepressant medications, Prozac, Paxil, and Zoloft, which increase the amount of serotonin in the brain's neural pathways by preventing the reabsorption of serotonin, have FDA approval for use by children. These medications have proven to be the most successful psychotropic (medications that affect the brain) medicines for reducing the symptoms of OCD in both adults and children.

Using a traffic analogy, a low level of serotonin causes the brain to fail in its activation of a critical stoplight. This malfunction allows too much traffic, in this case danger signals, to enter the intersection, creating the equivalent of a crash. Or, as Dr. Jeffrey Schwartz, a prominent OCD researcher at UCLA, dubbed it, "brain lock." As you watch your child struggle with an unrelenting need to count, clean, or touch, picture this unrelenting flow of traffic in her brain, with her stoplight locked on green. The result is an overdose of inaccurate information causing an overreaction to stimuli that should not threaten her, but does.

The Plastic Brain

How this so-called brain lock turns into the debilitating disorder of OCD has to do with the repetition and reinforcement of activity along this neural pathway. When a child responds over and over to an obsessive thought by performing a compulsive ritual, it reinforces the brain pathway associated with OCD. An axiom in neurology says, "neurons that fire together, wire together." This refers to the plasticity of the brain, meaning the brain can be changed by the ways people think and behave. This has important implications for OCD treatment, especially in children whose brains are even more plastic than those of adults. Treatment, by both cognitive behavioral therapy (CBT) and medication, actually changes the brain so that it functions more normally by weakening old patterns of neural pathways and forming new ones.

Working Hypotheses, Remaining Questions

Scientists initially came up with a working hypothesis about the role of serotonin in OCD by observing the clinical outcomes of patients taking antidepressant medications. They noted how the SSRIs (Selective Serotonin Reuptake Inhibitors) positively affected their patients with OCD, both adults and children, and concluded this result came from the ability of the medications to cause more serotonin to remain in the brain's neural pathways.

 **Fact**

> Brain scans performed before and after treatment show similar increases in the levels of serotonin in children and adults who receive SSRI antidepressants *and* in those who participate in Cognitive Behavior Therapy (CBT) for OCD. This finding underscores the plasticity of the brain and the benefits of both medication and therapy in treating this anxiety disorder. See Chapter 8 for more on treatment choices.

The fact that these existing treatments have shown some success does not mean more research won't lead scientists to discover other neurotransmitters or biological processes that may play an equally important role in OCD, and thus offer other avenues to find even better treatment. This is already indicated by the fact that not all children with OCD respond to SSRI medications.

The dynamic nature of ongoing research puts a great deal of importance on the expertise of the doctor treating your child's OCD.

Because data is constantly being accumulated, it's important to seek out the most knowledgeable practitioner in your region of the country. Doctors who are associated with university hospital research centers are among the most informed. It is equally important for you to keep abreast of new developments in anxiety and OCD research and treatment by making use of the resources listed in Appendix B.

Creating a Family Mental Health Genetic Scorecard

In an apparent contradiction, while OCD is a genetically transmitted anxiety disorder, not all OCD is traceable to genetic inheritance. How can both these things be true? Brain researchers now believe there are multiple genes (genetic mutations) involved with a susceptibility to OCD and other closely related anxiety disorders, especially Tourette's syndrome. At the same time, there are children with OCD who have no trace of the disorder in first-degree relatives (parents and siblings), putting much more emphasis in those cases on so-called silent genes and environmental triggers.

Family Studies

Family studies consist of interviews and clinical examinations with large numbers of patients with OCD (and other anxiety disorders), along with their first-degree relatives. In some of the most valuable studies, researchers have been able to study twins, identical and nonidentical, who were adopted. The advantage of these twin adoption studies where twins are separated at birth lays in the ability of researchers to rule out environmental factors as the primary cause in cases where both twins manifest a specific mental disorder.

Data from families where OCD is present is then compared to examinations and interviews done with control groups of individuals who do not have OCD. These surveys produce the sort of statistical data that can help predict the risk of OCD in parents, offspring, and siblings. To date, family studies demonstrate that from 18 to 30 percent of children with OCD have first-degree relatives who also have the disorder.

The Human Genome

More recent family studies—those done since the successful mapping of the human genome in 2002—add genetic information (genome scans) of related and unrelated patients with OCD as compared to the genetic scans of members of control groups to the purely statistical data garnered previously. This type of study is also called DNA linkage analysis. Genetic scans or blueprints (created from blood samples) are examined in minute detail for genetic similarities and differences in all study participants. The goal of this research is to find so-called genetic markers (a difference in a particular chromosome or part thereof that, by their unusual prevalence in the sample population, can be statistically associated with the presence of OCD).

With the advent of genetic linkage analysis, it is possible to go beyond statistical associations and potentially discover the genetic cause(s) of OCD and other disorders. While you are not likely to have any immediate reason to obtain a DNA analysis for your child, the working conclusions of these broader genetic analyses of patients with OCD and their families provide guideposts for the more accurate diagnosis and treatment of all children with OCD.

Similarly, there are important clues in your own family health history that, even without discovering their genetic underpinning, could potentially contribute to a diagnosis of your child's mental health problem by providing probabilities in one direction or another.

Researching Your Family Mental Health History

You may not have access to family members from previous generations or their health records. If they are still living and available to you, there may be reluctance on your part to broach a "touchy subject." However, if access to the people and information is possible, the mental health history of relatives who are further removed from your own immediate family, for example, uncles, aunts, cousins, or grandparents, can be helpful as you attempt to collect all relevant information prior to bringing your child for his mental health evaluation.

Why does it matter? Consider the possibility that your child's grandfather was known to be a notorious hand-washer. While this behavior may in the past have been considered innocuous, or simply eccentric, today it can provide a vital piece of information to assist your child's diagnosis. It also potentially opens up a conversation about other unusual behaviors family members may have noticed in this grandparent. You may be able to find out at what age Grandpa's excessive hand washing began. If this information starts adding up to the likelihood that this grandparent had OCD, and particularly if other sub-threshold OCD behaviors are present in you or your spouse, you would have more reason to closely monitor your child's behavior at an earlier age. Cynthia, a mother of two in her thirties, saw a pattern of anxiety disorders in her family after her seven-year-old daughter was diagnosed with OCD.

> My daughter has more obsessions than compulsive behavior. Because she didn't do the more common things, like hand washing or counting, I didn't see it right away. I just knew there was something wrong. She would have all these fears and unwanted thoughts. She'd scream and cry that she didn't want to go to school. Bedtime was terrible, too. Now I am diagnosed too, with depression and anxiety. And, when I look back, I can see it in my father, too. He was a hoarder. He couldn't get rid of anything. His house was totally full of stuff by the end. He could hardly walk. So I tell everyone, check your family history! You just might see some of the same behaviors in the past as you see in your kids. If it helps get your child's problem diagnosed faster, all of you will be better off.

In many families OCD or another anxiety disorder will be present in multiple generations. Take a few moments to consider whether that may be the case in your own extended family. Again, this has nothing to do with assigning blame to one branch of the family or another. The purpose of this exercise is to assess whether tendencies or vulnerabilities toward particular disorders may be the result of a genetic influence on your child or children.

Environmental Triggers

Some of the illnesses or events once considered possible causes of OCD have been redefined as environmental (also called *nongenetic*) triggers of the disorder. Environmental in this usage refers to nongenetic factors. This means that, while not a cause, they are capable of catalyzing symptoms of OCD in genetically susceptible children or adolescents. These can be events that occur inside the child's body (such as an illness or prenatal exposure), or in his immediate environment.

Because there are children who develop OCD without a known family genetic link, many scientists believe they'll eventually discover firm evidence of environmental factors that can alter genetic material and create the mutations associated with OCD. These mutations may or may not then cause OCD in the affected individual, but could potentially pass on a susceptibility to OCD to a subsequent generation.

The Streptococcus Throat Hypothesis

The most studied environmental trigger for OCD is streptococcal infection (streptococcus infection), also called Pediatric Autoimmune Neuropsychiatric Disorder (PANDAS). With this link, originally made by NIMH researchers in the early 1990s, scientists determined that for an estimated 20 to 30 percent of children who develop early-onset OCD, the disorder is triggered by the child's own immune cells attacking the basal ganglia in his brain.

Question?

Does streptococcus throat cause OCD?
Although not a cause, a strep infection is thought to be a trigger, meaning it can bring on the early onset of OCD. A child with strep throat, particularly if he has demonstrated any previous OCD symptoms, should be closely monitored for any subsequent muscle weaknesses or tics. Researchers believe that the child who develops OCD after a strep throat was genetically susceptible to the disorder prior to the onset of the OCD.

Trauma, Stress, and OCD

Other possible OCD environmental triggers that have received less study fall into the category of traumatic childhood events, such as the death of a parent or a change in the child's school or periods of sustained stress in a child's life. Many parents make a correlation between such events and the onset of OCD in a child.

Stressful events *are* likely triggers for aggravated symptoms in many children who already have OCD or a susceptibility to the disorder. And there is substantial anecdotal evidence among parents of children with OCD to conclude that high-stress times, such as the start of school, a family illness, or an accident, can exacerbate OCD symptoms in their children.

> With school back in session, my ten-year-old daughter's OCD is back in force. She's picking at her skin and pulling her hair out. This morning, her second day back, she refused to get out of bed, saying her OCD was telling her not to go to school.

> My son, who's seven, fell down and cut his leg at recess. The school nurse cleaned off the dirt and put a bandage on it, telling him to keep dirt out. Well, that

set off his germ fears big time! Now he's afraid germs are going to get him from everywhere.

My daughter just changed from middle school to high school and she's a wreck. I found out she spent half of the day hiding in the girl's bathroom. She was so afraid she'd pee in her pants in class, she decided she had to stay there just in case.

There are strategies outlined in future chapters to help both parents and children anticipate and cope with these high-stress times.

Identifying Culprit Genes

In the past fifteen years, genetic researchers have located seven different genetic mutations they associate with OCD. It is believed one or more of these genetic "mistakes" make children and adolescents more susceptible to OCD triggers in the environment. Most of this genetic research has focused on a specific mutation in the human serotonin supporter gene, named hSERT, found to an unusually high degree in unrelated family members with OCD, as reported in a 2003 study by the National Institutes of Health (NIH).

In the same NIH study, a second mutation in this same hSERT gene found in the same patients appeared to correlate with more severe OCD symptoms in those individuals. Interviews done with family members of those found to have this particular "double hit" of two mutations on the hSERT gene revealed that six out of every seven patients had a second anxiety disorder in addition to OCD, primarily anorexia nervosa, Asperger's syndrome, social phobia, or substance abuse.

Question?

What is a tic?

Tics are involuntary, repetitive speech patterns or physical movements including twitches, eye rolling, and head tilting associated with the neurobiological disorder known as Tourette's syndrome. Speech-related tics can cause a child to make repeated, involuntary comments or outbursts. Children with OCD are at a higher risk of developing tics.

The sum total of genetic research done thus far suggests that rather than a single gene expressing its DNA to create OCD, it is more likely that several genes participate in creating smaller effects. These effects then combine to cause a predisposition to OCD, with varying degrees of severity dependent on specific genetic combinations and nongenetic triggers. This is a rapidly changing field as government and privately funded brain research continues at a frenetic pace at several of the nation's leading research institutions.

CHAPTER 4

The Experience of OCD for a Child

"I was ten when an invisible robber broke into my head and hijacked my mind," says fourteen-year-old Janice in an OCD group therapy session. As Janice describes her experience of an unwanted obsessive thought, several group members nod in recognition. That's because Janice is describing the fundamental experience of OCD for a child: The feelings of powerlessness and fear when control over her mind and body is essentially lost to an illness she doesn't understand. Other children use the words "kidnapped" or "hostage" to describe their loss of self-control at the onset of OCD.

Perceptions and Misconceptions

Am I crazy? It's the most difficult and nagging question many young people with OCD say they face. And if by "crazy" the child means psychotic or delusional, the answer is *no*, he's not crazy. OCD is a neurobiological disorder that can be managed, often without medication.

Children with OCD, particularly those over the age of seven or eight, say they are aware of the fact that their obsessive thoughts and compulsive behaviors are irrational. They also know their behaviors can be construed as crazy.

 **Fact**

Few outside of the OCD community of caregivers, patients, and families realize that 80 percent of children treated for OCD experience significant improvement. A recent study confirmed as fact what common sense predicts: When a child's parents are actively involved in his (CBT) treatment, he has a much higher rate of success and remission of his OCD symptoms than if parents are not involved.

Your child with OCD wishes she could stop her compulsions. But she can't. And it's not for any lack of desire or willpower on her part. Neither does a child with OCD enjoy her rituals. If she did, you would see a sense of calm come over her when she finished counting or skipping over cracks on the sidewalk. And she wouldn't be trying so hard to hide her behavior from you or from her friends.

Among the most harmful misconceptions about OCD is the belief that the disorder is not treatable. Often people who don't know better (including the child with OCD) view OCD as a completely debilitating disease—as if everyone suffering from OCD grows up to be as bad off as the character played by Jack Nicholson in the movie *As Good as It Gets*. Rather than serve as the butt of jokes, children with OCD and their families would benefit from more accurate media accounts about the disorder.

In contrast to the common perception of the severely debilitated OCD sufferer as typical of those with this disorder, studies show there are more people with OCD at the lower and the middle point of the symptom severity spectrum than at the higher, more dysfunctional end. This is especially true as many more children and adolescents are being diagnosed earlier and successfully treated.

Essential

> Early treatment of your child's OCD is the best thing you can do to ensure her success in treatment. However, if a child doesn't know help is possible, she is much less likely to ask for it and more prone to hide her problem. Eighty percent of those who receive treatment for OCD make significant progress in managing the disorder.

OCD must be taken from behind the curtain of secrecy and embarrassment where it has long remained. Children with OCD are better served when there's an open ongoing dialogue about the disorder with parents, teachers, and friends. In the parlance of family therapy it's called "normalizing" the problem. In other words, this means letting your child know that her OCD is a medical condition like many others. She is not at fault for having its symptoms. Finally, she needs to know that you understand and accept the size of the challenge her OCD presents for the entire family, and you don't blame her in any way for this challenge. (For more on family dynamics, see Chapter 15.)

Limited Self-Awareness

If your child has OCD, he will do many things that won't make sense to you. What may not be as obvious is that these same behaviors often make no sense to him either. Even if he knows his compulsive behaviors are irrational, a child with OCD cannot explain why he keeps doing them. That's because from his perspective he's not "in charge" of his own behavior; to your child it's truly as if there's a foreign dictator in his head telling him to do these crazy things. Take the case of Josh.

JOSH'S WORLD

When overcome by the demands of his OCD, ten-year-old Josh often looks like he's daydreaming, off in a world of his own. The truth is that Josh is temporarily in a different, separate reality. This business of trying to deal with his obsessions by taking the "right" corrective measures can be enormously time-consuming. Look at what's involved in Josh's sitting down to dinner with his family.

Josh hears his mother call him, but he can't put down the book he's reading because he'll lose his place in his homework and have to start all over. He can't even stop long enough to tell her his problem. When she comes into his room and convinces him she'll help him find his place after dinner, he reluctantly agrees. He goes to wash his hands, and does it four times. Then he uses his sleeve to open the bathroom door so he doesn't get new germs on his hands. On the way to dinner, he walks carefully down the center of the stairway, not touching the banister as he walks.

Arriving at the dinner table, Josh is stunned to see new dishes on the table, and he stands still for several minutes, obsessed with the possibilities that fill his mind: These dishes are covered with germs from whatever store they came from. His mother didn't run the new dishes through the dishwasher. His sister didn't wash her hands before setting the table.

While Josh continues to stand in the same spot, his brother Scott bounds into the room followed by the family dog Scooter; Josh watches Scott pet Scooter before sitting in his seat, presenting a new concern to Josh about dog germs on his brother's hands.

When Josh's mom asks him to please sit down, Josh begs her to keep Scott from touching any of the food or serving bowls or plates before he gets them. And on and on it goes.

OCD in Children and Preteens

OCD can affect children as young as three and four years of age, but OCD symptoms look and sound different in a younger child than they do in the school-age youngster of eight or the prepubescent boy of eleven. For example, a younger child will often reveal more of his obsessive thoughts to his parents, even if he doesn't yet have the words to verbalize what he's thinking or the cognitive skill to understand the contradictions inherent in these thoughts.

A younger child's OCD-related fears can be particularly intense. The desire to cling to you may be strong, making the first day of school very trying. A younger child with OCD would also be more likely to try to enlist you in the performance of her compulsions than an older child might. She may, for example, ask you to clean off the seat of the car repeatedly before she'll sit on it. Or she may demand that you wear gloves before touching her food. Acquiescing to these demands will only reinforce your child's obsessive behaviors and increase their frequency. In later chapters, you'll learn better strategies for handling such situations.

How Does OCD Feel to the Younger Child?

Of course, every child is different, but the unwanted thoughts and compulsions caused by OCD often result from the same triggers and produce the same compulsive behaviors in different children. To a young child with OCD, offensive dirt and germs can dwell anywhere, whether visible or invisible to the naked eye. From mild to extreme, these fears often interfere with the most basic activities of the child's daily life. What follows are statements from children under the age of twelve who are dealing with OCD-related contamination fears.

- "I don't want to eat peas. They have bugs."
- "I hate having food mixed up on my plate, with everything touching. The worst is Chinese. I have to separate each piece if I'm going to count them. And I have to separate and count them before I eat any."
- "This glass isn't clean. Are you sure this glass is clean?"
- "I put my books in the microwave to burn off the germs that got on them at school."
- "You touched the dog. Don't touch the milk carton. Don't touch me!"

If your child displays any of these symptoms on a regular basis, then you know how easily they can disrupt her daily functioning and create chaos for the entire household.

Safety Fears

The dangers that any young child perceives may (to you) be nothing more threatening than an imaginary monster or ghostly presence. But it's important to realize that a child with OCD who experiences these fears believes he's in very real, immediate peril. And, as a consequence of this perceived danger, he feels he must act, often by performing a ritual or prayer to stave off ominous consequences.

- "As soon as I heard that stupid rhyme I couldn't get it out of my head. Now I have to count all the cracks in the sidewalk. Of course I never step on them. If someone talks and interrupts me, I have to start all over again."
- A girl's father, a fireman, died on a TV show. "Now, I know Daddy is going to die. I have to check on him all the time to see if he's still here."

Safety fears like these can prompt severe distress and crying fits in the child with OCD, especially if she is not able to perform the ritual she has designed to forestall the negative consequences she fears. As future chapters spell out in detail, the way to help your child conquer imaginary fears is not by telling her these fears are not real, but rather by assigning the blame for her fear where it belongs: to her OCD.

Ordering Fears

The need to create order in his environment reflects a child's desire for certainty in the face of what he perceives as chaos, which to a child with OCD can be a source of great anxiety. In some cases this desire can be harmless, even positive. A child with mild OCD may, for example, prefer to have the shirts in his closet and the socks in his bedroom bureau lined up by color. With this done, he hopes he can quell the anxiety that greets him every morning when the alarm wakes him up for school.

But, with more acute cases of OCD, ordering fears can interfere with the child's daily routines and his ability to learn.

- "I can't finish my math homework because I keep going back to the beginning and starting over."
- "I erased the answer on my paper so many times, now there's a hole in it."
- "I can't go to sleep unless the curtains are pulled together exactly in the middle of the window."

The key for you as a parent is to help your child determine where normal, helpful ordering crosses a line and becomes obsessive compulsive. Here a mother describes her fifteen-year-old son's ordering obsession as it relates to time.

> He can't do anything without timing it. From beginning to end of a movie, a song, a walk, he watches the clock or his watch. If we go out, he times it. Sometimes he'll time something down to the second. If his timing gets disturbed, it really throws him off.

OCD in the Teenage Years

With an adolescent's greater independence and opportunity for social interactions, his OCD symptoms will differ from those of the younger child with OCD. They can also be much more complex, hidden, and frightening to the adolescent involved. Following are statements from teenagers, all between thirteen and eighteen years of age, who are dealing with OCD.

Contamination Fears

These teens talked about their fears of contamination by germs, dirt, and disease.

- "I get down on my hands and knees and clean the linoleum floor with a toothbrush. If I do that, tomorrow will be a good day."
- "I spend an hour picking the lint off my coat before I go outside."
- "I can't touch the doorknob. Open the door for me."
- "I took eleven baths already that day. Then I took another one so I'd end up even."

Many young people with OCD say they feel the need to wash their hands anytime they become anxious—about anything! Excessive washing is probably the most pervasive OCD-related behavior, and, as a result, it's the easiest symptom for a parent to spot.

Ordering Fears

A child with an ordering fear attempts to deal with his inner anxiety by creating a sense of order in his environment. Here are some statements by children who experience this type of obsessive need.

- "Symmetry is omnipotent."
- "I have to have everything set up on my desk in a perfect rectangle or I can't start homework."
- "I couldn't get out of bed until the digital clock was on an even number."
- "I hate multiple-choice tests. Even if I know the right answer, I can't stop thinking about all the other choices and how they could be right too. So I never get to the end of a test."

These statements illustrate the OCD-related need for order, which is an expression of the affected child's need for certainty or control. This is also referred to as his need to make things "just so." The child cannot give a logical explanation for either the need or the criteria he uses when he puts things in "proper order." As a parent, you gain nothing by looking for logical explanations where they don't exist.

Safety Fears

Many OCD-related obsessions concern a fear of imminent harm coming to the child or to a family member as a result of something she did or did not do. These fears reflect the child's extreme self-doubt, which in turn often stems from her fear of being bad, sinful, or otherwise guilty of a wrong deed. A teen with this obsession will often make statements such as these:

- "If I don't get straight A's this semester, my whole family will die."
- "What if that bump in the road was a body? I'll have to drive back and check."
- "That guy looked at me on the bus. I'm sure he's following me now."
- "God is angry with me because I'm so bad. Mom, is God angry with me?"

This type of OCD obsession can become self-fulfilling. For example, the child who has extreme fear about the possible consequences of failing a school exam will be unable to concentrate properly while taking that exam and is therefore far more likely to fail.

Aggression and Avoidance

An avoidance compulsion in a young person often shows up as an intense, irrational fear that he will commit an aggressive act toward another person. Avoidance stemming from these fears in a teenager with OCD is frequently linked to difficult emotions, especially anger, or discomfort about his own evolving sexuality. But avoidance can also come from nothing more than his fear of experiencing certain "bad thoughts" (violent, aggressive thoughts) *in the future* if he were to find himself in a certain situation or in close proximity to certain people, for example, the opposite gender.

All these fears can lead to the young person's avoidance of any people, places, or situations that might escalate his anxiety. This vicious cycle of obsessive thoughts and compulsive behaviors can show up in girls and boys. Here's how some adolescents with OCD articulate their difficulties with anger, aggressive emotions, and avoidance compulsions.

- "Sometimes if I get mad at someone, the thought comes into my head 'I hate you.' Then, 'I want to stab you with a knife.' Then I'm so afraid that I'll do that so I have to stay away from them or anything sharp."
- "I have a tic that makes me have to say every thought in my head."
- "Did I just tell Aunt Mary she's ugly?"
- "What if I'm really gay? Even though I never felt that way, it could happen. I have to stay away from boys just in case."

As these statements illustrate, OCD thoughts and behaviors can and often do reflect fears that are a natural byproduct of growing up, for example, a preteen's developing sexuality. The problem for a young person with OCD comes when these fears reach an exaggerated, often harmful intensity and regularity, prompting extreme and disruptive avoidance behaviors.

What becomes quickly apparent about all young people contending with OCD is the sense of isolation they share. It can often feel to them like they're the only unfortunate victims of this illness. The first thing a parent can do to help a child with any of these symptoms is to reassure him that he is not alone.

Negative Coping Behaviors: Avoiding and Hiding

As a child with OCD matures, she wants what every other child wants: acceptance by her peers. To get that acceptance, she may go to great lengths to hide the symptoms of her OCD from friends, teachers, classmates, babysitters, and neighbors; in other words, anyone who might "expose" what feels to her like unacceptable weirdness in a social setting.

In addition to hiding his OCD symptoms from friends, your child may also be contending with an inability to cope with what he perceives as the filthy habits of his friends, siblings, and classmates. Tragically, his contamination fear causes him to adopt a hypercritical attitude toward others, including the very people he wants desperately to be his friends.

His social difficulties can be aggravated when he's in physical proximity to these peers. He may react to this trigger with a contamination fear or experience a flurry of "bad thoughts" containing images of violent acts or inappropriate sexual activities—with either causing an intense spike in his anxiety level. His fear that he might become contaminated or do something violent may result in a strong need to remove himself from the friend in question. If he can't remove himself, for example, because he's in the classroom or on a school bus, his anxious reactions may become particularly acute.

What Children with OCD Need Most from Parents

Your child needs your assurance that, despite her OCD, you still see and hear her, and, most important, that you still love *her*. Your assurance that you still remember who she is apart from the OCD telescopes the important message that you can tell the difference between her and the behaviors related to her OCD.

Once your child has learned that her OCD is something she can learn to manage, she needs to know that even though it will be a challenging learning process, she is not alone; that getting a handle on her OCD will be a team, or family, project. Your understanding should include an awareness of the daily toll OCD takes on your child's well-being. For example, if she must focus all her energy on "keeping it together" on the school bus, by the time she gets home she will be a very stressed out, hard-to-console child. She will then need your patience and understanding, as well your help, in developing a practical strategy for coping with her own stress.

CHAPTER 5

The Parent's Role in Identifying OCD

Perhaps you feel overwhelmed by the sheer amount of new information already covered, or you fear you're not adequate for the task ahead. Both are normal and reasonable reactions at this stage. However, you'll soon see that despite any feelings of inadequacy you may have, you *are* the best possible person to help your child come to terms with her OCD. That's because you are already the world's preeminent expert on your child. Secondly, you don't need to be an expert on OCD to help your child get control of it. Helping a child come to terms with OCD is a job best done by a loving, informed parent.

When Abnormal Becomes Normal

As a dedicated and conscientious parent, you love your child totally. You praise the positive things she does and use every opportunity to foster her self-esteem. You also set boundaries, rules, and expectations for her behavior at home and in the world, establishing consequences when those rules and expectations aren't met. At least that's what you try to do.

When OCD is present in a child, many of these "normal" rules for parenting are turned upside down. The dynamics created by OCD can throw your family and household into disarray. At times it seems as if your child is manipulating the rest of the family. The presence of OCD in a child can slowly and insidiously cause "normal" behavior to become so skewed that abnormal becomes the norm without your being cognizant of how this happened.

How Abnormal Becomes Normal

When you get caught up in your child's compulsions in an effort to calm him down or "keep peace" in the family, the abnormal can quickly replace anything resembling normality. For example, you attempt to head off his tantrums by meeting his requests, no matter how illogical. Think about whether any of these "peacekeeping" behaviors sound familiar:

- Do you regularly serve your child special foods?
- Do you wash his bedding on a daily basis?
- Does your child make his siblings wash their hands before "allowing them" to touch the remote?
- Does the process of getting your kids ready for school regularly break down as your child takes an inordinate time to wash and dress, thus making everyone late?
- Do you reassure your child each and every time he worries aloud about imagined threats to his own or your safety?

If these examples resemble some typical dynamics in your family, you should be aware of the likelihood that your child's OCD is now running your household.

The Temptation to Deny

Typically a child with OCD develops the compulsions associated with her disorder over many months or years before a parent recognizes what has happened. During this time, your child has no doubt made many gallant attempts to respond to or neutralize her own obsessions by performing cleaning or counting rituals, asking you and other family members for reassurance, or avoiding the triggers that provoke her.

In many instances, she's tried and failed many times to stop the recurrence of offending thoughts, and has accepted a certain sense of inevitability about them. After all these attempts to fight her OCD and, from her perspective, still losing that battle, a child may simply not feel up to trying again. That's when your encouragement will really count.

To begin the process of taking back your household from the domination of your child's OCD there are three primary "don'ts" for parents.

- Don't get caught up in the OCD.
- Don't clean up things that don't need cleaning.
- Don't let OCD take over *your* world.

From a busy parent's point of view, a child's intense new attentiveness to cleanliness can seem, well, normal, even a positive development. You may disregard the possibility of a deeper problem being present using some rationalizations that are not all that outlandish. For example, the self-evident fact that "Germs are real." Or, the assumption that "She'll grow out of it."

But for many parents new to OCD, there is also the temptation to deny reality when and if your child's OCD-related behavior goes beyond the normal fears and phases of childhood. You deny reality not because you don't care or notice the strangeness in her behavior, but because the possibility that your child has a mental health problem can be a very disturbing prospect for any parent.

Secondary Signs of OCD

In addition to the typical obsessions and compulsions associated with OCD (see Chapter 2), there are some indirect symptoms that may be red flags telling you that the disorder is present. In general terms these are negative behavioral changes, overt signs of worry and noticeable, frequent mood swings. Any one of these can be the initial issue that prompts a parent to bring a child to therapy. And while the behaviors listed below are associated with several different anxiety and mood disorders, if they exist in tandem with the symptoms of OCD, they are an important clue for parents and mental healthcare providers to test the child for OCD as well as the other disorders.

- Sustained periods of listlessness and withdrawal
- Sharp drop in self-esteem
- A sudden drop in school performance
- Unproductive hours doing homework
- Sleeplessness and irritability

It cannot be overemphasized that any or all of these behaviors alone do not signify or cause OCD. But they do sometimes co-occur with OCD.

The End of Denial

Parents rightly fear the stigma associated with mental illness. Unfortunately, the prejudice shown toward people dealing with mental health challenges exists despite the indisputable fact that disorders like OCD are neurobiological in origin, and no more the fault of the sufferer than other biological conditions such as diabetes or asthma. The fact that there's not a simple blood test for OCD does not in any way diminish its real physical symptoms or the suffering it causes. As more parents and children recognize and treat OCD, this ignorance and the resulting stigma of shame are more likely to fade away and eventually disappear.

Your Own Emotions

It does no good to deny your own fears and feelings of sadness over the possible signs of a mental health problem in your child. They are entirely appropriate. A sense of guilt is also common, particularly as you look back and begin to see signs of OCD that you may have missed earlier in your child's life. Take heart in the fact that you are now learning what you need to know to help him.

If he has OCD, you are identifying the problem early enough so that his prognosis is much better than if you had waited. Based on current treatment rates for OCD, it is highly likely that he can fulfill his potential in school and beyond. In other words, treatment works, while the cost of doing nothing can be very high.

 Fact

The obsessions and compulsions of OCD, if not treated, grow more severe as a child matures. Conversely, 80 percent of those treated with a combination of cognitive behavioral therapy (CBT) and medication respond positively to treatment. Treatment for OCD may be hard to find, and even harder to carry out, but not treating OCD in a child is far more problematic.

Fear of Medications

Another issue that may prevent you from taking appropriate actions to recognize and treat your child's OCD is your apprehension about psychotropic medicines. You may worry about the possible side effects of prescribed medications. This understandable concern on your part should be discussed with your child's pediatrician or with the mental health practitioner you eventually consult. One point that bears mentioning here is that the typical and recommended treatment for OCD includes both psychotherapy and medications, with therapy as the preferred initial approach, especially for the younger child.

In other words, you should not avoid seeking help just because you have reservations about the use of psychotropic medications in children.

There are specific situations when medication for OCD in children is strongly called for. Chief among these is when your child's symptoms are extremely debilitating, to the point where behavioral therapy is highly difficult or impossible. This may be a short or long-term measure. But medication is not a cure for OCD. At best, it reduces symptoms. Eventually, a child or young adult must learn the proven therapeutic techniques that allow him to "talk back to his OCD."

If You Suspect OCD

As you become more convinced that OCD symptoms are present in your child, you may fear that you'll upset him by asking questions about the suspect behaviors or by suggesting a visit to the doctor for testing. What parents discover is that the opposite is often true. Their children, who may have thought for months or years that they were the only ones with such strange thoughts or behaviors, are relieved to find out that other young people have been in the same boat, and, most important, that they've found a way out.

OCD is an anxiety disorder with discernable symptoms within a broad spectrum of severity, from mild to severe. Yet several things about OCD can make it hard to pin down.

First, its symptoms can come and go for weeks and months at a time. The intermittent appearance of symptoms may lead you to believe that your child's unusual behavior is simply a phase, now past. If her obsessions change, manifesting as different compulsive behaviors—such as changing from a need to wash repeatedly to a new pickiness about food—it may take you some time to process this new data and connect the dots between her symptoms.

Because OCD tends to occur in families, behaviors that might represent the norm in your household may in fact represent subclinical symptoms of OCD. When and if these behaviors start to occur more frequently or to a more severe degree, there is a danger that they may be more easily accepted or overlooked in your family than they would in another household where mild OCD is not present.

Essential

Don't focus on the content of your child's obsessions. Don't debate the logic of an obsession. Do focus on his process, and how he's feeling before, during, and after his OCD symptoms appear. High levels of anxiety before and after the performance of repetitive behaviors are clear indications of the presence of OCD.

Less Obvious Signs of OCD

Parents should be on the lookout for any of the following less obvious warning signs of OCD:

- A dramatic increase in laundry
- High, unexplained utility bills
- Repetitive questions
- An exceptionally long time spent getting ready for bed
- Constant checks on the health or safety of other family members
- A persistent fear of illness

If you see these behaviors in your child, it is time to begin monitoring how often you see them over how many days, weeks, or months. Along with this quantitative measure, pay special attention to his emotional temperature before, during, and after you notice the physical signs or observe him carrying out the new behaviors.

- Do you notice a spike in his anxiety level before meals or bedtime?
- How often is he concerned about your safety when there is no apparent cause for alarm?

As you gather this data, first casually, then, if need be, in the form of a written symptom log, you may begin to see patterns that suggest closer monitoring and testing are in order.

How to Help Your Child Take an OCD Self-Test

Before you take your child for a medical evaluation, there are some simple questions you can ask her to get a clearer picture of her obsessions and compulsions. The language you use should not include medical jargon. Try your best to use words that are familiar and age-appropriate. For example, you might ask any of the following questions:

- Do you think thoughts or have feelings over and over that bother you?
- Do you check the same things more than once or twice?
- Do you wash your hands more times than other kids?
- Do you collect things that others throw away? (hair, fingernail clippings, old food)
- Are there many times each day when you have to make things "just so" in order to feel okay?

Try to have this conversation in a familiar location, and make it more of a conversation than a clinical assessment. This exchange represents the beginning of what may become a long-term communication between you and your child about OCD. Therefore your child must always feel safe, something you can accomplish by letting her know that you are *on her side.*

If She Doesn't Want to Talk

If your child has developed a tendency to hide her OCD thoughts and behaviors, you may have to do some gentle prodding to get her to talk about them. One way to reassure her is to say something like, "Other kids have this happen to them too," or "You know there are things we can do to make your bad (or nasty, bothersome) thoughts go away."

If your child becomes visibly upset by the conversation, reassure her that she isn't in this alone, and if she opens up and talks about the problem, let her know that you can help her try and solve it. Or, if she's still not ready to open up, let her know you are there, ready to help if and when she does want to talk about it. Like adults, a child sometimes needs to pick the time for a difficult conversation.

As mentioned in earlier chapters, you should also be aware that in some young children the compulsive behaviors they perform might not be accompanied by obsessive thoughts (at least not any thoughts they are aware of). This can make the child less aware and less able to discuss her own OCD behavior. In this case, you may need to gently offer examples of behaviors you've noticed that your child is not conscious of.

Keep a Daily Log of Your Child's Behavior

As you begin this phase of monitoring your child's symptoms, you will feel a subtle shift in the role you are playing in your child's life. In addition to parent, you are becoming a facilitator in his diagnosis and treatment. Some parents look at the role more as their child's coach. Although it may feel new, trust that it's a positive and necessary step. As you become more informed about OCD and tuned in to his OCD-related challenges, you become a better advocate for him at home, at school, and in the medical community at large.

One-week OCD Symptom Log

Day	Activity	Trigger	Duration	Notes
M	hand-washing	dinner	40 min.	called 5x
T	ritual	school	25 min.	counting cracks
W	face-picking	school	15 min.	excess washing
TH	laundry	bed	30 min.	wouldn't accept sheets
F	after school	toilets	NA	wet pants

The most useful log will cover at minimum a week's time. You may then wish to expand this time period to multiple weeks or a full month. A weeklong log done every few months is also a good way to get a snapshot view of how your child is doing over the period of months or a year. All of this information becomes valuable data for you and for your child's treatment provider when you are ready for a formal diagnosis.

CHAPTER 6

Getting a Formal Diagnosis

If your child has any of the obsessions and compulsions typical of OCD, and if these symptoms last for a period of one month or longer, you have sufficient cause to seek out a formal diagnosis. This doesn't mean you are certain about the outcome, only that you are concerned enough to get it checked out. As a general guidepost for assessing your child's symptoms (detailed in Chapter 2) consider the following question: Is she able to control her behavior, or do her obsessions and compulsions appear to control her?

Where to Go for Help

If you believe OCD may be present in your child, and you've monitored her behavior for at least a month, it is time to get professional help. Because of the relatively short time that OCD has been understood both within the medical profession and in the culture at large, this could take some time and effort on your part. After reading this book and taking advantage of the latest information available online (listed in the Appendix B), start your search by bringing your immediate concerns to the medical professional who knows your child best. If you have a pediatrician or family doctor, begin with him. (If you don't have private health insurance, other options are provided in Chapter 18.)

Start with Your Pediatrician

By doing your homework, you'll be familiar with the terminology and diagnostic criteria used for OCD, and this knowledge will make any conversation with your child's doctor go much better than if you arrive uninformed. To further prepare, make a simple list of those OCD behaviors you've observed in your child, focusing on the ones causing her the most distress. Review the common obsessions in Chapter 2. Does her fear of contamination make touching things or people difficult? Are everyday routines often delayed by her need to order things according to her own impossibly precise standards?

Then consider which behaviors consume the most time and emotional energy, and detract the most from the conduct of her daily life. These will become your child's *presenting symptoms*, the evidence you'll need to focus on when speaking with the doctor. Be sure to include details about frequency and duration when describing your child's behaviors, and do your best to remain calm and avoid sounding distraught as you discuss them.

If you've kept a behavior log (discussed in Chapter 5) bring it with you, and share those results too. As you do, make a point to say what you recall about your child's state of mind when she performed the behaviors listed in your log. Was she more or less distressed after performing the compulsive behavior you noted? What about the effect of her behaviors on you and the rest of the family? A good pediatrician or family doctor is attuned to the whole child and family, making any serious disruption in your household a legitimate issue worthy of his concern.

If Your Doctor Doesn't See What You See

In spite of a doctor's good intentions, be prepared for the possibility that he may not be knowledgeable about OCD. If he hasn't seen or treated a patient with the disorder before, he may dismiss your concerns as needless worry.

Alert!

Physical symptoms such as chapped hands, rashes, hair loss, and stomach ailments may be overlooked if a doctor isn't familiar with OCD and doesn't connect these outer signs to the faulty OCD thinking and repetitive behaviors that can cause them. Do not assume your child's doctor will connect the dots between these symptoms and the possibility of OCD without more information from you.

Even after you've shared your observations with your doctor, she may not agree with your concern that your child has OCD. Having a doctor negate your view can be a trying circumstance for a parent. Self-doubt may set in. Rather than simply acquiesce, it's appropriate to ask for a referral to a psychiatrist, psychologist, social worker, or therapist, ideally an OCD specialist, to obtain an in-depth examination of your child using formal diagnostic criteria. If she doesn't know such an expert, try a simple request for the name of a psychiatrist (who works with children) whom she would recommend. Whether or not your doctor shares your concerns, she should be willing to refer you to someone who has more experience diagnosing or treating OCD and other childhood anxiety disorders. But if you don't get a referral from your doctor, don't despair. There are other options for getting specialized help.

Who Will Diagnose Your Child?

Your choices for obtaining an expert medical opinion on your child's possible diagnosis of OCD depend largely on where you live. For example, a medical school with a psychiatry department and teaching hospital often provide outpatient psychiatric services with staff doctors or psychiatric interns who can perform OCD testing and treatment. A call to the office of the chairman of the psychiatry department should yield information on staff specialties.

An advantage of receiving treatment at a university-affiliated research or teaching hospital is the greater likelihood that its doctors are familiar with the latest research findings regarding OCD treatment. You can also learn about which university hospitals are leading OCD research centers by reading online, especially the news and resources sections on the Web site of the Obsessive-Compulsive Foundation (OCF).

Sources of OCD Expertise

A private hospital, HMO, health insurance company, or medical group in your area may list practitioners who treat anxiety disorders in general, if not OCD in particular. If you've scoured local medical directories and asked other parents, school counselors, teachers, and therapists for suggestions, but still haven't located a qualified practitioner, it's a good idea to directly contact one of the national advocacy organizations listed in the Resources section of this book. For example, the Obsessive-Compulsive Foundation can be contacted by e-mail or toll-free telephone to obtain the name of the nearest doctor or therapist experienced in OCD treatment, or someone who has recently attended one of the foundation's regional OCD trainings, called Behavior Therapy Institutes. Other organizations with national and state level chapters that may provide referrals in your area include the Anxiety Disability Association of America (ADAA) and the Association for the Advancement of Behavioral Therapy (AABT). Fortunately, all these organizations and professional associations have Web sites and helpful information online.

Who Can Diagnose OCD?

A diagnosis is the essential first step before treatment for OCD (using CBT therapy and/or medications) can begin. There are five categories of credentialed professionals permitted to make a formal diagnosis of OCD and other mental disorders. In most states, the professionals legally approved to do so include the following.

- Pediatrician, psychiatrist, or other medical doctor (M.D. or D.O.)
- Psychiatric nurse practitioner or psychiatric intern or resident (operating under the supervision of an M.D.)
- Clinical Psychologist (Ph.D. or Psy.D in psychology)
- Licensed marriage and family therapist (LMFT)
- Social worker (MSW, LCSW) or other licensed counselor

While the professionals in each of these categories can legally diagnose OCD, not all of them have the specialized knowledge required to do so properly. In Chapter 8 there is a list of questions you can use to interview a potential doctor or therapist. Then there is the issue of medications. Regardless of a practitioner's specialized training or knowledge, only medical doctors (general practitioners and psychiatrists) and psychiatric nurse practitioners are permitted to prescribe medications.

What Does an OCD Diagnosis Mean?

The criteria for a diagnosis of OCD are set forth in a book called the DSM-IV, or *Diagnostic and Statistical Manual of Mental Disorders, Fourth Edition.* This manual, specifically, the fourth edition published in 1994, is created and updated by the American Psychiatric Association (APA). The purpose of the DSM-IV is to create uniformity in symptoms for all currently recognized mental health disorders. As new research sheds light on causes and symptoms for a particular disorder, the DSM-IV is changed accordingly.

Each disorder in the DSM-IV, including those under the heading of anxiety disorders (OCD, social phobia, panic disorder, eating disorders, general anxiety disorder, post-traumatic stress disorder and attention deficit hyperactivity disorder) are given a code consisting of three to five letters and numbers. This code then appears on all tests, clinical treatment records, and insurance records for a given patient.

There are four main indicators set forth in the DSM-IV that are to be used by professionals in diagnosing obsessive-compulsive disorder. Their application to a given child in order to come up with a yes/no OCD diagnosis is based more on the experience of the professional than an obvious correlation with the indicators as written. They're listed here for your informational purposes.

- Degree of control over the obsessive-compulsive behavior
- Amount of distress caused by the behavior
- Extent of impairment or interference with everyday routines
- How much time behaviors consume (more than an hour a day?)

Given the wide spectrum of severity in OCD symptoms, these criteria must be applied and interpreted individually for each child or adolescent being diagnosed. For example, it's possible your child is driven to perform rituals to appease his safety fears. At the same time he does not worry about dirt or germs. In his case, the total amount of impairment caused by his OCD would be based on time consumed by those rituals he performs that relate to his safety concerns and the interference they cause to his daily routines.

A child, on average, goes through four obsessions before reaching adulthood, and each may be very different than the one before. Again, the main issue when determining whether he has OCD is to what extent any of these behaviors seriously disrupt his everyday life.

Tests for OCD

There is no blood analysis, X-ray, or other medical test yet available to confirm the presence of OCD in an adult or child. As is the case with all other mental illnesses (with the exception of Alzheimer's disease), OCD must instead be diagnosed through the observation of behavioral symptoms and a comparison of those symptoms to the criteria for OCD listed in the DSM-IV.

Essential

Because you are with your child all the time, you may not be the first to notice her OCD symptoms. Someone who doesn't see her every day, such as a grandparent, family friend, coach, or teacher, may observe the behaviors before you do. It's important to be open to this kind of feedback, as it often speeds the process of recognition so that you can then take necessary action to find help for your child sooner.

When a suitable medical or mental health practitioner is found to perform your child's OCD diagnostic assessment, there may be a lengthy waiting period before you can schedule an appointment with that person. Once you do, the process of evaluation can take three or more appointments to complete. These appointments require participation by parents and children. Younger children are often tested with their parents present, while adolescents are more frequently tested separately.

Question?

What is the CY-BOCS test?
CY-BOCS is the most widely used clinical tool for making a diagnosis of childhood OCD. CY-BOCS stands for Children's Yale-Brown Obsessive Compulsive Scale. This test surveys your child's past and present OCD symptoms by rating their frequency on a scale of one to four. Clinicians administer CY-BOCS tests to patients and their parents, usually in the clinician's office.

A Baseline for Testing OCD Behaviors

Of the several behavioral tests developed by medical researchers to formalize the process of OCD diagnosis, the most universally accepted test is called the Yale-Brown Obsessive Compulsive Scale or Y-BOCS. An adaptation of the same test for children, called CY-BOCS, is used with patients between the ages of four and eighteen. In all cases, a clinician administers this test, with different versions of questions concerning the child's obsessions and compulsions addressed to both the parent and child. This is usually done in separate sessions except for the very young patient. The outcome of this test will set the baseline for your child's OCD, establishing the level of severity of her disorder.

Sample the CY-BOCS Test

Here are some sample statements about OCD behaviors from the CY-BOCS test. A patient or parent rates the relevancy of these statements using frequency as their primary criterion. Since younger children often have less self-awareness, a parent's answers can provide an important confirmation of the child's typical OCD behaviors.

The scale used begins with zero, for behaviors occurring the least often, and goes up to four, with four representing the most frequently occurring behaviors.

- Excessive cleaning of items such as personal clothes or important objects
- Checking that he or she did not/will not harm others
- The need to involve another person (usually parent) in ritual, such as asking a parent to repeatedly answer the same question, making mother perform certain mealtime rituals involving specific utensils
- Need to touch, tap, rub

Another commonly used test is a self-exam for OCD called the Leyton Obsessional Inventory or LOI-CV. Although it is considered helpful as a preliminary step for measuring OCD symptoms in adults, adolescents, and children, a recent NIMH study compared results from the two tests with later diagnoses of OCD and concluded the clinician-administered CY-BOCS yields more accurate data than the LOI-CV, especially when the LOI-CV self-test is taken by young people. One concern raised by this study is that the LOI-CV test, when used by children and adolescents without a clinician's assistance, tends to underestimate the prevalence of OCD. Still, while not replacing a clinical exam, the LOI-CV test can be a valuable diagnostic tool for parents and children to use at home.

Other Tests for Childhood OCD

In the process of obtaining a diagnosis for your child you may encounter other tests. Some of these will address other anxiety disorders that may be present in your child. One reason anxiety tests are often given to children presenting symptoms of OCD is the large percentage of young OCD sufferers who have at least one other anxiety disorder in addition to OCD. The well-established co-occurrence clinically referred to as *comorbidity* of OCD with other anxiety disorders often means that your child's treatment will address more than one mental health disorder simultaneously.

 Fact

Eighty percent of children and adolescents who have OCD also have one or more additional anxiety disorder. The most common second disorders seen in children with OCD are attention deficit hyperactivity disorder and social phobia. There is also a higher risk of depression in children with OCD.

One commonly administered test for anxiety disorders is called Screen for Child Anxiety Related Disorders, with the acronym SCARED. This test has a version for both parents and children. You will notice the questions in the SCARED test have a more general tone than the OCD tests described above. For example, the SCARED test presents a child with the following statements about himself to which he can respond "not true," "somewhat true," or "very true."

- When I get frightened my heart beats fast.
- I get really frightened for no reason at all.
- I follow my mother and father wherever they go.

In contrast to SCARED, the CY-BOCS test asks children to rate the applicability to themselves of far more OCD-specific behaviors.

The Moment of Truth: Hearing the Diagnosis

Even if you are fairly certain of your child's diagnosis of OCD prior to testing, hearing a doctor or therapist say the words, "Your son has obsessive-compulsive disorder" can still be an emotional, even traumatic, event. Perhaps you were hoping to have your suspicions proven wrong. Many parents describe this as a "moment of truth" when time appears to move in slow motion, resulting in whole parts of the conversation being missed or misunderstood.

If you are going to hear the news, with or without your child, it may make sense to bring another adult with you for this appointment. Your spouse, another family member, or close friend can offer emotional support and help you recall details you may otherwise miss. Another good idea is to bring paper and pen so that you can take notes during or immediately after the appointment.

Discussing Diagnosis and Treatment Options

Because the CY-BOCS test uses a scale to evaluate the severity of OCD symptoms based on their quantity and frequency, it's important to ask where on the scale your child's symptoms are located; at a high, low, or medium level of severity. As your test giver will likely explain, this initial test result will be kept in your child's clinical file and serve as an important reference point against which to evaluate the course of his OCD. The test can also detect the possible appearance of new compulsions, which can then be added to the list of behaviors to be tackled in exposure exercises should you move into a cognitive behavioral therapy (CBT) treatment phase.

 Fact

CY-BOCS test scores measure the number and severity of OCD symptoms, providing a detailed picture of the state of your child's disorder at a given time. The score is also used as an objective, quantitative measure of the progress of his OCD treatment. A lower score on a CY-BOCS test (indicating fewer, less severe symptoms) done three or six months after your child's initial assessment provides valuable feedback on the progress of treatment. When such reductions occur, it also provides cause for celebration and rewards for progress.

Seek Recommendations for Treatment

After receiving a diagnosis of OCD, there are some important options to consider regarding your child's treatment. At this stage you are only gathering information. A decision on how to proceed may be weeks, months, even years away. For now, you should obtain your therapist or doctor's thoughts on the suitability for your child of each of four options for OCD treatment.

- Monitor his behavior (Do not seek immediate treatment)
- Begin psychotherapy
- Begin medication
- Begin simultaneous therapy and medication

The primary issue guiding the choice of whether to treat or not, or to choose among treatment options, will be the severity of your child's symptoms. When and if you decide to obtain formal treatment for your child's OCD, the preferred treatment according to consensus guidelines published in the 1997 *Journal of Psychiatry* is a type of talk therapy called Cognitive Behavioral Therapy (CBT). This form of therapy is discussed in detail in Chapter 8. Because the medical practitioner (psychiatrist, other M.D., psychologist, or other licensed therapist) who diagnoses your child's OCD may not be the same person who eventually treats him, you should receive (along with your child's test results and diagnosis) the names and contact numbers of therapists or others who are qualified to treat OCD in your local area.

Alert!

If your child's OCD symptoms are extremely severe, a clinician may suggest an immediate course of antidepressant medication, an option that should be thoroughly discussed with the doctor (psychiatrist or other physician) who prescribes the medication and (if it's not the same person) the OCD specialist who makes the initial diagnosis. Potential side effects caused by medication need to be weighed against the possible dangers of not acting.

What if It's Wrong? Misdiagnosis Rates with OCD

Statistics point to an average of four doctors or specialists visited over a nine-year period for individuals who eventually received the diagnosis of OCD. Because this average reflects the recent past when OCD expertise was less common in the medical community than it is now, it is likely that this rate of misdiagnosis will fall rapidly in the years to come. However, there are still many reports from parents whose children have received erroneous diagnoses of bipolar disorder or who were told their child's problem was strictly behavioral, thus fixable by a different parenting style. Another common occurrence is a mistaken diagnostic emphasis on another disorder within the OCD spectrum (such as ADHD or social anxiety), which is not your child's primary presenting condition. This mistaken emphasis on a lesser problem can thwart treatment because the debilitating symptoms of OCD usually need to be brought under control before other treatment progress can be made.

Because diagnostic inaccuracy is so common in the mental health field, it behooves you as a health-care consumer acting on your child's behalf to be as vocal and persistent as you can in obtaining both an accurate formal diagnosis from the most qualified professional you can find and the best treatment for your child's OCD. For example, if your doctor states her preference for a type of therapy (other than CBT or its offshoot, Exposure Response Prevention, ERP) that is not usually recommended for OCD, you can press her for names and dates of studies to back up this recommendation. The results of the latest research studies are frequently available online on the Web sites of NIMH and other public sources for medical information listed in Appendix B.

Given the high level of comorbidity of OCD with other anxiety disorders and the similarity between symptoms associated with OCD and other disorders including autism and depression, a second opinion for your child may well be in order. The need to obtain another diagnosis to confirm or dispute the one you've already obtained should always be weighed against the emotional and physical toll that another round of testing will take on your child.

Talking about His Diagnosis

There are likely to be two different and contradictory emotions going on in your child when he receives a definitive OCD diagnosis. One will almost certainly be a feeling of relief, even liberation, from his conscious or unconscious fear that he's the only one suffering from this strange and unrelenting ailment. Now, at least, he has a name for what he experiences as relentless anxiety or excess worry. This is an important time to reassure by telling him there are effective treatments available for OCD.

Other useful points to make include the following:

- OCD is as common as diabetes in young people, a disease he's probably heard much more about.
- With a prevalence of OCD in children between 1 and 2 percent, there are likely to be at least four to five other students at his elementary school (given an average elementary school population of 400), and up to twenty if he's in high school, all dealing with OCD.

For more help in dealing with the implications of your child's OCD in the school setting, see Chapter 11.

How to Talk about Being "Different"

The flip side of his reaction of relief may be a new or increased fear of being different from other kids. In fact, he may balk at being given a label of any kind. This understandable reaction undoubtedly has to do with the social stigma surrounding mental illness in the culture at large. At school, kids with disabilities are often shunned or teased. Your child is no doubt aware of this negative behavior; he may have already suffered from some teasing at school. There is no question this behavior is insensitive and unfair, but you do your child no good by pretending it cannot happen to him. It's far better for him to be forewarned about this possibility, and to have a response prepared.

You can offer further reassurance by making the following points:

- Having OCD is not the same as being psychotic or insane. It's an illness much like asthma or diabetes. And like these illnesses, it can be managed with treatment and practice.
- Treatment for OCD can lessen and even eliminate most, if not all, of his symptoms.

- By getting to know other kids who are dealing with OCD in therapeutic settings, he'll learn strategies for dealing with the illness in public. He may choose to laugh about it, explain it, or ignore it. There are different tactics for different situations.
- Like anyone else with an illness, adult or child, he is entitled to privacy about his medical status, including OCD. It's up to him whom he tells and does not tell.

The bottom line for your child is the knowledge that whatever happens, he's not alone. The most important thing you can do is to let him know you are there for him and will be for as long as it takes to get a handle on the OCD.

OCD Is Not All Bad

You might also talk with your child about the benefits of OCD. Yes, you read that correctly. As discussed in Chapter 2, there is a wide spectrum of severity in the disorder called obsessive-compulsive, and at its lower end are the behaviors people often describe as those of a perfectionist. And, frankly, among these behaviors are some of the best strategies for success in life and work. Of course, this is a superfluous topic until and unless his worst OCD symptoms are tamed.

After he gets the upper hand on his symptoms, the tendencies created by this disorder can in certain circumstances help make your child's day-to-day life work better. This is true, if, for example, he has high standards for cleanliness and tidiness in his personal space and hygiene. And, you can point out it's a good thing to wash one's hands before eating or after using the restroom. Likewise, checking homework for errors contributes to good study habits, an excellent strategy for academic success. It's only when he has to perform any of these behaviors incessantly that they become onerous.

Isn't all this obvious, you ask? Although it may appear so, don't underestimate the power of positive encouragement in any form for a young person struggling to gain control over his OCD. Owning the part of him that "works" is as important as disowning the part that doesn't work!

CHAPTER 7

Differentiating OCD from Other Childhood Disorders

In its symptoms, causes, and treatment options, OCD has a great deal in common with several other neurobiological and anxiety disorders affecting children. If your child has OCD and you've seen reports about autism, for example, you've probably recognized the similarity between their symptoms, especially repetitive behaviors, restlessness, and emotional withdrawal. OCD can also look a lot like other anxiety disorders, including social anxiety, attention deficit hyperactivity disorder, and eating disorders. Because of these similarities, it's important to know basic facts about each disorder and the key symptoms that distinguish one from another. This knowledge will help you obtain a more speedy and accurate diagnosis for your child.

What You Should Know Before Seeking Help

As the parent of a child with OCD you will be greatly helped by learning the basic vocabulary used by medical and mental health professionals when discussing childhood mental disorders; for example, the word *comorbidity*, which refers to the co-occurrence of more than more disorder in a single patient. Another commonly used word is *neurotransmitter* (specifically serotonin and dopamine), meaning the brain chemicals whose malfunctioning is suspected in many of these disorders. Think of this new body of knowledge as a crib sheet or scorecard to have in hand as you begin a fast-moving new game with its own language and rules.

Before you read on to learn about several other anxiety disorders, it may help to address the use of the word *disorder*. Many parents get hung up on the idea that their child might be classified as having one, let alone two or more overlapping mental health disorders. A leading mental health professional in the OCD treatment field, Bradley C. Riemann, Ph.D., Clinical Director of The Obsessive Compulsive Disorder at Rodgers Memorial Hospital in Wisconsin, offers some insights into the use of the word *disorder* on the Obsessive-Compulsive Foundation teen Web site, Organized Chaos:

> Many times I see a confused or frightened look on [patients' and parents'] faces. You can almost read their minds thinking, "Oh my God, I have a disorder! Am I crazy?" The answer is "No." Having a disorder does not make you crazy. . . . The word disorder is simply the term doctors use to describe the interference or disruption that the obsessions and compulsions that you are experiencing are causing in your life. . . . The object of treatment for OCD is to reduce the obsessions and compulsions to a point where they are no longer causing interference or disorder in your life.

Out of necessity parents today are becoming much more involved with their children's mental healthcare, including diagnosis, treatment options, and related advocacy efforts. You may wish to join a parent support group as soon as you see indications of a mental health disorder in your child. Educational opportunities abound in these organizations; many are listed in Appendix B.

The Link to Anxiety Disorders

Anxiety disorders is an umbrella term for a related group of mental health conditions characterized by nervousness, worry, restlessness, and excessive difficulties in such areas as social interactions, eating, sleeping, and coping with stressful situations. OCD is one anxiety disorder. Researchers believe the same neurotransmitter malfunctions trigger OCD and several other anxiety disorders. There is also growing evidence that the specific genetic mutations linked to these illnesses may also overlap. And yet, each condition under the broad category of anxiety disorders has its own list of primary symptoms.

 Fact

More than one anxiety disorder occurring in the same patient is more common than not, especially in children. A study of children with OCD done in 2003 reported that only 26 percent of the children surveyed had OCD as their only diagnosis. When a child has another anxiety disorder in addition to OCD, her OCD can be more difficult to diagnose and treat.

Give yourself time to learn about these disorders. There is a lot to absorb, and you can't do it all at once. One excellent way to begin is by participating in an online support community for parents dealing with mental health issues in children, such as those offered on Yahoo Groups and other sites. When you hear from other parents about the symptoms and solutions they're confronting in their children, it can help shed light on what at first are just vague medical terms and diagnoses.

In addition to OCD, the other anxiety disorders include the following:

- Social anxiety disorder (SAD)
- Attention deficit hyperactivity disorder (ADHD)
- Eating disorders
- Body dysmorphic disorder (BDD)
- Panic disorder

- Generalized anxiety disorders (GAD)
- Post-traumatic stress disorder (PTSD)

Anxiety disorders are the most common mental illnesses in the United States, with an estimated forty million adults (18.1 percent) over the age of eighteen affected. More details on each disorder follow, with special attention paid to similarities and differences when compared to OCD.

Social Anxiety Disorder (SAD)

Also called social phobia, social anxiety disorder (SAD) affects an estimated fifteen million adults, 6.8 percent of the U.S. population. Of all the childhood anxiety disorders, social anxiety disorder is the most common. SAD also affects children at a younger age than any of the other anxiety disorders.

SAD is diagnosed in a child or teenager when she becomes overwhelmingly self-conscious in everyday social situations. Much more than a tendency toward shyness, the socially phobic child has an intense fear of being watched and judged by other people. She may become terrorized by her fear of making mistakes and becoming embarrassed. A youngster with social anxiety disorder may harbor dread about the start of school or a birthday party for days or weeks in advance. She may develop stomach ailments, feign an illness, or refuse to leave her room.

Because social phobia is one of the more deceptive anxiety disorders, affected children can appear fine on the outside, even friendly and occasionally outgoing, while on the inside they suffer a debilitating fear of negative scrutiny.

Their choice of activities may reflect this disorder. For example, a child with SAD may opt repeatedly for online role-playing games, rather than accept invitations for in-person socializing. They may also dislike talking on the telephone.

The child with SAD experiences silent suffering that may only become apparent to you as a parent when you notice your child opting out of social situations on a regular basis and, by choice, spending an inordinate amount of time alone.

Essential

The similarities between the social withdrawal common in kids with social phobia and the isolating behavior in OCD children are self-evident. What is not always as clear is whether OCD is the underlying cause of a child's social anxiety, or if her social anxiety adds additional issues to the OCD. Where SAD appears to be present with OCD, additional testing for this anxiety disorder will confirm that fact.

Supplementary treatment, especially Shyness Groups, an effective form of exposure response prevention (ERP) therapy focused on social anxiety, is often of value to a child with OCD who is also suffering from social anxiety disorder.

Eating Disorders

The eating disorders called anorexia nervosa (obsessive restriction of food) and bulimia (forced purging) tend to begin in the preteen years and worsen in later adolescence. The severe weight loss associated with anorexia nervosa and sometimes bulimia results from a young girl's distorted view of her body as overweight. Ninety percent of people with eating disorders are female.

Eating disorders can affect girls as young as seven years old. Many in the medical community have gone so far as to call the increase in eating disorders in the United States over the last two decades an epidemic. Many anorexic girls literally starve themselves, giving anorexia nervosa the highest mortality rates among all childhood anxiety disorders. Obsessive exercise often accompanies the girl's starving behavior and sometimes causes parents to overlook the destructive impact of the disorder, so it's important to look beyond the generally positive effects on children of regular exercise to whether your child is keeping a minimum body weight for her age and height.

As many parents are increasingly aware, the cultural messages being received by preteen and adolescent girls often overemphasize thinness as an ideal and ridicule curves and larger-sized females. This can put enormous pressure on any young girl as she enters puberty, but for the preteen girl with OCD the stress can be especially burdensome. This issue can be made even more difficult if the child is taking a type of antidepressant that can cause weight gain as a side effect. When confronted with this delicate situation, parents need to keep the lines of communication as open as possible with their children. If you believe your child is developing symptoms of anorexia nervosa or bulimia, it is a serious issue that requires therapeutic intervention.

Obsessions with Food

Studies confirm that teenagers with OCD are at a much higher risk of developing a co-occurring eating disorder. Like many young girls and boys with OCD, children suffering from eating disorders have an intense preoccupation with food. Sufferers of both disorders often insist on cutting up their meals into small pieces, often saving their food rather than eating it at mealtimes. Many also develop irrational fears about the food they eat. These fears often involve contamination. The child may imagine germs or parasites on the food, even if there is no visible evidence to support this suspicion.

With both OCD and eating disorders, a child's food obsession can lead him to eat substantially less than he should. Both disorders can also cause an extreme self-consciousness about appearance. More information on teens with OCD and their vulnerability to eating disorders is in Chapter 13.

Body Dysmorphic Disorder (BDD)

People with BDD are plagued by a serious, persistent dislike and concern about some slight or imagined aspect of their appearance, causing them significant emotional distress and difficulties. This disorder can affect anyone, male or female, and often begins in early adolescence. BDD frequently co-occurs with eating disorders, anxiety disorders, and OCD.

Body dysmorphic disorder (BDD) shares with OCD several symptoms including an obsession with appearance, avoidance of social situations, and many repetitive behaviors, including excessive grooming, washing, and tics.

Attention Deficit Hyperactivity Disorder (ADHD)

ADHD is the most commonly diagnosed mental disorder in young people today, affecting an estimated 3 to 5 percent of school-age children. ADHD is characterized by inattention, hyperactivity, and impulsivity. These children struggle with a lack of inhibition and an excess of activity. The similarities between ADHD and OCD include the child's tendency to make repetitive motions and talk incessantly. Both OCD and ADHD children are at higher risk to develop the motor and vocal tics associated with Tourette's syndrome.

One important difference between OCD and attention deficit hyperactivity disorder is their customary course of treatment. Whereas CBT, a form of behavior modification psychotherapy, is the preferred first method of treatment for OCD, followed by an SSRI antidepressant, children with attention deficit hyperactivity disorder more often receive a stimulant medication (examples are Adderal and Ritalin) and less frequently participate in CBT.

Other Anxiety Disorders

Because of the high rate of comorbidity between OCD and the other anxiety disorders, each of the less frequently occurring of these is listed below. Special attention should be paid to any characteristics of these disorders you've witnessed in your child in addition to those specific to OCD. If these symptoms continue longer than a month, make a point to add what you've observed to your discussion with the doctor or therapist who eventually evaluates your child's OCD.

Generalized Anxiety Disorder (GAD)

GAD is characterized by constant, extreme worry about everyday things, sometimes for no known cause. For those adults and children suffering from this disorder, worry goes on for the greater part of the day, and often into the night.

Physical symptoms of GAD include the following:

- Sleeplessness
- Stomach and digestive problems
- Irritability

The demeanor of a child with GAD is defined by pervasive worry. Her worries can attach to just about anything: personal safety, a natural disaster, parents' divorce, the family running out of money, and, perhaps most commonly, their own school failure. One salient difference distinguishing the worrying that characterizes GAD (from OCD) is the child's tendency to follow her fear in a more or less logical direction, for example, one failed test can lead to her not getting into a preferred college. The child with OCD taking the same test might take her fear in a wholly illogical direction; for example, the scary notion that one failed test might lead to a parent's death.

Post-Traumatic Stress Disorder (PTSD)

This anxiety disorder can affect children as well as adults. PTSD is connected to traumatic events, which, in a child, may include sexual or physical abuse that has caused him intense fear, helplessness, or horror.

Like OCD sufferers, those with PTSD experience intrusive, incessant images and disturbing thoughts. In both disorders, commonplace events and things in the environment, including being bumped in a crowd, loud noises, and public restroom facilities, can trigger compulsions. With OCD, many parents report that traumatic events, such as the loss of a parent, physical illness in the child or the family, or an accident, have triggered the onset of OCD in their children. When OCD and PTSD are both present, it is usually necessary to treat both issues. However, when both conditions are present, special concern must be taken to not conduct CBT exposures relating to triggers that connect too closely to the emotional areas most traumatized earlier in the child's life. This special requirement for treating PTSD necessarily makes its treatment come first.

Panic Disorder, Specific Phobias

Panic disorders are more common in adult women than any other group, but they are also seen in teens and less often in younger children. Panic disorder is characterized by sudden physical symptoms, including dizziness, increased heart rate, cold sweats, headaches, and trouble with breathing. The so-called panic "attacks" that result from this disorder are associated with specific triggers or with an unknown cause. Panic disorders have a high comorbidity rate with depression.

Specific phobias are outsized fears of a specific place or thing, including water, heights, or a more generalized fear of the outdoors. Phobias frequently lead the sufferer to an extreme avoidance of the thing he fears.

Given the tendencies within each of these disorders for the sufferer to strenuously avoid the objects of her obsession, a parallel exists with avoidance behaviors commonly associated with OCD. Treatment for panic disorder and specific phobias is also often the same as that provided for OCD, especially the use of habituation and controlled exposures to the fearful things as a way for the sufferer to lesson her fears.

The Autism Spectrum

Autism Spectrum Disorder (ASD) is an increasingly common diagnosis (affecting anywhere from 1 to 2 children per 500 to 1 per 100) in children involving neurological impairments in the processing of information, communication, and social interaction. Autism Spectrum Disorder, unlike OCD, is not classified as an anxiety disorder.

There is an ongoing debate about whether the prevalence of ASD is exploding in the population or whether it is simply being recognized more frequently. Symptoms of autism vary from the very mild to severe. More boys than girls are diagnosed with Autism Spectrum Disorder, especially Asperger's syndrome, which is sometimes called "high-functioning autism," but is, in fact, a distinct disorder. Because it does not involve significant developmental delays, Asperger's often goes undiagnosed until a child reaches adolescence or young adulthood.

Alert!

Asperger's syndrome is considered part of the autism spectrum, but unlike classic autism it does not involve significant delays in language or cognitive development. It is marked by impairments in nonverbal interactions such as eye contact and facial expressions. Children with Asperger's have trouble making friends and exhibit an unusual preoccupation with one or more stereotypical interests (frequently quantitative or mechanical) and parts of objects.

An autistic child appears overloaded by sensory stimuli and frequently retreats into "a world of his own." In addition to developmental delays, the most common area of difficulty for a child with autism is his interactions with others, including family, teachers, and peers. Eye contact is often a problem. There can be significant problems in speech and other cognitive milestones, and an absence of emotions and imaginative play. Frequently, an autistic child displays an intense focus on a particular subject, activity, or object.

What if My Child Has Autism and OCD?

As may be immediately apparent to you as the parent of a child with OCD, there are similarities between the core symptoms of OCD and autism. Chief among these are the affected child's repetitive behaviors and excessive need for order. Children with autism and OCD will frequently be seen lining up toys and other objects in their environment. The co-occurrence of these two disorders in children is not uncommon. In fact, it's unusual for someone with autism to not exhibit some OCD behaviors. What is more problematic is if a child who has been diagnosed with OCD exhibits some of the symptoms of the autism spectrum, but these go unrecognized and untreated.

Both of these disorders require serious attention. If you have an intuitive sense that your child's symptoms go beyond OCD to those more closely associated with autism, you should bring this concern to the attention of your doctor or mental health professional as early as possible. By doing so, you may be able to take advantage of many recent advances in the early detection of autism in infants and toddlers. Researchers have been able to identify autistic tendencies, such as avoidance of eye contact or the lack of a startle response to noises, in infants as young as six months old.

Early intervention with infants and toddlers with autism has been demonstrated to have a positive effect, in many cases enhancing a child's ability to sustain social interactions through targeted therapy encouraging eye contact, touch, and verbal development.

Alert!

In 2007, the American Pediatric Association initiated new autism testing guidelines for infants and toddlers. These guidelines reflect the consensus in favor of the advantages of early testing and therapeutic intervention for autism. Pediatricians were instructed to test for signs of autism at well baby visits a minimum of two times before the child reaches the age of two.

Tourette's Syndrome (TS)

Involuntary and often repetitive motions or verbalizations called tics characterize Tourette's syndrome, or TS. There is no question that Tourette's syndrome and OCD are linked and frequently comorbid. A child may have the tics associated with Tourette's syndrome for many years without you realizing it. There is a wide range of symptom severity with Tourette's. Some of these common tics are fairly invisible to others:

- Eye-rolling
- Coughing
- Forehead touching
- Frequent intakes of breath
- Head turning

Frequently, a parent and even the child with OCD will become aware of the presence of these tics only after they are defined as tics and brought to their attention. Other tics are more obvious and disruptive:

- Incessant laughing
- The need to say whatever comes into her head
- Jerking a hand or arm into the air

For the child with OCD, these tics are often the most noticeable aspect of his disorder and the most difficult to control. Here's how J.Z., age seventeen, described his experience on the OCF Chicago teen Web site:

> Tics come and go, and I had quite a parade: sniffing tics, grunting tics, slurping, whistling, humming, tics in my hands, legs, and neck, and even a shrugging tic that gave me whiplash. . . . In sixth grade the mental anguish of OCD joined the physical torment of Tourette's. I had scrupulosity (fear of hell, compulsive praying), and contamination obsessions. I couldn't sleep because my mind swirled with dread of hanta virus and eternal damnation. I couldn't eat for fear that chemical residue from science class might be on my hands. The grades took a nosedive.

Fortunately, J.Z. found help for both his OCD and Tourette's syndrome from ERP exposures. As he summed up his experience of therapy, "ERP works. I learned how to manage the OCD and get on with my life."

How Depression Plays a Role

If your child suffers from OCD (or any other anxiety disorder), he is at an increased risk for developing depression. It is important to note however that the appearance of symptoms of depression more frequently result indirectly from the stress of dealing with his OCD rather than as a direct manifestation of this mood disorder. For a parent, it is often difficult to differentiate between these two possibilities without the involvement of a mental health professional. Psychological testing is one way to determine whether depression and anxiety—or any other pair of anxiety disorders—is the child's primary presenting issue.

Depression is a serious clinical condition characterized by hopelessness and lethargy that can only add to your child's difficulties in dealing with his OCD. Other primary symptoms of depression include the following:

- Persistent sad mood
- Feelings of guilt or worthlessness
- Fatigue or decreased energy
- Sleep disturbances
- Feelings of helplessness or hopelessness
- Changes in appetite
- Irritability
- Difficulty concentrating or making decisions
- Memory problems
- Thoughts of death or suicide

For a quarter of children with OCD, depressive episodes are severe and frequent enough to be considered major, chronic depression requiring treatment. Given the additional difficulties faced by the OCD preteen or teenager trying to fit in and succeed at school, and the natural moodiness of adolescence, any amount of depression is an issue of concern for the parents of the older child with OCD, particularly teens.

Learning Disabilities

Learning disabilities are neurologically based information processing problems that tend to arise in a child's elementary school years. These problems interfere with his learning of basic skills, including reading and writing or math. They can also add difficulties to his higher-level skills, such as organization, time management and abstract reasoning. The most common learning disability is dyslexia, which affects language and reading.

Common symptoms of learning disabilities include:

- Short attention span
- Poor reading and/or writing ability
- Poor memory
- Problems telling right from left and telling time
- Difficulties with sequencing
- Reverses letters
- Delayed speech development, immature speech

While the child with OCD may have difficulty finishing his homework or concentrating in school because of the demands and distractions caused by his obsessions and compulsions, a learning disability is a separate issue that could require therapeutic intervention. If your child with OCD frequently displays symptoms of a learning disability, he should be tested separately for this possibility. As is the case with many childhood disorders, specific therapies have been developed to help a child cope with learning disabilities. And as is frequently the case, the sooner they are addressed, the better for your child. Fortunately, many school districts have developed tutoring programs for learning-disabled students. See Chapter 11 for guidance on accessing these programs.

Common Dual and Multiple Diagnoses

By the sheer volume of overlapping symptoms for the disorders discussed in this chapter, it has no doubt become more apparent why the diagnosis of your child's OCD is neither a simple nor speedy matter. If you take one message from this chapter, it's the frequent comorbidity of OCD with other anxiety disorders in young children. If your child has the symptoms of, for example, social anxiety in addition to OCD, your doctor's treatment choices, including a specific course of therapy and medications, would differ slightly than if the symptoms of ADHD were also present. As you become more informed and conversant in these disorders, symptoms, and treatments, you will become the best advocate for your child's care.

CHAPTER 8

Deciding on Treatment: CBT

After you've obtained a definitive diagnosis of childhood OCD, your child is much closer to getting the help she needs. The doctor or therapist who makes the diagnosis will in most cases also give you a recommendation for her treatment. Any direction you receive on treatment should reflect the guidance provided in 1997 by the American Psychiatric Association, which issued its *consensus guidelines* in favor of Cognitive Behavioral Therapy (CBT) as the preferred first course of treatment for OCD. You may also be referred at this time to a psychiatrist for a medication consultation. The question of medication for childhood OCD is covered in depth in Chapter 9.

How CBT Works

It is important to know right from the start of your child's treatment that the specific type of cognitive behavioral therapy for the treatment of OCD is not the same as traditional psychotherapy or what is sometimes called "talk therapy." Cognitive behavioral therapy was first employed in the treatment of OCD in 1996. The *cognitive* in cognitive behavioral therapy refers to the thought process behind a person's behavior. In cognitive approaches to therapy, a therapist works to change his client's belief system so that unproductive behaviors will be dropped. The process by which a cognitive therapist tries to change the patient's thoughts in order to change her behavior is sometimes called "reframing." The word *behavioral* addresses the actions that result directly from someone's thoughts. If, for example, your child washes her hands six times before dinner, the belief behind her behavior is the mistaken idea that only by excessively washing will she avoid depositing dangerous germs she picked up in the course of her day on her meal.

CBT therapy for OCD goes one step further than simply aiming to change a client's thoughts in order to influence her behavior; using Exposure Response Prevention techniques (ERP), it exposes the OCD sufferer to the things he fears in order to gradually reduce his levels of anxiety.

In this process, OCD sufferers are given exercises where they agree to touch or focus on the things that trigger their anxiety in the form of an obsession. By gradually increasing time and contact with a feared thing or situation, they become *habituated* to their fear to the point where it no longer causes them the level of discomfort it once did. These structured exposure exercises are the foundation of the type of therapy adults and children with OCD use in order to manage their disorder for life.

For example, many children with OCD experience anxiety when they use public toilets. As a result of this anxiety, a contamination obsession takes over the child's mind whenever she's faced with the possibility of using a toilet outside of the family home. To deal with this particular obsession, CBT treatment involves the child in gradually increased exposures to public toilets. She might first go near a public restroom without actually using it. Next, she might stand next to it for longer periods. Then she might go inside and touch the toilet. Finally, she would use the toilet and do so without compensating with a compulsive prayer or ritual. This process is also called habituation. The goal of a CBT exposure is to give your child both the tools and practice to help her fight back against her OCD by confronting the anxiety behind her OCD in whatever manifestation it may take.

Unlike other forms of therapy, CBT for the treatment of childhood OCD should involve homework in the form of exposure exercises done outside of the therapist's office. With childhood OCD, this homework will necessarily involve one or both of the child's parents. Given the importance of ERP homework, the therapist you choose should be available between weekly appointments to take your phone calls or e-mails in order to answer any questions that may arise in the course of home ERP therapy.

Finding the Right Therapist

The main criteria to use when choosing a therapist for your child with OCD is whether he has had prior experience treating OCD using cognitive behavioral therapy (CBT), specifically the approach known as exposure response prevention (ERP). Because the preferred first course of treatment for OCD is psychotherapy, you are not restricted to psychiatrists or psychiatric nurse practitioners (the only mental healthcare providers who can prescribe medications) when choosing the provider with whom your child will learn CBT. But caution is advised.

In the following, Dr. Michael Jenike explains what he considers the essential things a parent must know in order to choose a behavioral therapist to treat childhood OCD. Dr. Jenike is Professor of Psychiatry, Harvard Medical School, and Associate Chief of Psychiatry and Research Psychiatrist and Director, Obsessive-Compulsive Disorders Clinic and Research Unit at Massachusetts General Hospital.

> You will need to ask the therapist what technique he or she uses to treat OCD. If the therapist has never heard of exposure and response prevention or is vague about discussing these treatments, it may be best to look elsewhere. You need to know what these techniques involve to interpret what you are being told. The exposure part of the therapy involves actually confronting the source of the anxiety and/ or discomfort. For example, a person afraid of contamination from public bathrooms will be asked to go with the therapist to a bathroom and touch some

"contaminated" item in the bathroom. The response prevention part of the therapy occurs when the patient does not wash her hands while feeling contaminated. Over time and with repeated sessions, the discomfort diminishes until the contaminated item no longer produces anxiety or discomfort. The behavior therapist then will have the patient similarly tackle an even more stressful situation until all of the fears have been confronted. This gradual process of exposing oneself to a fear situation and then not giving in to the ritualistic response is therapeutic for the patient. For many patients, pretreatment with medication makes the process less anxiety provoking and hastens or facilitates the overall improvement.

Parents are advised to learn as much as they can about developments in OCD treatment using CBT and ERP before selecting a mental healthcare provider to treat a child's OCD. Psychiatrists, psychologists, social workers, marriage and family therapists, and psychiatric nurse practitioners are all licensed to treat childhood OCD. As important as a license, however, is the issue of whether the provider under consideration has experience treating childhood OCD. To make sure, ask. Remember, ineffective treatment can be worse than no treatment at all, especially if it turns your child off from getting further help.

Asking for Referrals

When you ask for referrals from a pediatrician or from other parents, you cannot assume the referrer is familiar with the exposure response prevention methods you are looking for to treat your child's OCD. Someone may give you the name of an excellent psychotherapist who works with young people, but that person may not be a good fit for your child's current needs. To find out if a provider does the most appropriate form of CBT, you will have to ask specifically about his training and approach.

Even if there are other anxiety disorders or mental health conditions present, your child's OCD will likely need to be the focus of treatment until she gets her symptoms under control, depending on the severity of the OCD symptoms and the symptoms of the other disorders. A focus on OCD would then exclude (at least for the time being) other forms of psychotherapy, including family therapy, play therapy, "holistic" therapy, or psychoanalysis. Once her debilitating OCD behaviors are addressed, it's an excellent idea to bring the entire family together in family therapy to identify negative patterns of relationship among parents, siblings, and your child with OCD, and then work with a family therapist to change them for the better.

Questions for Therapists

When interviewing a potential therapist for your child's OCD treatment, there are several important issues to address. Your interview can take place in person or by telephone, but be sure to ask as many of the following questions as time permits:

- How many children have you treated successfully for OCD?
- What assessment tests do you do to determine OCD as her primary condition?
- Do you perform cognitive behavioral therapy with exposure response prevention?
- Can you teach my child to do ERP at home?
- How long should we expect treatment to take?
- Are you available between sessions for phone calls or e-mails?
- What is your opinion on the use of medication for childhood OCD?
- How do you involve parents in treatment?
- Would you consult with my child's school staff and other treatment providers?

Fact

Cognitive behavioral therapy has been successfully used to treat children as young as eight. One study of children with OCD showed that those whose parents were actively involved in CBT treatment made substantially more progress than those without strong parental involvement.

After you've gotten answers to your questions from a potential mental healthcare provider and you've determined the individual's technical competence, the final factor to consider is his "bedside manner." Is his style agreeable to both you and your child? You will have to trust your intuition on this. A good therapist should emanate warmth and reassurance while providing strong guidance on long- and short-term goals and methods to be used in your child's therapy. He should be patient and thorough when answering your questions and not overly dogmatic when discussing related topics.

Essential

Since you are going to openly discuss many intimate aspects of your lives with your child's therapist, the bottom line is for you and your child to feel safe with this person. There will be ups and downs and frustrations before treatment begins to pay off. Make sure this is someone who makes you feel very comfortable in saying whatever must be said.

The use of cognitive behavioral therapy including ERP for treatment of OCD was first developed for adults. Over the past twenty years, it has been refined to treat several anxiety disorders in addition to OCD, including social anxiety, PTSD, and phobias. It has also been adapted for children, largely through research and clinical work done by John S. March, M.D., of Duke University.

Dr. March calls his kid, and parent-friendly program "Talking Back to OCD," and he has a published book with the same title (see Appendix C). Many other mental healthcare providers are now using the Talking Back approach. One of its strengths is the specific guidance it offers parents on how to work with children at home in order to reinforce and expand upon techniques learned in formal sessions with therapists.

Exposure Response Prevention (ERP)

The specific CBT therapeutic technique used with OCD is called exposure response prevention or ERP. *Exposure* occurs when an OCD child allows herself to be exposed to the things that ordinarily trigger a compulsive response, be it the idea of germs on clothing, an imperfect (wrinkled) bedspread needing smoothing, or a situation where the child seeks constant reassurance from her mother about her fears regarding her mother's safety. It is these compulsive responses to specific triggers that the exercise is intended to prevent, thus the words *response prevention* in ERP.

Alert!

As you prepare to help your child with his CBT homework exercises, it's important to bring all other outside obligations for both of you to an absolute minimum. This means curtailing or stopping his sports, your PTA, late work hours, or whatever else might rob you of valuable time you need to help reinforce and monitor his progress with the challenging process of exposures and response prevention.

As in traditional cognitive behavioral therapy, the therapist using ERP identifies the specific faulty thinking behind behavior such as excessive hand washing. But he then adds the element of *habituation* to the therapeutic process. Habituation means the taming of obsessive fears by gaining the child's consent *to be exposed* to a particular trigger and then gradually decreasing the number or degree of compulsive behaviors it provokes with each exposure—thus *preventing* the response in the future.

Two examples of ERP in action: A twelve-year-old girl with a contamination fear agrees to decrease the number of times she washes her hands before dinner from twenty to ten, then she cuts back to five, four, and three, until she is able to wash only once. A seventeen-year-old boy with an obsessive fear that he's gay avoids all social contact with boys his own age. In his exposures he introduces brief periods of contact with male peers into his daily life, beginning with walking in the school hallway while other boys are also in transit, then building to joining a sports team.

In each of these cases, the child, in consultation with his therapist, selects each of these exposures. He then keeps a log of his progress in preventing the compulsions that normally result from the selected trigger and discusses what happened at his next therapy session.

As with most things, it helps to break the ERP process down into simpler parts. Your child, with your encouragement, does the following steps.

Identify the Problem

First, she charts the OCD triggers, noting the obsession behind each trigger and the compulsive behaviors linked to it. This can take the form of a list that makes a one-to-one correlation between each fearful thought and the "must do" action that will be addressed with ERP.

ERP Chart

Trigger	Obsession	Compulsion(s)
Family dog	Contamination fear	Put on gloves before petting
		Wash hands after touching
		Walk six feet away

Attack the Problem

After identifying an area of obsession and the compulsive behavior that she's ready to work on, your child decides on an immediate goal for her exposure. In this example, the child gives herself the goal of touching the dog without gloves, or not washing her hands after petting the dog's head. If both of those possibilities are still too scary for her, she can break her exposure target down into even smaller parts; for example, washing only twice after petting the dog.

Chart the Outcome

The outcome of each exercise will be the comparison between what she had to do previously to satisfy her compulsion, and what she does after the completion of her exercises. Especially as you begin exposure practice at home, it's important to keep a written record. This record should note each exposure target, the number of times each is practiced, and the outcome of each exercise.

When your child works at home on her ERP assignments, she gradually does each exposure long enough to reduce the anxiety level formerly associated with that particular OCD trigger. Compare it to staying seated in a very hot tub until you've habituated to the temperature. But, unlike the bathtub analogy, your child must repeat each exposure often enough so that she loses the anxiety from the start of her assignment and thereafter.

Question?

What does the habituation process in ERP feel like?
Bradley C. Riemann, Ph.D., compares the habituation that goes on in ERP therapy to the experience of sitting down in a tub of very hot water. At first, the temperature feels extremely hot, perhaps too hot to stay seated. However, if you stay put, you will become *habituated* to the hot water, to the point where you may believe the water temperature has cooled down. The fact is it hasn't. You've simply become habituated to the heat!

What to Expect When Therapy Begins

Although the principles of CBT are relatively simple to understand, the therapy is not easy to do. Exposures such as those described require huge changes in a child's thinking and behavior. And, like their adult counterparts, children resist change. Even if a child's OCD symptoms are oppressive and painful, and even if he's relieved to find out he's not the only child to have this disorder, the world of OCD is currently his "known world." Remember the old saying, "The devil you know is better than the one you don't." It's hard to let go of the devil you know.

Because of his natural resistance to the unfamiliar, your child may react to his treatment with a new burst of even more severe OCD behaviors than had been his norm. Think of this display of symptoms as a protest against the difficulty of what he's about to take on. It can also stem from his fear of failure. Children who have tried unsuccessfully for months or years to get a handle on their OCD symptoms on their own can have a very defeated and demoralized sense of what's possible.

You may find that your child suddenly drops the masks he'd been using to disguise his OCD symptoms from you. It's also likely that you're not aware of all the rituals he'd employed to get through a day at school. This new burst of visible OCD behaviors may give you the false impression that his OCD has gotten worse just as he begins therapy. True or not, your job is not to overreact to the (out) burst, no matter what form it takes.

Letting Your Child Take Charge

Particularly with children under the age of ten, ERP exposures can be a good fit with a child's age-appropriate desire to be "the boss." Younger children tend to like the notion of *talking back to OCD* even more than some of their teenage counterparts. Parents should seize on this bossiness as an asset in the therapeutic process.

Question?

How do I begin ERP therapy at home?
One of the first steps you can take at home (before visiting a therapist) is to encourage your child to pick a name for her OCD, something like Ms. Perfect, Mr. Pain in the Butt, or whatever appeals to her. The goal in naming the OCD is to create a sense of distance from it. In other words, to reinforce the idea that *she is not her OCD*; OCD is something she can separate from and gain control over.

Once she sees the OCD as separate from her core self, your child can acquire the detachment needed to objectively look at which behaviors she'd like to change. Only then will it be possible for her to get down to work.

One Therapist's View: Roxie's ERP Session

What follows is a simulated account of an ERP exposure session for a fictional fourteen-year-old client named Roxie. Roxie is a girl who suffered from untreated OCD for approximately five years before beginning CBT therapy.

> Whenever Roxie came to a closed door, she had to bow down in front of it, and then pry it open with her foot or elbow. Her contamination fear dictated that she could never touch the doorknob with her hands. Roxie had been opening doors this way for as long as she could remember, so long that no one at home even noticed anymore. But now Roxie was getting embarrassed at school when she had to go through a closed door. She wanted her rituals to stop.

> In order to make them stop, I told Roxie she would have to tell me in therapy exactly what would happen if she opened a door and didn't use her rituals—the bowing down and using elbows and feet and whatever else she used to stave off the disaster she feared.

> When I asked Roxie whether she'd rather go through the rest of her life using feet and elbows to open doors, she got visibly upset and began to cry. I asked her again to say what would happen if she touched the doorknob with her hand, and she reluctantly agreed.

> With tears falling down her face, Roxie began to describe her worst fear: how she'd come to the door to the gymnasium at school, and as soon as she touched it with her fingers, invisible germs would jump onto her from the doorknob, then these "creepy crawlies" as she called them would crawl up her arm, and infect her with AIDS. She then described a picture of herself lying in a hospital bed, her body emaciated and covered with sores. In this, her worst-

case scenario, Roxie's AIDS would quickly lead to her death, and her mom and dad would be sorry they'd ever made her go to school. Roxie's visualization ended with her tearful parents standing at their daughter's funeral casket. After she finished describing this scene, Roxie was exhausted, breathless, and perspiring.

After she'd recovered her breath, I congratulated Roxie for getting through this part of the exposure and asked her to notice the fact that she was quite alive and well. I then asked her if she was up to the task of performing the same visualization at least three times a day, every day, until our next session. She begrudgingly agreed.

Roxie returned the following week and reported her success at performing this exposure exercise for each of the seven days since I'd last seen her. I congratulated her again and then asked if she felt ready to do the very thing she feared—touching a real doorknob. Most difficult of all, Roxie would open an actual doorknob without using any of her usual rituals, no bowing down, no using feet and elbows, no counting, no prayers—nothing but her bare hands.

Roxie started at home, opening the front door, the door to the bathroom, and the door to her own room without using rituals. Her mom helped her keep a chart of her progress. But the real test came at school, where Roxie, on her own, finally got to the point where she could open the gymnasium door without using any of her old rituals. It was a major achievement.

Now Roxie can open doors at school and anywhere else she needs to. Not that it's always easy, she says. But if she gets into trouble again, Roxie knows what to do. She can go back to her exercises, picture her worst fear until the anxiety subsides, and then open a door the way everyone else does.

Although simulated, Roxie's story is entirely authentic. It's based on several clients who faced and defeated exactly the same level of fear and paralysis as the fictional Roxie.

Continuing Exposure Exercises at Home

Before trying your child's first ERP home exercise, the two of you need to come to an agreement about your role (and the roles of other family members) in his ERP process. Does he want you to record his ERP responses on a chart? Does he want to do them alone? Some of both? Even with this discussion, there will undoubtedly be tensions and difficulties as you begin the ERP process at home. Expect his fear level to rise as he approaches each new ERP exercise. Respond to his anxiety and frustration with calm and encouragement.

 Essential

Your most important roles are to support and be a cheerleader for your child in the ERP process. Any and all efforts he makes in attacking his OCD are to be applauded. Give him tangible rewards and praise at regular intervals as they are earned. Do not be his critic or scorekeeper. The child with OCD does plenty of self-criticism all by himself.

It is important to retain flexibility at all times when doing home ERP exercises. Your child's efforts are the key, not necessarily reaching a specific goal, as goals may need to be changed, broken into smaller parts, or simply deferred. There is additional advice on structuring exposure exercises and the best ways to use rewards, praise, and discipline in Chapters 14 and 16.

How Long Does Therapy Last?

The length of time needed for professional therapy varies depending on the severity of your child's OCD and his response to treatment. An initial course of CBT for OCD will usually last a minimum of twelve weeks of forty-five-minute sessions and may require up to twenty weeks.

If your child takes quickly to the ERP process and is diligent at recording his progress and monitoring his own behaviors, he may not require additional one-on-one therapy after twelve sessions. After an initial period of regular therapy, your child's therapist should remain available to you for regular (typically every three to four months) follow-up sessions, or for an "emergency" session in the event of a major slip or if a new obstacle comes up in your child's independent progress.

This is an area where the perfectionism of OCD can be turned to good purposes. That is, if it doesn't go too far. A sure way to sabotage progress in treating OCD is by having an all-or-nothing attitude. Conversely, one of the sure signs of success is when a perfectionist decides something is "good enough for now." And then there's the strong likelihood, make that a certainty, that he'll have slips and regressions in his progress along the way.

When You Live Far from Treatment Centers

If you are unable to find a competent therapist in your local area, you may have to change the timeframe in which you schedule treatment. Instead of arranging therapy on a once or twice a week basis, you can schedule several sessions over a shorter period of time. There may be a potential treatment provider located within traveling distance, for example, two to four hours from where you live.

In this case, you can set up several appointments with this provider over one to two weeks, with a goal of learning and practicing the techniques for exposure response prevention in the presence of the therapist. You and your child would then commit to doing the exercises at home, returning at regular intervals for further evaluation and re-testing with the provider.

If Your Child Refuses Treatment

There are several reasons why your child may resist treatment. With teenagers, there is a potential power struggle built into the equation. Namely, if it appears that sixteen-year-old Alex's parents want him to get better more than Alex does, therapy is far less likely to succeed. Unfortunately, it may not even begin.

Another area of difficulty concerns your position in relation to your child's OCD. You may begin this process as a parent who is enmeshed in your child's OCD behaviors. If he wants his clothes washed and dried multiple times before he puts them on in the morning, you've accommodated his request in order to "keep the peace" in your household. While this is an understandable and common response, it doesn't help your child deal with his OCD. To then suddenly have you stop enabling his compulsive behaviors could feel very threatening to your child. It can feel as if he's being forced to go "cold turkey" and become a completely different person than he's been all his life.

Your job at this juncture is to reassure him that his therapy will only go as fast as he can handle. In fact, be sure to let him know that he is completely in charge of what OCD symptoms will be tackled, in what order, and how fast the process will go.

Why Treatment Fails

CBT treatment for OCD is not easy. And there are many reasons why it may fail at various points in the process. Here are some of the typical reasons for failure or resistance to treatment, especially CBT therapy.

- The presence of comorbid disorders, such as major depression or bipolar disorder, interferes with your child's ability to participate in CBT therapy.
- Lack of open, effective communication between the child and his therapist.
- Insufficient number or frequency of therapy sessions.
- Inadequate or insufficient exposures at home to reinforce what is learned in therapy sessions.
- Family interference or lack of support for CBT treatment.
- Wrong therapy provided (research does not support the use of treatments such as hypnosis, psychoanalysis, EMDR, homeopathy, or hypnosis for treatment of OCD).
- Lack of parent and/or child support by others facing the same challenges.
- Lack of health insurance or funds to cover treatment (see Chapter 19 for other ways to get treatment if your insurance doesn't cover CBT or medications for OCD, or if you don't have health insurance).

If your child is having problems in his treatment for OCD using either CBT therapy and/or medications, consider whether any of these issues may be playing a role.

A Report Card on Individual Therapy Outcomes

Even with successful treatment, your child's OCD will never go away completely. OCD remains a chronic, lifelong condition that comes and goes throughout one's lifetime. However, your child's OCD symptoms can go into varying levels of remission.

 Fact

CBT therapy for OCD has an 80 percent success rate. In many cases, improvements start to become apparent after five sessions of CBT therapy. However, for the 20 percent of patients for whom ERP exercises prove too difficult to manage, or whose symptoms are too severe, other treatments may be necessary.

According to the national advocacy organization Mental Health America's most recent compilation of available outcomes data, here is what is known about success rates with CBT and ERP:

- As many as 25 percent of patients (adults and children) refuse CBT
- Those who complete CBT report a 50 to 80 percent reduction in OCD symptoms after twelve to twenty sessions
- People with OCD who respond to CBT usually stay well, often for many years

As more treatment data and meta-analyses of this data become available, there will no doubt be an even more compelling picture of the benefits of treatment for OCD. Keeping informed about this research is easier than ever today. You can sign up for e-mail newsletters and alerts from a number of organizations that monitor this topic; many are listed in the resources section of this book.

CHAPTER 9

Deciding on Treatment: Medication

Childhood OCD is commonly treated with a combination of cognitive behavioral therapy (CBT) and medication. The advantage of avoiding the possible side effects of psychotropic medications in children is a compelling reason to follow the American Psychiatric Association's consensus guidelines, which recommend first trying CBT alone when treating children and adolescents with OCD. However, there are exceptions and good reasons to combine approaches or to even begin with medication. Responses to different forms of treatment vary from person to person, making the choice of when and if your child should take medication for her OCD a very individual decision.

When Medication Is Necessary

The primary circumstance when a psychotropic medication is immediately prescribed for a child diagnosed with OCD is when the child's symptoms are severe and debilitating. What does severe mean? There may be different answers for different parents and children.

The inability of a child to adequately eat, sleep, and function at school probably represents the "bottom line" for most parents. Her symptoms may have your child so bound up by her OCD that it's difficult for her to find an entry point into CBT therapy. Rather than skip therapy altogether, a doctor will often recommend a course of medication to tamp down her symptoms and give CBT a chance to work.

 *Fact*

> Both CBT and medication can effectively treat childhood OCD because both affect brain chemistry, which, in turn, affects your child's behavior. Medication can regulate serotonin, reducing obsessive thoughts and obsessive behaviors. The SSRI class of antidepressant medications targets serotonin directly and has been shown to dramatically reduce OCD symptoms in two-thirds of the adults and children who take these medications.

Another reason why medication might be prescribed for your child with OCD is if a course of CBT does not sufficiently lessen her symptoms or if psychotherapy is simply not working for your child, which is the case for approximately 20 to 25 percent of children who try it.

Your child may be too young or immature to understand the concepts and apply the techniques of CBT. Or she's suffering from additional neurological conditions, which then aggravate her OCD and make therapy more difficult. Any decision made about medication at the outset of treatment can be revisited at a later point when your child's age, situation, and/or symptoms change.

In addition to lessening a child's OCD symptoms, medication can ease the depression and anxiety often accompanying OCD. Although no cure-all, and not immediate in its effect, medication often works, faster on a child's OCD symptoms than psychotherapy alone.

Serotonin and SSRIs

The primary medications used for OCD are the same ones doctors most frequently prescribe for adult and childhood depression, the SSRI (Selective Serotonin Reuptake Inhibitors) class of antidepressants. These drugs act on serotonin by blocking its "reuptake" by brain neurons, thus leaving more of this chemical in the pathways of the brain's neurotransmitter network. The first SSRI antidepressant medication—called Fluoxetine, brand name Prozac—came on the market in 1986, with several others released in the two decades since.

In this time, the effectiveness of SSRI medications for treating mood and anxiety disorders (including OCD) has been well established. Although there are side effects associated with SSRIs, they cause fewer and less severe side effects than caused by most other classes of psychotropic medications.

There are seven medications currently being prescribed for OCD in adults and children (brand names are listed first, followed by generic names).

- Anafranil (Clomipramine)
- Prozac (Fluoxetine)
- Zoloft (Sertraline)
- Paxil (Paroxetine)
- Celexa (Citalopram)
- Luvox (Fluvoxamine)
- Lexapro (Escitalopram oxalate)

All of these medications are SSRIs except Anafranil (Clomipramine), the first medication developed to treat OCD, which is in a category called *tricyclic antidepressants*. Unlike the SSRIs, a tricyclic affects other neurotransmitters in addition to serotonin, primarily norepinephrine and dopamine.

The Massachusetts General Hospital Mood and Anxiety Disorders Institute Resource Center (MADI) 2006 public information on medication for children and adolescents with OCD made the following comments on medication choices and dosage decisions:

> Sometimes larger doses of antidepressants (up to four times the standard antidepressant dose) are prescribed to reduce OCD symptoms.

There is no "best" medicine to treat OCD, and it is important to remember that medicines usually reduce, rather than eliminate, symptoms. Different medicines or dosages may be needed at different times in a child's life or to address the emergence of particular symptoms.

The MADI handout also emphasized the need for parents and physicians to pay special attention to special situations, which arise when there are comorbid disorders with a child's OCD. Among the disorders that complicate medication choices are bipolar disorder, where standard SSRI antidepressants can increase manic symptoms, and autism spectrum disorders, where lower dosages of antidepressants (for example, one mg of Prozac) are also needed.

From this list of seven antidepressants commonly prescribed for OCD, three have FDA approval for treating OCD in children.

- Anafranil (Clomipramine) for age ten and up
- Luvox (Fluvoxamine) for age eight and up
- Zoloft (Sertraline) for age six and up

What does *approved for use by children* mean? The Food and Drug Administration (FDA) requires pharmaceutical companies to perform additional studies on drugs that are already approved for adult use before they are authorized for children. However, doctors will often prescribe drugs for children with OCD prior to those medications receiving this approval. This practice is not uncommon and the medications are not considered unsafe for children; it only means that the drug companies involved have not yet completed all the lengthy FDA testing for the final stage of approval. The use of a medication for OCD by doctors prior to final FDA approval often reflects a doctor's successful use of the particular drug with adults with OCD, and/or new research studies demonstrating its effectiveness or promise for treatment of OCD.

Medication Side Effects

All OCD medications can cause side effects, although most (but not all) side effects occur in the first weeks of a patient's use of the medication and decrease with time. The most common side effects include drowsiness, insomnia, dry mouth, nausea and upset stomach, perspiration, nervousness, rash, changes in libido, changes in appetite, and weight gain.

 Essential

The psychiatrist who prescribes your child's OCD medication will usually schedule monthly follow-up appointments to monitor his response to the drug and any side effects it may cause him. It is not uncommon for a doctor to advise a lower dosage to offset a bothersome side effect. If there is no improvement in your child's symptoms, he may increase a dosage in order to enhance the drug's effectiveness.

Less common side effects that may require a doctor's immediate attention include any extreme degree of those side effects listed above, heart palpitations, seizures, and any suspected serious drug interactions.

Atypical Antipsychotics

This is a class of medication that is typically used for diagnoses of bipolar disorder, severe depression, and schizophrenia where the symptom of *thought disorder* is a significant issue. Thought disorder refers to the person's illogical association and sequencing of ideas, thoughts, and words as a result of brain malfunction. This symptom can make it sound as if the beginning of a child's sentence does not match its second half, for example, "The sun is out today; I'm going to be punished." When a psychiatrist prescribes an atypical antipsychotic drug for someone with OCD, it is usually done in small doses with the specific goal of improving reality testing for abnormal beliefs. These medications are sometimes prescribed for short-term use for older children with OCD. However, they frequently bring more severe side effects than an SSRI medication. A common side effect is weight gain. Among the common brand names associated with this antipsychotic category of medications are Zyprexa and Abilify.

Alert!

Never try a psychotropic medication on your child without a doctor's prescription. It's equally important not to stop a medication or change your child's medication dosage without discussing it beforehand with your child's doctor. Hearsay benefits of a particular drug for another child will not necessarily be replicated with your child. In fact, there could be a harmful interaction with a medication he is already taking.

Always ask your child's treating physician about a new medication if you would like to know if it might be suitable for your child. It's also important to let your child's doctor know about any psychotropic medications that you or another family member may have taken in the past or are now taking that have brought benefits for OCD or another anxiety disorder.

FDA SSRI Advisory: Weighing Medication Risks

In October of 1993, the FDA responded to anecdotal reports of a small number of suicides by teenagers who were taking antidepressants (primarily Paxil) for depression by issuing a public health advisory about the possible link between the use of SSRIs and adolescent suicide, stating that "antidepressant drugs could increase the chances of suicidal thoughts or actions in children and teenagers." This warning received much attention and appeared to have substantial impact on parents and doctors by inhibiting prescription of antidepressants for children and adolescents.

This impact was underscored by a report released in September of 2007 by the U.S. Centers for Disease Control and Prevention (CDC) which documented an increase in the number of suicides in children and young adults ages eight to twenty-four during 2003—the year following the placement of a warning on the use of antidepressants by adolescents. The increase in suicides amounted to 8 percent, from 4,599 or 6.78 per 100,000 in 2003 to 7.32 deaths per 100,000 in 2004, representing the largest rise in child and adolescent suicides in fifteen years. It's also significant that this rate had fallen consistently over the previous thirteen years when diagnoses of teenage depression and anxiety and antidepressant use by adolescents had sharply increased.

Many mental health professionals subsequently voiced their strong concern, saying that under-prescribing antidepressant medications for teenagers was the greater of these two potential dangers.

Another point frequently made in this ongoing debate concerns the urgent need for and frequent lack of careful monitoring of a child's response to antidepressant medication in the weeks and months after beginning its use. For parents facing a choice about Paxil or any other antidepressant medication for an adolescent or child, discussing the relative risks involved and staying in close contact with your doctor during treatment is a vital cautionary strategy.

Questions about Medications

Parents have many questions about which, if any, medications are right for childhood OCD, how long they should be taken, how medication works with CBT therapy, and what to do about side effects. All of these are important matters to discuss with your child's prescribing doctor, whether that is her pediatrician or a psychiatrist.

The following frequently asked questions address many concerns parents have when considering or beginning a course of medication for a child or teenager's OCD. These questions and answers should not replace your discussion with your child's doctor.

How Long Until Medication Works?

With most of the SSRI antidepressant medications, there is anywhere from a two- to four-week waiting period before any positive effects of the medication are felt. In contrast, side effects usually become apparent much sooner, although they often fade in days or weeks. The improvement in your child's mood and a decrease in his OCD symptoms are usually a gradual and subtle process. It can take up to three months for the full benefit of medication to take hold. It's not uncommon for a child to be unaware of changes in his own behavior. You might notice and point out a positive change to him, saying, "Did you notice you only washed twice before dinner tonight?" He may be pleased to hear the feedback. At the very least, he'll be more likely to notice his own changed behavior the next time.

Are SSRIs Addictive?

Antidepressants are not considered addictive since they don't produce a euphoric reaction, as painkillers and sedatives do. Rather, their purpose is to alleviate negative symptoms. However, the process of stopping an antidepressant medication can be unpleasant for a short period of time. Some temporary side effects, including drowsiness, headaches, and a dip in mood, are common.

What Happens When He Stops Taking Medication?

The APA's consensus guidelines for OCD treatment call for a minimum one- to two-year course of antidepressant medication after a patient's OCD symptoms are stabilized. Only then should a gradual tapering off be considered. If there is not a combined CBT and medication approach, it is very common for OCD symptoms to reappear after the child stops taking an SSRI medication for his OCD. If the cessation of medication causes a severe relapse of symptoms, many adults and children suffering from OCD opt for a longer-term or life-time use of SSRI medication.

What if Medication Doesn't Help?

For reasons not yet understood by psychiatrists, different people respond positively and negatively to different SSRI medications. This reality often necessitates trying more than one antidepressant before you find the right drug for your child. One drug may cause bothersome side effects, prompting your doctor to try another. In some cases the use of more than one medication at a time, up to three or four, will bring the child greater improvement. This process of trial and error can be difficult for your child, and can cause you additional worry. Unfortunately, until research yields more clues shedding light on why a drug works best for a given patient, there is no better way to go about treatment with psychotropic medications.

 **Alert!**

Children and parents can fall into the trap of thinking of medication for OCD as a cure-all, when it is much more likely to be just one tool in a larger tool kit for dealing with your child's OCD. With the best results, medication doesn't eliminate all OCD symptoms, making CBT and exposure response prevention (ERP) techniques an important adjunct for the majority of children and teens with OCD.

Here's how author Amy Wilensky describes the different ways she feels after beginning an SSRI medication in her book *Passing for Normal, A Memoir of Compulsion.*

> For me, once it finally took effect, Prozac was no miracle cure, brought no transcendent revelations, or reversals of thought. The best explanations I can provide of its do-good-ing is that it has effectively turned

down my volume, alleviating my tics and especially my rituals to a manageable extent. . . . Such shifts sound diminutive in scale, I know, but there's no gift quite as gracefully received as additional hours in the day.

Whether or not to use a psychotropic medication is a highly personal and individual decision for a parent on behalf of a younger child with OCD. There are many fears about possible short- and long-term side effects to be carefully considered. This is one of the areas where it is most important to have an open line of communication with your child's prescribing doctor. A doctor should be available by telephone in between visits for consultations about your child's potential need for a dosage change or to discuss any side effects that may arise. Teenagers will more often make their own decision about starting or stopping medication; it should always be made with your parental consent and a doctor's consultation.

A Report Card on Medication and Psychotherapy

Studies show that OCD symptoms are reduced substantially after two months of treatment with SSRI medications in about two-thirds of children who take them. Of all medications tried with children, all of the SSRIs have shown fewer side effects than the tricyclic antidepressant Anafranil (Clomipramine) and the antipsychotics. However, the remaining unknowns about possible long-term side effects of antidepressant or any other psychotropic medications on children make many parents uncomfortable enough to opt for an initial approach of CBT alone, deferring the use of medication until later if deemed necessary.

This is an area where regular reading of OCD-related Web sites and newsletters is highly valuable. A parent can learn about a new medication, or about a study conducted with a different combination of medication and therapy, and then ask a mental healthcare provider whether the new approach might be appropriate for their child.

Studies also confirm that a combination of CBT therapy and SSRI medications is more often the most effective approach for treating children and adolescents with OCD, with the combined CBT and medication approach yielding the longest duration of reduced symptoms. It has also been demonstrated that over half of children with OCD will have a reduction to minimal symptoms after just twelve weeks of combined (optimal) treatment.

The Pediatric OCD Study (POTS)

The most significant of these studies was funded by NIMH, carried out by John March, M.D., at Duke University and Edna Foa, Ph.D., at the University of Pennsylvania, and reported in the October 27, 2004, *Journal of the American Medical Association (JAMA)*. Called POTS, it involved ninety-seven seven- to seventeen-year-olds with OCD who completed twelve weeks of either CBT, the SSRI Zoloft (Sertraline), a combination treatment, or a placebo.

Combining CBT and the SSRI Zoloft proved to be more effective than either treatment alone. CBT alone was superior to Zoloft alone, which, in turn, showed better results than a placebo.

Alert!

It is very common for children with OCD to be afraid of taking medications. Most of the time, these fears have to do with swallowing a pill rather than the effects of the medication. Some medications come in liquid form; others can be pulverized before taking. Speak to your prescribing doctor before you begin any course of medication for OCD if your child has a fear of swallowing pills.

When Treatment Doesn't Work

About 20 to 25 percent of children and adults with OCD show no improvement after treatment with either CBT or medication. If your child falls into this category, you should not lose hope. Your child may have a different result when trying either approach at a later time, when she's older or perhaps more receptive to treatment. Advances in research and new medications are announced on a regular basis. Stay connected to sources of news and new resources about OCD by joining one of the support organizations noted at the back of this book.

Summary of Expert Guidelines on Childhood OCD Treatment

In what are called "The Expert Consensus Guidelines" for treatment of OCD, edited by John S. March, M.D., Allen Frances, M.D., Daniel Carpenter, Ph.D., and David A. Kahn, M.D., and formulated as "The Patient-Family Handout," preferences for first- and second-choice strategies were offered for different age groups of patients diagnosed with OCD and OCD spectrum disorders. Among the panel's findings for adolescents and prepubertal (younger) children were the following recommendations for "first line" and "second line" strategies. "SRI" in this list refers to a serotonin reuptake inhibitor medication, including: Comipramine, Fluoxetine, Fluvoxamine, Paroxetine, and Sertraline. CBT refers to cognitive behavioral therapy, as described in Chapter 6.

Adolescent OCD

- First line for mild adolescent OCD: CBT first
- First line for severe adolescent OCD: CBT + SRI
- Second line for mild adolescent OCD: CBT + SRI
- Second line for severe adolescent OCD: CBT + SRI, SRI first

Prepubertal OCD

- First line for mild prepubertal OCD: CBT first
- First line for severe prepubertal OCD: CBT first
- Second line for mild prepubertal OCD: CBT + SRI, SRI first
- Second line for severe prepubertal OCD: CBT + SRI, SRI first

In this set of guidelines, the authors describe mild OCD as causing distress but not necessarily dysfunction; this diagnosis is associated with a score of 10 to 18 on the Yale Brown Obsessive Compulsive Scale. Moderate OCD causes both distress and functional impairment (YBOCS score of 18 to 29). Severe OCD causes serious functional impairment requiring significant help from others (YBOCS score of 30 or above).

The following information is also included:

- These experts recommend combined use of cognitive therapy and exposure response prevention as the "optimal treatment" for OCD. They add that cognitive therapy may provide "additional benefit" by directly targeting distorted OCD "beliefs," meaning pathological doubt, aggressive obsessions, and scrupulosity or other OCD beliefs, as contrasted with an OCD "urge-like symptom" such as arranging, or touching rituals, where they suggest ERP treatment as most helpful.
- When comorbid conditions are present with OCD, other classes of medications may be used, including the classes known as psychostimulants and mood stabilizers.
- Guidelines suggest thirteen to twenty weekly individual CBT sessions for the typical patient, with home exposures done between sessions; in severe cases, they suggest a daily regime of CBT sessions for a three-week period.
- For the maintenance phase of treatment, CBT visits can be reduced to a monthly basis. Medication can be discontinued gradually under a doctor's supervision. If severe relapses occur, medication use can be reconfigured on a long-term basis.

These guidelines are presented here to give parents an overview of what are considered "best practices" in the treatment of childhood OCD, not as a substitute for consultation or treatment with a medical professional. The complete "Patient-Family Handout" is available online at *www.psychguides.com*.

CHAPTER 10

Other Therapeutic Choices

If you think of this book as a tool kit for helping your child manage her OCD, this chapter adds some fine-tuning to the standard treatment—CBT and ERP therapy with or without medication—and some treatment alternatives when standard approaches are not possible or viable. In cases of severe childhood OCD, or when a family lives too far from an outpatient OCD treatment provider, intensive inpatient treatment is one such option. Group therapy, including group ERP, has been effective for many older children and teens and is gaining increasing popularity. Mindfulness training and neurofeedback for OCD symptom management are two other practices being employed by mental healthcare providers.

Group Psychotherapy Using ERP

The most immediate benefit of group OCD therapy for children and adolescents is the support your child feels as she sees and hears from other young people who are dealing with the same issues she's struggled with on her own for so long. There is an immediate emotional lift felt, especially for preteens and teens, when the loneliness they've experienced is replaced by camaraderie.

Another common positive response that can come from the group therapy experience is your child's realization that she's not "the worst off." No matter how bad she feels about her own symptoms, there's inevitably another child who seems worse, at least to her. Then there's the very real possibility that your child can help at least one other member of her group by providing a mirror or a model for that child's struggle. The power of identifying and communicating with others coping with the same relentless burden cannot be overestimated for young people with OCD.

Amy Wilinsky describes her first meeting with someone like herself in *Passing for Normal, A Memoir of Compulsion:*

> When Bryant described how his father had always reacted to his tics—with an initial confusion that grew quickly into anger and shame—it was as if I'd discovered a twin from whom I'd been separated at birth; I'd never even imagined being able to describe how that particular rejection felt to anyone else.

How Group CBT Therapy Works

The techniques of CBT exposure and response prevention used in individual OCD treatment are transported to therapist-facilitated OCD therapy groups with measurably positive effects. Some HMOs, such as Kaiser Permanente in California, offer these groups for OCD and other anxiety disorder as a primary means for treating these conditions. These always involve a licensed therapist or psychologist who usually requires both a commitment by participants for a fixed number of sessions (usually twelve) and the payment of a fee for his time.

The main difference between individual and group CBT is the ability in groups to have fellow group members participate in ERP role-plays. These are exposure exercises designed to replicate the actors and circumstances that make up each group member's obsessions and compulsions in real life. For example, the child who fears shaking hands upon meeting a new adult, his teacher for example, can act out this exposure with a peer playing the new teacher. He performs the exposure multiple times until he's able to shake hands without using his usual compulsions of praying, counting, or going out of his way to avoid this sort of physical contact. Equally important is the support he receives from other group members, many of whom have the same contamination fear he does.

 Essential

There's power in numbers. Each group member is given an individual CY-BOCS test at the beginning and end of his twelve-week CBT therapy group experience. This score measures changes in symptoms reinforcing a youngster's progress with a quantitative measurement of where his OCD symptoms stood "before and after."

In the course of a twelve-week CBT group each group member is in the spotlight—performing his own exposures—every third or fourth session. In other sessions, he participates by playing a role in other members' exposure exercises. There is a great therapeutic value gained on both "sides" of these CBT group role-plays.

Other Types of OCD Peer Groups

In addition to the formal CBT group therapy facilitated by a professional therapist, there are two other types of OCD support groups, both less formal than the CBT therapy group. Many OCD preteens and teenagers attend these groups to support each other in managing their OCD. Neither type of group charges a fee.

The first is the mutual support group, which is frequently facilitated by OCD sufferers who are older, and have their OCD symptoms under control. These mutual support groups are informational and inspirational in nature but not specifically therapeutic. They often include speakers, including college-age individuals who are in recovery from OCD as well as medical experts who speak on subjects related to OCD, such as research and treatment advances. These support groups meet monthly or on a more frequent basis. A good way to find out about an adolescent OCD mutual support group in your area is to contact the OCD foundation and check Web sites or newsletters of the organization's state and local chapters.

Obsessive-Compulsive Anonymous (OCA) Groups

The second type of OCD support group approach is the twelve-step method used by the network of Obsessive-Compulsive Anonymous (OCA) groups throughout the United States. These groups use self-help principles originally developed by Alcoholics Anonymous (AA) to help people dealing with alcohol addiction. Foremost among twelve-step principles are a commitment to the anonymity of group members, an acknowledgement by each group member that his problem (OCD) has made his life unmanageable, and a commitment to trust a "higher power" (God to some) to help him recover from his problem. Many of the basic self-help slogans advocated by twelve-step groups such as "One Day at a Time" and "Take It Easy" have a special appeal to OCD sufferers of all ages. A list of OCA groups can be obtained from OCF headquarters by calling 516-739-0662.

Inpatient Treatment for OCD

In the last decade, a handful of hospitals, usually those with established outpatient treatment centers for childhood OCD, have added inpatient programs to treat young people with OCD. These residential programs employ a very low staff-to-patient ratio, with a team of medical doctors and nurses, psychologists and psychiatrists, therapists and social workers on call on a twenty-four-hour basis. They present a viable alternative for children with severe OCD symptoms and those with comorbid conditions. These programs often have the benefit of state-of-the-art treatment expertise, because of the presence of OCD researchers in the same or connected hospital facilities and psychologists who are leaders in the field of OCD treatment.

One such program, led by noted OCD specialist Dr. Bradley C. Riemann, opened in 2007 at Rogers Memorial Medical Center in Wisconsin. The initial program will have ten beds, serving children ages eight to twelve. According to Dr. Riemann, "We are anticipating getting kids with severe OCD or other anxiety disorders with significant comorbidity and complex presentations. Severity is determined by how much the OCD impairs a child's functioning. If the OCD is keeping him from going to school, being social with friends, and creating behavioral challenges in the home, this program may be what they need."

According to Dr. Riemann, treatment in the program will combine CBT/ERP and medications, and will have large family therapy and parent education components. According to the program's medical director, Dr. Peter Lake, the goal of the program is to return the children to their homes with a reduction in their anxiety symptoms and improved daily functioning. A child's stay at a residential OCD treatment program may last anywhere from one to three months. Inpatient treatment programs are usually highly individualized and therefore by necessity flexible. Because these programs involve parents in regular, often weekly or bi-weekly family groups or individual family therapy sessions, a child's parents will either remain in the geographic area of the program or travel back and forth from home as needed.

To find out more about other residential programs for treatment of childhood OCD, contact the Obsessive-Compulsive Foundation.

Diet, Nutrition, and Supplements

There is no scientific evidence to prove any benefits gained from herbs or nutritional supplements as an effective treatment of OCD. There are, however, potential harmful effects from interactions between certain SSRI antidepressants and, for example, the herbal remedy St. John's Wort, which can result in a dangerous condition known as serotonin syndrome.

Still, many parents who have used vitamin and other supplements for their children with OCD offer anecdotal reports of improved mood states and reduced symptoms. Among the nutritional supplements they (and some psychiatrists) recommend are B complex, omega 3 fish oil, and calcium/magnesium. The potential use of any vitamin supplements and herbal medicines for your child's OCD should be discussed with your doctor.

If your child or adolescent is dealing with OCD, there are clear benefits to be gained from cutting down the amount of highly sugared and caffeinated products in his diet. This includes candy, cookies and cakes, sodas, coffee, tea and other "energy boosting" bars or drinks containing high amounts of sugar and caffeine. These products can increase anxiety and nervousness in a child with OCD, ADHD or social anxiety. A balanced diet with all food groups represented is an important element in the home care of a child with OCD. Also important is an adherence to a regular routine for three meals a day.

Neurofeedback Therapy

Used first to treat epilepsy, Attention Deficit Hyperactivity Disorder (ADHD), and other anxiety disorders in children, this is a newer treatment technique based on technology and principles first developed in the 1960s and '70s for *biofeedback*, a self-monitoring method designed to help adults to lower their own stress levels. Neurofeedback therapy employs electroencephalography (EEG) brain waves, and involves placing electrodes as brain wave sensors in various places on a child's head and forehead in order to show him how to directly train his own brain functioning. Typically, the child is placed in front of a video screen where a picture of his brain activity is displayed. This is often done in the child-friendly form of a video game. He then changes what's on the screen by changing the ways in which he responds (emotionally and mentally) to verbal stimuli from interactions with his therapist and to his own brain feedback as measured on screen.

Essential

One recommended book about the use of neurofeedback therapy, primarily with younger children who have a diagnosis of ADHD, is *A Symphony in the Brain: The Evolution of New Brain Wave Biofeedback* by Jim Robbins.

Although this approach is being increasingly tried for treatment of childhood anxiety disorders and depression in the United States, it is only recently being subjected to controlled studies to determine formal outcomes and applicability to various disorders. At this time, a small number of psychologists and psychotherapists have incorporated neurofeedback use into their practices.

CHAPTER 11

OCD at School

Teachers and school counselors can play an important role in identifying your child's OCD. Many parents don't realize that several pieces of legislation enacted since the 1970s make it a requirement for public schools to provide assessment and learning aids to school-age children with emotional and neurological disorders. The public school can now be another significant point of access to treatment for your school-age child's mental health needs. But sufficient knowledge and services for students with OCD are not available in every school district and school. In order to obtain this assistance, you should know your child's rights and become his advocate.

Typical Learning Problems for OCD Students

Beyond the many difficulties often involved with just getting a child with OCD dressed and ready for school in the morning, once she's at school, her OCD can make academic success extremely challenging. Students react in different ways to these challenges. Some are able to keep their OCD hidden during the school day, performing well in the classroom and working around fears related to coming into physical contact with their peers and the school environment, only to emotionally collapse from the stress of all that effort once they get home. More typically, students with untreated OCD tend to get bogged down at school by the same obsessive thoughts and compulsive actions that affect them at home.

Her need to have things "just so" can make your child's school-work go slowly or stop altogether. She can bring OCD-related problems that began at home into the school setting. If, for example, she stayed up late worrying about something or someone she may encounter the next day in the classroom, or if food issues have kept her from eating proper meals, she may be too tired or hungry to perform at school. In another common occurrence for the student with OCD, her exaggerated fears about harm coming to those she loves can become inappropriately attached to how well she does on a test, causing her to perform rituals to stave off that outcome. In the process she may become distracted from test taking, ensuring the very outcome she dreads.

Contamination Fears at School

Whereas a youngster may believe she has some power to avoid contamination at home, she's likely to be cognizant of the fact that germs or other sources of contamination at school are beyond any semblance of her control. All this can trigger her OCD and make the stress of a typical school day feel overwhelming. Contamination fears can disrupt class in many ways, including:

- Janice stayed up until 3 A.M. worrying about whether the boy who sits in front of her in homeroom would push his chair back into her desk, releasing germs from his unwashed hair onto Janice's desk and person.
- Twelve-year-old Steven was unable to sit still at his desk. He kept turning around to rummage through his backpack in order to check whether he'd brought his clean uniform for gym class, lest he be forced to borrow unfamiliar and potentially contaminated gym shorts.
- Stasi, fourteen, became distraught and distracted when she felt the need to urinate in the middle of her third-period math class, since her fear of using the girls' restroom would make it necessary for her to "hold it in" for the remainder of the school day.

Many parents observe that their child's OCD symptoms become more acute as stress at school increases. It may peak at the beginning of the school year, and reoccur after winter or spring breaks. Added stress also comes with tests and grading periods, or it can result from social pressures from other students.

> Tonight my fifteen-year-old son wanted to get a head start on studying for a history final on Friday, to help him feel more in control tomorrow, and more prepared for the in-class review. Not fifteen minutes into it he began panicking again and just couldn't pull himself out. He had another panic attack. I convinced him to come with me in the car (I had to pick up my husband at the train station), and by the time the drive was over and the cold air blowing in his face he had started breathing again and the attack passed. This was just terrible to witness. He kept saying he couldn't breathe and he can never go back to school. I dread tomorrow morning. I don't know how I'm going to get him there. As a mom you just want to protect your kid, but it's so hard to protect them from themselves.

When he suffers from OCD-related obsessions about schoolwork having to be perfect, a youngster can be set off into states of panic. The same fears can cause the student to sabotage his test or assignment or go to great lengths to avoid the situation by refusing to go to school at all.

How Perfectionism and Procrastination Sabotage School Success

A common learning problem associated with a child with OCD and those with sub-clinical cases of OCD relates to perfectionism: The need to reach an unobtainable state of perfection in school assignments. A need for certainty and a fear that he cannot achieve the perfection he craves can keep your child from even starting an assignment. Rather than begin, he procrastinates, doing his best to avoid facing this inevitable wall of uncertainty. To a teacher, these stalling and avoiding behaviors can look like simple disorganization, daydreaming, disinterest, or resistance. Once he does get started, the student with OCD often feels compelled to erase and re-do, re-read, and re-compute everything he does. After completing the work, he will often throw it away and start over from scratch.

Beyond the emotional and academic toll it takes on affected students, these OCD tendencies toward perfectionism and procrastination put a great strain on teachers. When a child repeatedly seeks reassurance by asking the same questions over and over, or when he refuses to move on in his classroom work, his behavior can negatively impact the entire class and disrupt a teacher's schedule. If a teacher is not familiar with the symptoms of OCD, she may incorrectly assume that your child is simply incapable of completing the work at his grade level. Or, she may alternately conclude—mistakenly—that his behavior is willfully disruptive and defiant then decide he's in need of detention or some other negative consequence to deter him from such behavior in the future.

When Safety Fears Enter the Classroom

Despite the fact that most children with OCD have average or above-average intelligence, a child who devotes a large percentage of her attention and memory to obsessive thoughts and OCD-related rituals has little energy left over for new classroom learning. A child dealing with obsessive fears and rituals in the classroom setting may:

- Use only certain "lucky" numbers or avoid "unlucky" numerical combinations.

- Count a certain number of times before turning a page or completing an answer on a test.
- Make unusual movements, patterns, and gestures as she enters or exits the classroom or gets in and out of her seat.
- Refuse to speak or go to the blackboard because of her dread of being watched by other students.

Even if he manages to keep them hidden from teachers and other students, these fears and ritualistic compulsions can cause a student major learning problems. Hidden or not, the behaviors will almost certainly harm his ability to concentrate and perform.

Forging a Partnership with School Staff

It is not uncommon for the first recognition of a child's OCD symptoms to come from her teacher. Because OCD is thought to be present in one out of every 100 school-age children, a teacher with several years' experience is likely to have seen one or more previous cases in her classroom. Given the fact that federal laws have mandated special attention to the needs of students with OCD and other emotional and neurological problems since the mid 1970s, school principals, teachers, counselors, and nurses should be gaining more experience with OCD and other common childhood mental health disorders with each subsequent school year. All of this puts teachers and other school personnel in a prime position to help you identify your child's OCD.

There are a variety of situations that make assistance from your child's teacher or school less forthcoming. If, for example, your child's OCD symptoms are not obvious or the most commonly known, such as excessive hand washing, her other OCD behaviors may not be seen for what they are. A child who manages to hide her OCD at school but then comes to class with incomplete homework or does poorly on exams may be incorrectly assumed to have poor study habits. Finally, school personnel may simply not be as informed as they should be about OCD. Whether the conversation about your child's OCD-related learning challenges is begun by you, or by your child's school's staff, it is a vitally important dialogue to begin and continue throughout her school years. Many parents solve this information gap by making an annual ritual of bringing OCD basic information kits to all of their child's teachers.

Question?

Who is eligible for school-based mental health services?
Any child in the U.S. public school system with an emotional and/or neurological disorder is covered under the *Individuals with Disabilities Education Act* (IDEA) and *Section 504 of the Rehabilitation Act of 1973*. These laws require public schools to provide a free and appropriate education in *the least restrictive environment (LRE) to all students,* regardless of family income. This includes any assessment, counseling, remedial services, and learning accommodations required for him to achieve the educational success that matches his abilities.

Privacy Tradeoffs

Sooner or later, you are likely to face a time when it makes sense to engage your child's teachers or other school staff in a conversation about her OCD. For the younger child, in preschool through second grade, it is often sufficient to tell him that his teacher now knows about his "problem," and remind him that the teacher is someone he can call on for special help—should he need it.

For the upper elementary, middle, and high school student, it is far better to enlist his cooperation before any decision is made whether to inform school personnel about his OCD or withhold information. The tradeoffs between these two options should be weighed carefully with him. From your child's point of view, the disadvantages of telling are likely to concern the possibility of bringing him embarrassment and teasing by other students—should knowledge of his OCD be commonly shared. From the parent's perspective, there may be fears of your child being labeled and stigmatized or denied future educational opportunities.

 Essential

Know your child's privacy rights. As the parent of a minor with OCD you must sign an official release before information about his mental health history goes to other healthcare providers to whom you may be referred through his school. Information about his OCD cannot be released to colleges or other educational programs to which he may be applying without parental permission if he's a minor.

The advantages of telling usually win out over not telling for most students and their families. Once the school is informed of your child's OCD-related needs, you will be better able to obtain referrals for support and treatment options in the community. It is equally important for many students with OCD to get learning accommodations. A therapist or an older student with OCD can be helpful in discussing the plusses and minuses of telling versus not telling, if the discussion becomes too fraught with emotion between parent and child.

How and What to Share

Presenting school personnel with information about your child's OCD challenges can be an intimidating process. This is true especially if school staff members are not as informed as they should be about OCD. On the other hand, many teachers are quite familiar with OCD-related learning issues and are very supportive of the needs of students who must contend with the disorder at school.

Essential

A "safe person" can make the difference between your child staying in school and staying home. A safe person is a school counselor, a teacher or teacher's aide, nurse, or coach who is informed about your child's OCD and to whom he can go "no questions asked" if he is going to have a meltdown at school. A few minutes with a safe person allows him to catch his breath, vent his immediate issue, and ask for advice.

When approaching all of your child's teachers, it helps to prepare a brief written summary of her case, essentially stating her most pressing symptoms and triggers, as well as short-term solutions that would be applicable in the classroom. If you have already secured a diagnosis from your child's mental healthcare provider, present a copy of that written diagnosis to his teacher. Here is the experience of a mother who went the full-disclosure route with her child's teachers.

> I noticed an uneven amount of knowledge about OCD among my child's teachers as she got up to the fifth and sixth grades. Some knew a lot, some nothing. So, I took to bringing in a notebook of information I'd copied and collected from Web sites and other places, along with a history of my daughter's symptoms and progress with her moderate OCD. Then when she got to middle school my daughter didn't want anyone to know about her OCD and asked me not to do my notebook thing anymore. Well, that was okay until she was in the middle of a math test, and the kid next to her borrowed a pencil, only to sneeze and hand the pencil back. This just sent her to Mars . . . she got up and ran out of the class. She came home in tears because her teacher wouldn't let her take the test after school or at another time. Finally, I

convinced her to let me tell the teacher. When I did, he was very understanding and arranged to have her take the test alone the next day.

This parent's experience illustrates the benefit of not waiting until a crisis strikes to develop an action plan with your child's teachers and other school personnel to arrange for her support at school.

How to Obtain School Services and Accommodations

To ensure that your child succeeds at school while coping with OCD, the most important information for you to become intimately familiar with are the detailed rights accorded him under the relevant educational disability laws. The differences between the IEP and 504 plans have to do with the classification of your child's disability, and can have an impact on the quality and degree of services made available. In most states the classifications of mental health disorders include the following categories:

- Emotionally disturbed (ED) or Social Emotional Disturbance (SED)
- Other health impaired (OHI)

While in the past children with anxiety disorders were typically given the label *Social Emotional Disturbance (SED)*, as more schools now recognize anxiety disorders (including OCD and Tourette's syndrome) as having a neurobiological basis, they have been placed in the category of *Other Health Impaired* (OHI). The category of Emotionally Disturbed (ED) is becoming increasingly outmoded as research points to a neurobiological basis for most mental disorders. (It is provided here as a reference, since some school districts still use ED as a category.)

Be advised that these classifications have different implications in different states, and in many states they've become increasingly politicized as they relate to local school funding decisions. As a parent, it is useful to become educated about these issues in your state so that you can be a better advocate for your child's education.

The *least restrictive environment* (LRE) wording in the law requires that learning accommodations be made that allow your child to remain in his school and classroom to learn among his peers, for example, by having a dedicated teacher's aide present in the classroom to assist him. If that is not possible, because your child's symptoms are too severe for him to remain in the classroom at this time, the school may provide a certain number of hours of homebound instruction by a teacher on a weekly basis.

Many schools have specialized programs for children with mental/emotional health problems that are separate from regular classrooms but are still within a public school campus. This option is typically utilized prior to using an at-home tutor or sending the child to a specialized school. Alternately, the school will obtain admission for your child at another, more appropriate school, at the school district's expense.

Essential Services

Learning services and educational resources guaranteed by federal legislation can make the difference between your child's success and failure in school. Here are some of the special accommodations and services offered for students suffering from OCD or other anxiety disorders in many school districts across the country:

- Longer time periods for homework and test taking
- Reduced homework and class participation expectations
- Abbreviated school days
- Excusing students from high-anxiety-producing events: fire/safety drills, field trips, assemblies, and other large group activities
- A "cool-down pass," meaning permission to leave class as needed, along with a designated "safe person" to whom to go in such times

- Space accommodations in the classroom, such as special seating
- Homebound learning, in which a teacher visits the child's home for one-on-one teaching a certain number of hours each day or week
- Teachers working with parents to coordinate a child's part-time classroom learning with home schooling

These services and accommodations are among the most common and productive of those offered under IEP and 504 plans for your child's education.

The Nuts and Bolts of IEP and 504 Education Plans

Whereas an IEP necessarily involves school district or school board consent and involvement, a 504 plan can be initiated and written by and with a child's teacher(s). Both plans will require documentation of your child's diagnosis and disability. When you ask for special educational services for your child at school, there are two types of formal procedures and possible plans, each relating to a separate law. Although the specific options and services are similar under both plans, the process by which they're obtained and managed differs with each.

IEP Plans

An IEP plan outlines the specific special education services your child needs, which are covered under the Individuals with Disabilities Education Act (IDEA). It requires a formal evaluation of your child's OCD, meaning testing and diagnosis with documentation of his OCD symptoms and their adverse effects on his ability to learn. In order to take advantage of IDEA, which is funded at the national level, the student must qualify for *Special Education* classification. The student then receives an Individual Education Plan (IEP) prepared by his school district. This program requires parental involvement, allows for parental appeals to decisions made by school staff and offers more accountability than a 504 plan.

504 Plans

The intent behind this law is to "eliminate barriers for every child's education and create a level playing field" for all students. A 504 plan does not require a Special Education classification, and it's appropriate for children who don't qualify for an IEP plan. Having a 504 plan in place makes it easier to request special services from your child's school. 504 plans are more general in terms of who is covered, allowing for in-school and at-home assistance for any student with an "impairment that interferes with his learning and socialization." Unlike IEP plans, parental involvement is not required, although it is permitted and has become common practice. 504 plans are generally faster to obtain than IEP plans and are viewed by many parents as potentially less stigmatizing for a child.

There are some potential disadvantages of a 504 plan if your child has severe and debilitating OCD symptoms. Services provided under a 504 plan do not receive federal funding, and must depend on state, county and school district resources. As a result, these plans tend to be more informal and can offer less accountability to parents. Still, by parents and teachers working closely together on behalf of children with special needs, these plans are being made to work in school districts all across the country.

Because a 504 plan begins with your child's teacher(s), her teacher is the obvious person with whom to begin the process of inquiry about in-school resources and accommodations for your child with OCD. A parent's initial request for a child's 504 plan must be made in writing, but, unlike an IEP, the 504 plan does not require formal testing in order to be completed and acted upon.

Here's one parent's experience with a 504 plan for her middle-school daughter, Jessie.

> We've had Jessie's 504 plan approved. She'll have a place to go, either a counselor's office or the library,

when she needs a break from the classroom. She'll agree to a certain number of times a day to go the bathroom, which will change as her treatment progresses. If she gets hung up with an in-class assignment, trying to be perfect, or needing to ask too many questions, her teacher will use a code word, something to let Jessie know they can talk privately about it later, but she should keep going for now. It's only been a few weeks, but I already notice she's a lot more cheerful getting ready in the morning. There's hope!

Each student's 504 plan will be individualized for the child's unique needs, and it will by necessity remain flexible as the child's OCD symptoms improve or worsen, or simply change.

Here are some additional differences and comparisons between the two types of education plans.

- An IDEA *Individual Education Plan (IEP)* derives from the Individuals with Disabilities Education Act. It has a more narrow definition of disability and involves a more formal process to obtain services.
- Since IDEA is a special education provision, in order to qualify for its services a child must be evaluated and "labeled" as a special education student. Although this by law remains a confidential matter, some parents don't wish to have this label attached to their child's record.
- A *504 plan* refers to an article from federal rehabilitation legislation protecting the civil rights of children with disabilities.
- For families who don't want their child to go through the formal special education evaluation process, or if the child's school is not recommending this, they can go the route of a 504 plan. This law defines disability more broadly and often provides the most appropriate model for a school's management of a student with mild to moderate OCD.

If you find knowledge about your child's OCD lacking on the part of her teacher and/or school administration, the next option is to take the proactive step of providing some background about the disorder. In addition to presenting information about OCD in general, offer specific information about your child's learning needs in writing for your child's teachers and administrators.

Your written OCD summary might include the following items.

- The definition of OCD as a disorder causing unwanted and uncontrollable obsessions (thoughts and images) and compulsive actions
- Your child's current OCD symptoms: For example, worries about contamination; excessive hand washing; fear of physical contact with books other than her own, other students or their clothing; or her fear of using a public restroom
- What responses help your child: Giving her extra space around her desk, or more time to get work done. Offering gentle re-direction when she gets distracted
- Specific accommodations you are requesting as part of her 504 plan: More time for tests, in-class assignments, and homework; the last in line for cafeteria and gym class

Much of this information can be gleaned from your own daily symptom logs and other documentation of your child's treatment you either have at home or can prepare. It's important to view a 504 plan as a work in progress. Flexibility must be maintained in order to reflect your child's progress, possible relapses and ever-changing needs.

 **Question?**

Do all schools provide the same resources for dealing with OCD?

Special education resources vary from one community to the next, as does the speed in which individual schools are able to respond to your initial request for a 504 or IEP evaluation. There is often a lengthy waiting list for services. Your success in getting your child the care and learning accommodations he needs will require persistence, patience, and a commitment to becoming and staying informed about new resources for treatment in your own community.

Your Child's Case Manager

The selection of a case manager for your child's IEP or 504 plan helps forge an effective home-school partnership for managing your child's OCD. The case manager can be his teacher, the school nurse, counselor, or any other qualified school staff person. The case manager will then keep all of those involved with your child's education and health/mental healthcare, both those within the school and any outside mental healthcare providers involved with your child, informed of any key developments in his care, capabilities, and new challenges; for instance, a change in symptoms.

In many cases, the child's teacher is responsible for writing the IEP or 504 plan and other team members contribute the sections that pertain to their area of specialization. For example, the school nurse might write the section on physical health needs, and the school counselor might contribute the section on behavioral and emotional needs. Having your child's teacher act as his case manager is often the most effective structure for coordinating his education under these circumstances.

Getting an OCD Diagnosis from the School District

If your child has not received a formal diagnosis of OCD from a private mental healthcare provider, and the school or school district does not have an on-staff psychologist who can render one, you should ask the school for an outside referral.

In addition to a formal diagnosis of OCD, in order to complete a 504 plan or IEP your child will need an assessment of her special needs in the school environment. This may require a referral (ideally by the teacher or administrative staff person who is her *case manager*) to a school district psychologist or another mental healthcare provider in the community with whom the school contracts for this specific purpose. This assessment will determine what school and/or community-based services your child requires, and provides those referrals. With this assessment permanently in your child's school files, her present and future teachers, counselors, and therapists will have a case history and baseline reference for her symptoms, academic capabilities and limitations, and treatment progress over time.

Redefining Success Beyond Grades

As a parent you are naturally concerned about your child's school performance as measured by her grades. In addition to academic progress, changes in her grades can be an important indicator of progress being made in her OCD treatment. Conversely, it can also indicate new flare-ups of OCD symptoms, thus providing a "red flag" to point you in a particular direction so that you can see what is triggering her new symptoms.

While grades can provide an objective indicator in these areas, they don't paint the whole picture of how a child with OCD is doing at school. It's important to remember that perfectionism can be as much a burden to your child as it is an incentive to do well in class and on homework assignments. It may be more helpful for your child to develop a *good enough* standard for her school performance. This different standard may result in a temporary drop in grades while bringing about an overall improvement in her ability to resist the underlying anxiety that triggers her OCD. With her therapist, you can help her identify milestones for this progress beyond grades, for example, the number of class sessions or homework assignments she completed without "do-overs."

Become an Advocate for Your Child's Education

In order to take a holistic view of your child's education, you must keep abreast of all aspects of his school day, including academic progress, physical safety, and social and emotional needs. The process of developing and executing an IEP or 504 plan with school personnel will represent a major commitment of time, self-education, and follow-through on your part. In this process, many parents also find themselves drawn into community initiatives and advocacy efforts to support increased funding for school-based mental health services.

Local Compliance with Federal Laws

According to the U.S. Department of Education, a full 90 percent of school districts are not in full compliance with the relevant laws covering services to students in need of special education services. In the same federal survey, over half of schools surveyed (55 percent) used contracts or other formal agreements with community-based individuals and/or organizations to provide mental health services to students. The most frequently reported outside resource was the school district's county mental health agency.

Funding for these school-based services comes from IDEA grants, state special education funds, and local government allocations. State Medicaid funding is the most common source of financial support for a school's mental health services. However, one-third of school districts reported that funding for these services had decreased since the 2000–2001 school year, while two-thirds reported that demand for services had increased in the same period.

Protecting Your Child from Peers

Depending on your child's age, you will need to find ways to monitor his social and academic progress without acting like an overly protective parent. This can be a tricky balance when your child has OCD. As your child matures, you will naturally have more concerns about peer influences, and you may worry that his OCD may make him more susceptible to teasing and bullying. Parental initiatives for "Zero Tolerance for Bullying" in public schools are an increasingly common solution to teasing and bullying as more awareness is spreading on this difficult issue.

The single most important resource for parents dealing with OCD in a child is a formal or informal network of other parents who are also dealing with OCD or other mental health issues in their school-age children. The support, information, and advice of other parents can be invaluable. More information on parent support groups and resource networks can be found in Chapter 16.

The Home Schooling Option

An increasing number of parents of school-age children with OCD are opting to teach their children themselves, or in partnership with a child's teacher(s)—at home. As the home schooling movement grows in the United States, there is more support available for parents in the form of home school curricula, teaching resource materials, and cooperative parent arrangements. Schools will often provide home schooling curricula materials for children who cannot attend classes. Where other parents are engaged in home schooling in their local communities, many parents share teaching duties, tips, and encouragement for what can be a challenging undertaking.

Why Home School?

One of the primary reasons parents cite for home schooling is to protect a child with OCD from teasing or bullying encountered as a result of his "being different" at school.

Many other parents whose children are having OCD symptoms that are still too severe for them to go to school, or those who have not yet seen sufficient improvement from medication, feel their child cannot cope with the school environment. Some parents begin home schooling as a temporary measure to keep their student engaged in learning until he's ready to return to the public or private school setting.

The success or failure of home schooling depends on many factors. First, there is the issue of limited time availability for the parent who's juggling part- or full-time work outside the home, and the needs of other children in the family. Most parents who do home schooling must learn their new teaching skills "on the job" and then teach a wide variety of academic subjects. While some parents adapt fairly easily, many find it a daunting task. It's important to take your own ability to cope with the demands of home schooling into account before deciding how to handle your child's OCD-related learning needs. Each parent and child is in a different situation and must make the best decision for her family.

Integrating Home Schooling and Homebound Instruction

In many cases, a combination of home schooling by a parent and a certain number of hours each day or week of homebound instruction by a teacher works best for the parent and child with OCD. Here are some different parental accounts demonstrating different solutions and the tradeoffs of in-school versus home school learning for a child with OCD.

> My son is fourteen with severe OCD symptoms, and, after having problems with him getting picked on by other kids at school, he's being taught at home by me and by one of his teachers from school. I get the books and lesson plans for what I teach (right now English and American history) directly from his school. Then his math teacher comes to teach him algebra and give him tests. In order to get his

homebound instruction, we had to have a letter from his doctor sent to the school board. Some of his teachers really didn't understand much about OCD, so I brought some of the books I had to school for them to read. This is the second year we've done it this way, and he passed last year okay, so I feel this is best for him right now.

My son just can't handle public school right now. As a single mother I can't afford private school and I find it hard to manage teaching him on top of everything else I have to do. It's really hard to do at night after a long day. But the main problem with home schooling is that it seems to just add a lot of tension to our relationship. Sometimes, he just won't do the work I give him. Right now, he's got homebound instruction with a teacher coming to the house a few hours a day. He seems to do much better with that. He does the work for this teacher, maybe because he thinks of her as "the teacher" and not Mom. This is not enough for the long haul, but it's the best we can do for now.

Learning about all the options available to meet your child's educational needs is the most important first step for a parent facing the issue of schooling a child with OCD. Again, no solution is right for every child. Likewise, each child's needs change as he matures and as he gets a better handle on his OCD.

CHAPTER 12

Special Issues for Younger Children and Preteens

The younger child who meets the recognized criteria for OCD is said to have pediatric-onset, or early-onset, OCD. This raises practical issues and implications for parents dealing with the younger child who has this disorder. A younger child will often express his OCD symptoms differently than an older child. Younger children tend to have different comorbid disorders with their OCD, and they require a simpler language in order to "talk back" to OCD. This chapter covers issues of particular relevance to the age groups of three- to eight-year-olds, identified as the younger child, and nine to thirteen, here called preteens.

Pediatric-Onset OCD

Noted OCD researcher Dr. Daniel Geller of Massachusetts General Hospital reported in the medical journal *The Psychiatric Clinics of North America* (2006 June) that pediatric OCD has a peak age of onset in *pre-adolescent childhood*. Geller advises mental health professionals that pediatric OCD patients will often demonstrate poor insight into the nature of their obsessions, which, combined with their limited verbal ability, can make diagnosis difficult.

Dr. Gellar points to some other key differences between pediatric- and adult-onset OCD:

- More boys than girls have pediatric-onset OCD, although the numbers of males and females with OCD is about even, or leans slightly toward females, by adulthood.
- Patients with pediatric OCD show a higher rate of tic and mood and anxiety disorders.
- Children with OCD show more ADHD and oppositional behavior disorders.
- Family studies show that pediatric OCD is highly familial, and new data supports prior findings that childhood onset of the disorder is associated with a markedly increased risk for familial transmission of OCD, tic disorders, and ADHD.

If a parent and child both have OCD it often complicates the recognition and treatment of the child's OCD symptoms. One mother who spent much of her day in silent prayer to ward off imagined disasters from striking her family had trouble seeing her daughter's terror at rain and lightning storms—expressed by the child as tears, screams, and trouble breathing—as anything out of the ordinary. Another mother who emptied and rearranged her kitchen cabinets several times a day didn't think it odd that her four-year-old son went through a doorway several times before he felt he'd done it "just right." Of course, none of these behaviors by themselves are necessarily symptoms of OCD. However, in these cases, both children were later diagnosed with the disorder.

 Fact

A child seven or younger may not realize that his OCD is unusual and will not try to hide it. He may get angry when a parent or caregiver does not go along with his rituals. Or, he may be fatigued but unable to sleep due to all the stress of his daily worries and repetitions.

The things that trigger OCD in children tend to be similar across different cultures, ethnic groups, economic classes, and family types (one or two parents, young or older parents, and so on). Many parents of children who developed full-blown OCD in childhood say they first noticed symptoms during the child's infancy and toddler years.

First Signs of OCD

Younger children with OCD tend to show a fascination for details at a very early age. They have a strong need for order and repetition, and show severe upset reactions when interruptions and changes occur in their routines. They often demonstrate abnormally intense fears about germs, bugs, blood, fecal matter, genitals, separation, strangers, changes in routines, and the dark. Of course, the fact that many of these fears are common and age appropriate for younger children can make it difficult for parents to detect a problem without the benefit of hindsight. Here are some examples of OCD symptoms in young children and preteens:

> Even as an infant, Lisa had to have her covers, food, and good night rituals a certain way, or she would scream and cry.

> At three, Jared built his Legos so they were just right, and then refused to take them apart. They had to stay exactly the same way for months at a time.

> A four-year-old had to go around and check that every light switch and electronic appliance in the house was turned off at night before he'd go to bed.

> At five, Bobby had a constant fear that there was "poop" in his pants. He would check his underwear at least eight times a day.

Eight-year-old Jamie feared that her underwear would fall down at school. She ended up wearing a bathing suit under her clothes to avoid that possibility.

Lisa, at ten, had to count everything around her, even if she was talking or while someone spoke to her. She counted cars, people on the street, words spoken to her or read on the page.

Justin, as a toddler, would do a puzzle over and over, fifteen or thirty times. If he did something wrong, he'd get angry and allow no one to help him.

A twelve-year-old won't use his pencils or crayons because if he does, they won't align evenly in the box.

Parents Share

These reports on the onset of their children's OCD symptoms come from parents. They reflect the most common childhood obsessions; namely, a fear of contamination and the need for order and certainty, along with the most frequently seen compulsive rituals and behaviors that often go along with these obsessions: washing, checking, avoiding, counting, and ordering.

As discussed in Chapter 2, sometimes an ordering compulsion takes the form of a need for "perfect" symmetry. To many young people (and adults) with OCD, this takes the form of making things even. Many with OCD call this symptom "evening up" or "lining up." Here Paula T., a mom, describes the advent of her son's "evening up" symptoms at age eight in an account titled "Managing OCD for Life" published on the OCF Chicago Web site.

For several years we didn't know Dan had OCD because he was symptomatic at school but not at home. . . . Dan retraced letters that looked uneven when he wrote, and if he touched something with his right hand, he had to touch it with his left hand, too. Dan also had to "even up" conversation by silently repeating backward everything he said and heard. . . . Dan is now thirteen, and dealing with his OCD is one of many things he does. Dan knows his OCD never really goes away, but with the training he received from his therapist, and refresher sessions as needed, he has the tools to manage his OCD for life.

My six-year-old son was climbing on my lap when his leg accidentally bumped the coffee table. He promptly got off my lap, went back to the table, and purposely bumped his other leg. Groan. I knew! He couldn't get into the kitchen, because he couldn't get both feet to touch the threshold at the same place and for the same amount of time. Back and forth over the threshold he would go. It was terrible to watch . . . I recognized that my eldest also had some of these symptoms and I recognized how much of this I had struggled with myself over the years.

This second account, from Nancy G., posted on the OCF Chicago Web site, illustrates OCD as a family affair. See the complete accounts and more at *www.ocfchicago.org*.

Many parents describe young children who manifested an early symptom of OCD by speaking constantly, often repeating the same word(s) over and over. These mothers describe how this symptom developed at a very young age.

My daughter is six and an incessant talker. It can be awful when I'm stuck in the car with her; sometimes she'll have things I have to say back exactly the same. "We're going to the store" is one. Then I have to say, "Yes, we're going to the store," right away, over and over or she'll have a meltdown. She even talks in her sleep.

My four-year-old daughter wants us to ask her the same questions all day long. She'll tell us to say, "What are you doing?" and then she'll answer, "Playing." Then she'll want to repeat it until she's done with that activity (sometimes a half hour to an hour). This was cute when she started it at two, but now it's driving us crazy.

Incessant talking can be an early sign of OCD. But it can also be a passing phase, or a symptom of another disorder such as ADHD. Continued monitoring is your best first step, noting how long the behavior lasts and the co-occurrence of any other symptoms you may note. Then discuss your observations with your child's pediatrician.

 Fact

From 10 to 50 percent of pediatric-onset OCD patients experience total or substantial remission of their OCD symptoms by late adolescence when they receive proper and effective treatment.

Helping the Younger Child and Preteen Battle OCD

Younger children and preteens need different things from their parents in order to do battle with OCD. In addition to playing a larger role in home exposure exercises, you will need to tread carefully as you change your own behaviors, which may be tangled up in your child's OCD. For example, don't withdraw reassurances abruptly if your child is the kind who is always asking for it. And don't quit participating in your child's rituals without warning.

Essential

Sometimes it's necessary to let your child go all the way into an obsession before he can summon the will to resist or let go of it. A good way to handle this is to structure a "worry time" into his day. In the ten, twenty, or thirty minutes allotted, he can let the obsession rule by worrying as much as he wishes to about any given trigger. Chances are, after the allotted time has transpired, he'll be bored with his obsession, and will then have a much better chance of beating it.

If a younger child has OCD, it is especially important to discuss any planned change in your interactions with him before making the change. Surprises and spontaneity do not go over well with a child with OCD. The concept of weaning is a good one to employ here. And, with the younger child, this approach is especially useful.

Still, despite all such attempts to smooth over transition times, the younger child with OCD typically has difficulty separating from her parents. Separation anxiety can go on for a longer period of time in the child with OCD as compared to other children at the same developmental age, and it can show up in unexpected places.

My daughter is six and has OCD. Her separation anxiety is one of the worst things for her and my husband and me. She cries every day when she goes to school. I have to tell her over and over again that I won't forget to come back and get her at three o'clock. But, she even does it in our house. If I leave her in the family room and go to the kitchen, she will scream and cry; she's afraid I'm going to leave her alone in the house (something which I've never done).

For a parent facing this extreme separation fear in a young child, exposures can be structured to have the child practice being alone in another room, beginning for very short periods, and gradually building up to longer times. Rewards often work well to reinforce each small success achieved.

Dealing with High-Stress Times

Different times of the day present different challenges when dealing with a child with OCD. Probably all parents would agree that the two most problematic time periods, in order of difficulty, are mornings and bedtimes. Preparation the night before can help take the stress out of school days.

Try doing these activities the night before the morning of your child's school day:

- Choose and lay out clothes
- Pack book bag and put it by the front door
- Take care of all special logistics (permission slips, outings, changes in pick-up times or persons)
- If your child has morning- or evening-based rituals (such as hand washings), set a timer to an established amount of time
- Employ a previously agreed-upon reminder system for your hurry-ups; for example, "We have to leave in ten minutes"

With your child's consent, place morning and end-of-day triggers at the top of her priority list for exposure exercises, and be sure to offer praise and rewards when goals are met.

Meltdowns and Tantrums

In your role as assistant coach in your child's battle against OCD, you are often called on to offer feedback, re-direction, and praise for his efforts. You also have to help him locate and pay heed to proper boundaries for his behavior. As you know, each developmental age has different cognitive and emotional processing abilities. Therefore the specific words and tone used should differ when dealing with younger children versus preteens. This can become particularly important if your child is facing a great deal of frustration and acts out with a tantrum, or a fit of crying and screaming.

Dealing with tantrums and fits is never easy; they always seem to come at the worst possible times. There are different methods to defuse these situations depending on the age and developmental level of the child.

- For the younger child who acts out, your goal is to help him wind down his tantrum. To do so, it helps to say in a slow, calm voice, "When you can talk to me in a regular voice, I can help you."
- A preteen will usually have more pride about how he's addressed. Then it might work better to frame your statement with that in mind: "Don't lose your cool," or, simply, "Slow down and tell me what happened."

Re-occurring tantrums are more common in a younger child with OCD. An older child dealing with the disorder may display more defiance and quieter forms of resistance.

Tantrums can be especially trying for any parent.

> For me my daughter's emotional outbursts and tantrums are the most exhausting part of my day. If she misses one arithmetic problem, she howls and screams as if she's in extreme pain. And I guess she is.

When dealing with tantrums or tears of frustration in a child with OCD, it's important to react with calm. If you need a moment to take a deep breath before dealing with your crying or screaming child, by all means take a few minutes to be by yourself. Whatever words are used, when your child is freaking out when things are not "just so," or he's having difficulty with a home exposure exercise or is stressed from a hard day at school, the most important message you can communicate to him is that *you're on his side.* Following from this basic premise is the statement that both you and he are united in your battle against the OCD.

 Essential

Targeting parents of younger children with OCD and other anxiety disorders, Worry Wise Kids is a terrific new online resource for parents who need help. Affiliated with the Children's Center for OCD and Anxiety Disorders in Plymouth Meeting, PA, the Web site offers a wealth of online resources for managing OCD in young children at home and at school. Go to *www .worrywisekids.org.*

As a parent of a child with OCD you often have to shift your attention from one symptom to another as your child's disorder waxes and wanes or transforms from one set of obsessions to another. In order to stay one step ahead of the OCD, it helps to keep learning about the disorder from other parents and the resources available online and in your local library or bookstore.

The Beginning of Scrupulosity

Defined as a hyper-religious or moralistic expression of OCD, the preteen who judges herself harshly, often for the very "bad" thoughts that are a result of her OCD, is said to be displaying scrupulosity or religiosity. The child often acts out a compulsive need to apologize, pray, or both to stave off the terrible consequence she fears will come to her or others as a result of her "badness." The incessant prayer is done openly and secretly.

> "I have to pray for everyone I know before I go to bed," says one preteen girl.

> "I was afraid to hurt the feelings of plants, even inanimate things like rocks," said a young boy.

This expression of OCD is another aspect of a child's obsessive need for certainty, such as doubting. She questions everything: the weather, what she said seconds before, whether she cheated on a test, if she burped at the table, or whether she was rude to her parents. In what is one of the most painful expressions of this symptom for a parent to witness, the child will often question something quite ordinary she just did, such as passing the peas at the dinner table, and then be horrified that she "left someone out" and thus offended him.

Given its often-broad swath in a child's personality, scrupulosity can be a difficult symptom to approach in OCD treatment. As with any exposure, the first step is to label the specific behavior (apologizing, incessant praying) as the OCD, not the child. It then helps to break your child's target symptoms down into as many smaller triggers as possible. An exposure for scrupulosity can take a counterintuitive form (to a parent) when the exercise appears to promote intentional rudeness or disrespectful behavior in a child.

For example, a child may be encouraged to keep things to herself (not share) when interacting with family members, and not apologize for this apparent lack of generosity on her part. She may give herself permission to interrupt others or burp intentionally at the dinner table. She then may struggle to let her guilty feelings pass without doing a ritual, such as a prayer or apology, no matter how much she feels the compulsion to do so.

If you are a parent with strong religious convictions, and you find yourself dealing with a child experiencing scrupulosity obsessions of a religious nature, you may find yourself confused about how to support her religious beliefs without triggering her OCD. This topic is covered further in Chapter 13 in the section on adolescent scrupulosity.

Dealing with Tics

Because so many younger children and preteens with OCD also suffer from the tics associated with Tourette's syndrome (TS), it's important for you as a parent to know about this disorder because its symptoms may also be present in your child. Tourette's syndrome is characterized by involuntary movements, motor tics, and involuntary sounds, vocal tics. These sounds and movements may not be bothersome to your child, or it's possible that his tics are so much a part of your child's demeanor that neither of you recognize them as symptoms of a disorder.

However, for many young OCD sufferers, tics are a cause of embarrassment and a barrier to social interaction. Some say they exhaust enormous energy on a daily basis to try and hide their tics from others, often without success. Three quarters of those suffering from TS are male. Some common tics include:

- A head or eye twitch
- A jerking arm, the motion and its negation
- A sniff, blink, swallow, or foot tap
- A word or statement repeatedly shouted out
- A burp, oink, or part of a word

Verbalizations such as those above are tics when they are involuntary and reoccurring in the same way as the physical tics operate, for example, as involuntary movements. Many young people with OCD will also use "tic" as shorthand for an even wider range of OCD compulsions.

Tics and Shame

Many children with tics view these involuntary actions and verbalizations as *mistakes*. The child carries a lot of shame because he believes his tics are something he should be able to will away. Exposure exercises can be used to dampen the high levels of anxiety that accompany tics, but it's important that your child understands that tics are not mistakes; tics result from the same OCD that causes his other symptoms. As such, they are things his brain and body cannot control. Your child may or may not decide to explain his tics to friends or teachers. But you may wish to point out to your child that this kind of openness with people he encounters on a daily basis often works to his advantage by getting those people on his side.

Too Much Touching

One behavior associated with Tourette's syndrome and OCD, which is sometimes defined as a *tic,* is the nearly constant need of some children to touch things, often in a ritualistic manner. One boy with a touching compulsion couldn't walk through the school hallway without putting his hand on the top right corner of every locker. Another child had to touch things that caused him pain, including stove burners and straight pins. For many children, these touching tics can be alleviated or eradicated through the use of ERP exposure exercises.

Although they affect older children as well, touching compulsions are especially common in younger children with OCD. Here is one mother's account of her son's touching compulsion, and another mother who watched her daughter's incessant touching turn into a "just right" ritual.

> We noticed my seven-year-old son's frequent touching started after the death of his grandmother. He wanted to touch his father and me—all the time. At first I thought it was just to ask for reassurance. But it's been a year and it's gotten worse, and there are other OCD symptoms, too. We've started to work with

the CBT by having him limit the number of times he touches us.

My daughter Tiffany always has to touch people or things a certain way, and if she doesn't think she's done it right, she'll do it over and over again. She used to do the same thing with doors. If she didn't walk in or walk out in the correct manner, she'd have to go back in or out until she got it "just right." This is what showed me that rituals don't go away, one just changes into another.

Hair Pulling

Given the clinical name trichotillomania, hair pulling is a compulsive activity (like hand washing, ordering, and counting), which occurs within the OCD spectrum of behaviors. A 2005 study at Harvard McLean Hospital showed that hair pulling tends to affect females and younger children with more severe cases of pediatric-onset OCD. Those with comorbid hair pulling are also likely to have tics.

Hair pulling is often one of the least conscious compulsive actions—many young children are completely unaware they are doing it. Since it, too, is a reaction to anxiety, the best way to approach it is by attempting to find the trigger for the child's anxiety. Does she have a contamination fear in the classroom? Is she worried about having to speak in class? These are the sorts of triggers to help her locate and attempt to deal with through exposure exercises.

Our daughter who is five was diagnosed with trichotillomania when she was three years old and just starting nursery school. I noticed when she stopped pulling her hair, she started incessant talking, specifically, counting everything in sight, all the time.

Skin Picking

This OCD symptom affects boys and girls equally and often begins in childhood. Like hair pulling, the younger child tends to have less conscious awareness of her compulsive skin picking. Here a mother connected her daughter's compulsive skin picking to the start of a new school year when her daughter was to enter the seventh grade.

> It's back-to-school time and my child's OCD and skin picking is back in full force. There are new sores on her face, and on her neck and arms. One way I've dealt with it is to have her wear long sleeves. But then she tried to stay home from school, and when I wouldn't permit that, she screamed and cried. I think she can get through it if she hangs in there, and I'm trying to work with the teacher to lessen the stress with breaks from class and early dismissals.

From Amy Willensky comes this description of skin picking as a symptom of her comorbid OCD and Tourette's syndrome, from *Passing for Normal:*

> There are still days when I want to rip off my fingernails or sit on my hands to keep from making an initial gratifying gouge. . . . [When] I imagine my body as a skinned tomato.

A child's skin picking is often among the first OCD symptom that a parent notices. If you observe a young child skin picking, monitor her closely. She may attempt to hide it from you, and she may well have some shame and embarrassment about her sores and raw skin. Tread carefully, and always let your child know you are on her side.

Social Difficulties

One of the great payoffs of starting OCD treatment with younger children and preteens is its potential to give them a much easier time with peers. Prior to treatment, friendship can be a minefield for a child with OCD, with much of the child's time and energy spent hiding his rituals and tics, and resisting his inner perfectionist's urge to criticize what he perceives as his friends' sloppy habits. In his autobiographical novel, *Not as Crazy as I Seem*, George Harrar depicts such a moment from the perspective of a young boy with OCD.

> [Harrar's character as narrator describes an incident with a new friend:] We go inside and he takes me upstairs to his room, which is the messiest place I've ever seen. There are piles of clothes in one corner and all kinds of sneakers in another. Under the window there are rows of Sprite cans three deep and ten wide. . . . His bed is stripped to the mattress and the covers are bunched up at the foot. The boy's friend invites him into the room, but he declines, saying, "Maybe I better go. It's getting late."

A child with OCD who has a contamination fear is facing a daunting barrier to his ability to have and keep a friend his own age. As this fictional vignette demonstrates, the child's avoidance of potential friends is often the result.

For the younger child, it may be helpful for you to speak to the playmate's parent before your child spends time at her house. You can simply inform the parent that your child has OCD, that she's in treatment, and, in the meantime, there are things your child may do that could be unsettling to someone who does not understand her problem. For example, you may wish to mention her need to wash more than once before having a snack, or discuss any special foods you may need to send with her. Until your child is further along in treatment, it may make the most sense to invite her friend(s) to your home.

CHAPTER 13

Special Issues for Teens

As preteens become teens, their expression of OCD changes to reflect their greater cognitive, physical, and emotional development, as well as their maturing personalities. The adolescent with OCD often faces more challenges than his younger counterpart, as he carries his interests, as well as his OCD symptoms, out into the world beyond his parents' view. Obsessions that appeared first in the preadolescent years may now become more problematic, including scrupulosity and violent thoughts. There is often an increase in obsessions about sexuality and a propensity for adolescents with OCD to develop eating disorders—all of this making the teen years a trying time for parents.

Adolescents with OCD at School

Because academic and social issues play such a major role in your adolescent's day-to-day life, OCD issues will be magnified when he enters high school. By the age of fourteen, if his OCD has been present for some period of time, the youngster may have formed many OCD-related behavioral patterns and avoidance strategies which, though they may have worked when he was younger, do not stand up to the pressures of adolescence. One reason why this is true is that parents are less able to shield their children from the social and academic consequences of a child's OCD behaviors in the high school setting, where more independence and accountability are required for the student to succeed there.

Some OCD-related issues, which may take on added weight in high school, include the following:

- Difficulty concentrating, following directions and completing assignments in class; concentration can be hindered by the adolescent's persistent, repetitive thoughts, which often take on higher stakes with the added pressures of standardized tests.
- Social isolation or withdrawal from peers is often made more intense by the more complex social interactions between boys and girls at this stage.
- Low self-esteem in social and academic activities can hamper a student's success in high school.
- Medication side effects can sometimes be as debilitating and distracting as the OCD symptoms.
- Learning disorders that are often overlooked as the treatment for OCD takes precedence can become especially detrimental, as academic subjects in high school require greater and more sophisticated reading, writing, and presentation skills.

Many of the accommodations and school interventions introduced in Chapter 11 take on an even greater importance as the student with OCD enters high school. These are some of the school strategies that help older students:

- Allow more time to complete homework and in-class assignments.
- Accommodate late arrivals when there are problems at home.
- Allow the student to tape-record homework if he has trouble writing.
- Give the student a choice of projects if he has difficulty beginning a certain task.

- Allow the student to change the sequence or numbering of items in homework assignments if he has problems involving odd or even number sequences.
- Adjust the homework load (stretch it out or change sequence of due dates) to reduce likelihood of the students becoming overwhelmed.
- Break up school attendance with at-home independent study to offer breaks.
- Negotiate expectations for transitions within school hours, for example, between classroom assignments or between classes.

How can a parent help the secondary school student with OCD? Encourage your student to change her own expectations of her school performance to bring them more in alignment with her OCD treatment progress—thus far. Cheer her on with success stories you gather from other mothers. Flexibility needs to be applied to attendance, grades, social success, and other standard measures of high school performance. The rest of this chapter focuses on specific areas of OCD symptoms that can be especially troubling for adolescents, and some strategies for handling them.

Dealing with Aggressive Thoughts

Affecting both boys and girls with OCD, unwanted violent images and thoughts are a particularly troubling and common adolescent symptom. For parents, this OCD symptom can produce enormous worry because of fears that the teenager may act on his aggressive thoughts and harm another person or himself. In the vast majority of cases, this fear is unwarranted. The youngster's imagined scenes, in which he inflicts harm through his deeds or thoughts, are no more "real" than any other type of OCD obsession.

Because obsessions involving violence and aggression are so common in teens with OCD, it's important for you as a parent to be prepared for their likely appearance in your teenager, if they aren't present already.

> One fourteen-year-old boy says: "I'm mad at my little brother for messing up my room. Then I see him getting hit by a car. When a car hits him, it will be my fault. I'm afraid I'm going to kill my little brother."

A violent thought of this variety brings a great deal of fear and shame to the teenager that experiences it, especially as the thought is replayed over and over in his mind in the course of a day, or longer. His shame can then get in his way when he tries to carry out an OCD exposure exercise focused on the recurring "bad thought." Before he can begin, he may have to allow himself to sink into his feelings of shame, letting it "take over his mind," so the obsession gets neutralized or, put another way, until he becomes bored with it.

Teen Sexuality and OCD

As many as 25 percent of teenagers with OCD have intrusive thoughts of a sexual nature. Again, this happens to both girls and boys. When these involuntary thoughts assault a teenager with OCD, they often bring the sufferer shame, embarrassment, and confusion. Obsessions of this type can be triggered in the teenager when she sees something as simple and innocent as two people expressing appropriate affection in public, like hugs, kisses, or holding hands. Similar scenes in movies and on television can have the same effect.

> I can't even look at a girl or really have much in the way of relations because of obsessive fears being triggered. Every girl I find attractive, my mind will immediately go to an image of my sisters or my mother. I will conclude that they resemble them in some way, and thus it's immoral to pursue this. I can't indulge in any kind of sexual expression or activity because of this.

Sexual anxiety can also be triggered in the OCD teen by his internal thoughts, with or without a stimulus. For example, when the image of a pretty girl occurs to a teenage boy, his OCD can cause him to imagine that girl engaged in "disgusting" or inappropriate sexual acts. The main point for parents to understand is that these obsessions, like any other OCD symptoms, are involuntary; your teenager has no control over when and if these thoughts come into his mind. Neither does he have the desire to engage in the acts that are causing him so much anxiety. Most often they are repellant to him. As the thoughts keep recurring, his shame and discomfort intensify.

Gender Instability

A heterosexual teenager with OCD will often develop an irrational fear that he is, or may become, homosexual. This very common obsession for teenage boys with OCD can prevent an adolescent from joining a sports team or any activity that puts him in close proximity to his peers. Locker rooms can be an especially trying environment for boys dealing with this issue. Here is one heterosexual thirteen-year-old boy with OCD sharing his experience dealing with his sexuality obsession and the resulting avoidance compulsion.

> If I looked at a guy's butt, groin, or face, I'd get a picture in my mind of kissing him, or having sex with him. So I looked away, or at the ground. A friend of mine asked why I always did that. I said because I'm shy.

Some of the other issues relating to male gender roles that provide fodder for teenage boys with OCD include fears of their own physical inadequacy, intellectual inferiority, and potential subordination to women. If a teenage boy with OCD has a belief system that includes a very "macho," ultraresponsible model of manhood, he may be more susceptible to self-doubts and fears in this area.

Since adolescence is already a time of huge emotional and hormonal growth and changes, it should not surprise parents to learn that gender roles and sexuality issues are common areas for OCD-related obsessions.

OCD specialist and psychologist Dr. Fred Penzel, author of *Obsessive-Compulsive Disorders: A Complete Guide to Getting Well and Staying Well*, addressed this issue on the OCF Teens' Organized Chaos Web site in an article titled, "The Boy Who Didn't Know Who He Was":

> One of the really maddening qualities of OCD is that it can make a person doubt the most basic things about himself—things no one would normally doubt. Even one's sexual identity can be questioned. . . . Doing compulsions, such as repeated questioning, avoiding things, looking for reassurance, and checking can work in the short run, [but] this is what keeps the problem going. By staying away from the things that make them anxious, sufferers only keep themselves sensitive to these things. . . . A favorite saying of mine goes, "If you want to think about it less, think about it more."

Religiosity and Scrupulosity

One way a teenager who has sexual subject matter as a dominant theme in her obsessions may manifest these intrusive thoughts is with compulsive actions and rituals reflecting her belief that she is a bad person or a sinner. If she has this issue, she'll often live with an unrelenting terror that she will be punished for her sins in life and/or go to hell. Incessant needs to pray or seek forgiveness from those around her are two common manifestations of this obsessive type.

Religiosity (also called *scrupulosity*) affects young people of all religions and cultures. For many OCD sufferers, these obsessions begin in childhood or during the preteen years. This does not mean that a family or individual's religious beliefs *cause* a religious obsession in a child with OCD. It may be more useful to view religion as another container available to this predatory disorder; just as any other part of the OCD sufferer's belief system can be warped by the wide-reaching brain malfunction the disorder inflicts, so can her religious beliefs. In an article from the spring 2007 OCF newsletter, therapist Laurie Krauth, M.A., recounted religiosity themes present in her preadolescent, teen, and young adult OCD clients:

> A nine-year-old girl obsesses that she once spelled "God" without capitalizing it and avoids stepping on the floor stains that look like Jesus.

> We are cutting shapes out of construction paper at the table and I'm thinking the devil will make me lose control.

> A chaste Christian college freshman obsesses that his close dancing with a girl is "bad."

In the same article, Krauth reports on the positive outcomes for these and other clients after they received treatment using CBT and ERP treatment for their religious obsessions.

 **Fact**

A 2004 study done by the Mayo Clinic showed that college students with OCD who described themselves as highly or moderately religious reported they did more compulsive hand washing and held more beliefs about the importance of their thoughts than was reported by OCD sufferers who were not so religious. The religious OCD sufferers also believed more often that their thoughts could influence someone else (usually negatively).

If your teenager displays tendencies toward scrupulosity or religiosity in her OCD expression, it should be recognized and labeled in the same manner that you would treat any other OCD obsession and compulsion—not as a part of your teenager's core self, but rather as OCD hijacking her brain and speaking through her. Remember the mantra: "It's not me, it's the OCD." At the same time, if you are a person with strong religious beliefs, you may feel some conflict about the fact that your child's faith has become intertwined with her OCD symptoms. This is a natural reaction for a parent.

Joseph W. Ciarrocchi, Ph.D., of Loyola College in Maryland pinpointed some of the issues that can arise in this aspect of the therapeutic treatment of OCD in his paper titled "Religion, Scrupulosity and Obsessive Compulsive Behavior." It appears in the book *Obsessive-Compulsive Disorders: Theory and Management.*

> Researchers and clinicians now agree that the more intractable symptoms in OCD often fall under the rubric of overvalued ideas. Overvalued ideas occupy a midway point between reality and delusion: ideas firmly held but with a tinge of uncertainty as to their truth. Religious obsessions and compulsions, because they involve the ethical dimension for people, frequently fall into this category of overvalued ideas. People with OCD may sense the irrationality of their anxiety-driven religious behavior, yet cannot give themselves permission to act against the religious compulsions.

In his chapter on OCD and religiosity, Dr. Ciarrocchi discusses the potential resistance in a religious person with OCD who is attempting to challenge and change his own religious compulsions. But he also points to the ethical responsibility of the therapist to continually hold and show respect for a client's religious beliefs, and not to in any way disparage or reduce the role of religion in a client's life.

Balancing the importance of faith in the religious OCD sufferer's core belief system, and helping him remove any obsessive thinking that has infected his religious belief system, is a delicate, sensitive process for a client and therapist. If you are concerned about this aspect of your child's OCD treatment, it is a good idea to discuss your concerns openly with his therapist. If your adolescent with OCD sees his therapist without you, you can encourage him to address it in a one-on-one conversation with his therapist.

Many parents of children with OCD rely on their faith to help them get through the arduous day-to-day challenge of keeping hope alive as a child's treatment continues. There is no reason why religion and treatment for a child's OCD should in any way conflict with each other in the long term for either parents or children with OCD.

Eating Disorders

Both OCD and eating disorders in adolescence revolve around the teenager's need to control her body and what goes into it. Of course, given the fact that healthy eating is essential to your teenager's health, this area can become a source of tremendous conflict between parents and teenagers with OCD. Because eating disorders already affect so many teenagers, the parents of teenage OCD sufferers must stay on high alert for any symptoms that appear to cross the line from OCD to the more extreme behaviors associated with eating disorders. Among the symptoms of an eating disorder is a complete or near complete refusal to eat, binge eating, the repeated throwing up of food, also called purging, or an "inappropriate compensatory behavior."

According to the Anxiety Disorder Association of America (ADAA), OCD is one of the most common anxiety disorders to co-occur with eating disorders. Here's how ADAA summarizes the overlapping symptoms of these two disorders:

> Eating disorders and OCD share many of the same features. Females with anorexia may suffer from obsessions with exercise, dieting, and food. They often develop compulsive rituals such as weighing every bit

of food, cutting food into tiny pieces, repeated checking of weight, or mirror checking. There are also similar characteristics between bulimia and OCD. Like the compulsions in OCD, binges are difficult to resist and hard to control. While binges provide some immediate relief to the sufferer, like the compulsions characteristic of OCD, this relief is short-lived and temporary.

Anorexia Nervosa

This disorder is marked by an intense fear of gaining weight or becoming fat, even if the sufferer is substantially underweight. Infrequent or absent menstrual periods (the absence of at least three consecutive menstrual cycles) in females who have reached puberty is one alarm signal for parents of a teenage girl that anorexia nervosa may be present in addition to OCD.

Teenagers with anorexia may repeatedly check their body weight, and many engage in other techniques to control their weight, such as intense and compulsive exercise, or purging by means of vomiting and abuse of laxatives, enemas, and diuretics. Teenagers with anorexia nervosa who regularly engage in binge eating or purging behavior are considered to have the binge-eating/purging type of anorexia nervosa. For the behavior to be clinically defined as a disorder, the binge eating and inappropriate compensatory behaviors must both occur, on average, at least twice a week for three months. Because purging or other compensatory behavior follows the binge-eating episodes, young people with bulimia usually weigh within the normal range for their age and height. However, like individuals with anorexia, they often fear gaining weight, desire to lose weight, and feel intensely dissatisfied with their bodies. People with bulimia often perform the behaviors in secrecy, feeling disgusted and ashamed when they binge, yet relieved once they purge.

Fear of Vomiting

Not necessarily associated with an eating disorder, many young people with OCD have an extreme fear of vomiting. The idea of throwing up can prompt the child with this obsessive fear into a panic attack or other OCD ritualizing behaviors. Some may not exhibit other obvious symptoms of OCD, but may show more subtle avoidance behaviors; for example, a fear of going near anyone with any sort of illness (past or present) or disability, refusal to go on buses, on long car rides or amusement park rides, or into public places with dank smells.

Exposures to deal with a fear of vomiting would bring the child into contact first with images of her trigger, and then with the actual places and smells associated with the same trigger in order to habituate her to these things and slowly free her from the underlying obsession.

Body Dysmorphic Disorder (BDD)

A body image disorder with the clinical name body dysmorphic disorder, or BDD, is another condition that co-occurs frequently with OCD in teenagers. This disorder is characterized by a general dissatisfaction with the body, or parts of the body, causing the teenager recurring obsessions that cause severe emotional distress and interfere with his ability to function. BDD develops most frequently during adolescence and affects about one percent of the general population.

Many of the symptoms of BDD overlap with OCD, particularly the teenager's extreme self-consciousness about appearance, which causes teens with both disorders to check themselves repeatedly in mirrors, pick at their skin, groom excessively, and change outfits often. Both also attempt to hide these behaviors from others. Despite their similarities, OCD and BDD are considered two separate disorders. If you notice a concentration of these symptoms in your teenager, bring the question of a comorbid or co-occurring diagnosis to the attention of her mental healthcare provider.

Alcohol, Drugs, and Teens with OCD

Between 10 and 20 percent of adolescents have alcohol or drug problems. The illegal drugs being used by young people include the perennials, alcohol and marijuana (pot, weed). Other newer or less common dangerous substances include ecstasy (E), Ketamine (Special K), Mescaline (Mesc), amphetamines (Meth, speed), and cocaine. There are also reports of the use of cough medicines, prescription sedatives and painkillers, glue, and other aerosol products that reportedly give users a temporary and very dangerous high.

Given the reality of widespread drug abuse among young people, there are likely to be peer pressures impacting your child at school or in other social interactions that may encourage him to use alcohol and drugs, pressures that affect all teenagers. But teens with OCD face even higher dangers from these substances than young people not dealing with a difficult mental health disorder.

Young people dealing with OCD are particularly vulnerable to *alcohol and drug use* as a strategy for numbing their relentless OCD-related anxiety—even though their illegal drinking or drug taking *does not* provide the relief they seek.

Self-medication is the term used when young people take it upon themselves to use alcohol, illegal drugs or prescription medications prescribed for someone else in order to ease the bad thoughts, difficult feelings, and physical discomfort they experience as a result of OCD. The same temptation to self-medicate can affect teens who are already receiving treatment for OCD with medication and/or CBT therapy, as well as those not in treatment. This is true especially at particularly high-stress times or when teens feel their treatment is not providing the relief they crave from their OCD.

There are special dangers for the teenager with OCD who uses illegal drugs or alcohol. Abuse of these substances can cause depression in young people who are already at a higher risk for depression as a result of their OCD. Unknown drug interactions can lead to overdoses or significant medical complications. Abuse of prescription drugs can also reduce the effectiveness of the medications your child has been prescribed for his OCD.

Other Dangerous Teen Behaviors and OCD

Teenagers with OCD are especially vulnerable to negative peer pressures. Their uncomfortable feelings about being different and a desire to fit in can make teens with OCD go to great lengths to appear "cool" in front of those whose approval they seek, even when these peers introduce them to risky, self-destructive behaviors. The other issue that comes into play is the added vulnerability of teens with OCD to become obsessed with a new idea or activity, no matter how harmful it may be for them. "Cutting" (the deliberate piercing of skin to experience a feeling of pain) and sexual promiscuity are two such dangerous and potentially obsessive behaviors. Here a mother discusses how these temptations affected her teenage daughter.

> My daughter spent years spent in the relative safety of smaller, private elementary and middle schools before she got to the temptations of the high school social scene. Once there, she got into some really worrisome self-medication and sexually promiscuous behaviors. I think she was trying to connect with her new "friends" at any cost, particularly one friend who was into drugs and cutting, who my daughter really wanted to have like her. It's getting better now that she's in treatment for her OCD, but I see how easy the temptations come to her. I guess it's just true that most things are going to be harder for her, at least for now. And that's true with social life and friends, too.

While a teen without OCD may be able to experiment with drugs and other negative behaviors and walk away, the teenager with OCD is much more inclined to get stuck and not have the same ability to stop after starting.

Overcome Fear Through Support

All of these special concerns for parents of teenagers with OCD can make the adolescent years a lonely and fearful time for both the parents and teenagers involved. But, even with all these tricky age-related issues, you can take heart in knowing that both medication and CBT treatment will alleviate the symptoms of OCD and reduce the heightened vulnerability of adolescents with OCD to these dangerous behaviors. It bears repeating that multiple studies support the reality that treatment works best if you and your teenager work together *to talk back to the OCD.*

Of course, if your teenager is in treatment for his OCD, hope can be derived from each new goal mastered. Given the particularly high stresses that accompany this developmental period, parents and teens alike often find their participation in peer support groups and online networks to be the best source of solace, practical assistance and strength.

Help Your Teenager Find His Passion

One of the best forms of therapy, some would say the "best medicine" for any teenager who feels lost and alone, is for a youngster to find her own individual passion. What is a passion? Music, dance, reading or writing, spoken word poetry, gardening, animal care (pets can be the best therapy for many kids with anxiety disorders), knitting, crafts, stamp or coin collecting . . . the list goes on and on. And that's just the point. A passion is whatever moves your teenager to get out of her own way and into her best self. There is absolutely no reason why a teenager with OCD cannot find her own passion. There is actually even more reason for her to do so.

As a parent, your job is to support whatever she finds that can offer individual fulfillment. And if her OCD makes it harder to find that one thing, you might be able to help guide her to different choices based on your own special knowledge of what makes her happy despite the rigors of her disorder. Here is one mother's example:

My sixteen-year-old son Jamie just danced in his school's opening night performance of *West Side Story*. I cried when I saw him up there, looking so happy in his body, so free for those few moments of his OCD. Later he told me he loves dancing, but that I shouldn't tell anyone, in case he can't do it anymore. That made me sad but all I could do was to encourage him to think positive. That if he made it through opening night, the rest would be easier.

As is often the case with parenting, the greatest opportunities to be a good parent arrive spontaneously—in the car on the way to school, in the middle of the night when your child can't sleep—and depend on your own intuition. All that this book, or any other source of information on OCD, can do is help inform your own best instincts as a parent.

CHAPTER 14

Supporting Your Child

To use a sports analogy, if your child is the newest player on the "Beat OCD Team," then her therapist is head coach and you are *assistant coach.* Your number-one responsibility in this role is to support your child's treatment by helping him with exposure exercises at home. You also have to figure out how much involvement on your part is too little or too much until you discover what is just right for your child. The end goal for you as a family is to help the child impacted by OCD to better manage and recover from the debilitating effects of his disorder. For such a large and complex battle, it's important to have the best strategies right from the start.

Encouraging Self-Acceptance

As you assist your child in the battle against OCD, one of your first tasks will be to encourage her self-acceptance. With self-acceptance, or by accepting *what is*, she can have a starting place for her own growth and healing. If she resists what is real and true about her own mind and body, she can get stuck in denial, frustration, shame, or any number of unproductive emotions. The issue of acceptance can come up in crucial areas for your child and hamper progress in significant steps she must take, including accepting the fact that she's got a serious problem, believing that she can change for the better, and accepting the limitations, even if only temporary, that the disorder will place on her capabilities.

Essential

As a partner in your child's battle against OCD, you can be her objective mirror. In this role, you provide gentle feedback when you observe an increase in her anxiety level. You can also offer reminders when she's off track during an exposure exercise, trying especially hard not to nag or criticize. No one says your job is easy, just essential!

In order to help your child reach self-acceptance, you'll have to first work through any of your own feelings of guilt or shame that may have arisen upon hearing her diagnosis of OCD, or after beginning treatment. Only when you are clear of these negative feelings, and when you can keep your own frustrations out of the way of her treatment, will you be in a position to encourage your child to think positively about herself and her ability to tackle the difficult road that lies ahead.

Self-acceptance for a child with OCD comes when she does these three things:

- Recognizes she is separate from the OCD
- Decides she is capable of beating it
- Commits to doing exposure exercises on a daily basis

Again, none of these things can happen unless, or until, she knows and accepts her own strengths and limitations, and, with your help, makes a conscious plan to strengthen her weaker aspects. Only then will she be able to make OCD a smaller, perhaps even a nonexistent, part of her future.

How Parents Sabotage a Child's Efforts

For a parent standing on the sidelines, the most excruciating part of watching a child do battle with OCD is coming to terms with the many times you cannot and must not help him. This is a tough thing for many parents *to see and not do.* Many parents say they need to learn this lesson over and over again. Helping can actually hinder your child's progress in treatment for OCD. *The more you do for him, the less he'll do for himself.* It's that simple, but not simple to put into action. Here are several things not to do:

- Don't get involved in his rituals (for example, opening doors for him).
- Don't make excuses for your child.
- Don't assist (even if it's hard).
- Don't reassure or comfort him when he's confronting something.
- Don't change the rules without consulting him.
- Don't take over his treatment.
- Don't criticize his efforts.
- Don't overpraise, or praise him for doing nothing.
- Don't encourage him to avoid the hard things.

When parents step in to help when self-effort by a child is called for they are engaging in what can be called a "fix-it attack." If you're having a fix-it attack, you should stop what you're doing. Another word for this kind of unproductive intervention is *enabling.* Borrowed from the twelve-step program for dealing with addictions, enabling means doing for someone something they should do themselves, cleaning up after someone's messes, or not challenging someone who is hurting himself and others by his actions or lack of action.

How to Help Your Child Create Success

Research has demonstrated that children in treatment for OCD who have a parent's active involvement in at-home exposure exercises do better and show greater improvement than children who don't. There are tried-and-true techniques for doing OCD exposures exercises at home. In terms of general guidelines, each exposure exercise should routinely take from thirty to sixty minutes per day, and perhaps shorter to begin with. Each target behavior (trigger) should require an average of two to three days to deal with effectively. If progress is not made within the allotted time, your child's target may be too difficult for her at this time. In that case, break it down into smaller goals, so that you can build small, regular successes into the process.

Here are five things you can do to support your child:

- Do help him recognize OCD triggers.
- Do let him face the difficult things.
- Do keep life simple with regular meals and bedtime.
- Do practice self-calming techniques.
- Do offer praise for his efforts.

Eventually your child will be educating *you* about OCD. For better or worse, he is the resident OCD expert in your family, and he'll become an even more informed authority on the subject as he develops the self-awareness that is an inevitable byproduct of his treatment.

Recognizing and Dealing with Triggers

A trigger is something that raises the anxiety level of a child with OCD and prompts his compulsive response. You can help your child identify his triggers and offer warnings when a trigger may be about to materialize—without subverting his progress. For example, you can forewarn your child about the upcoming visit of someone he doesn't know if the visit of a stranger is something that usually pro-vokes anxiety and prompts his OCD symptoms.

Alert!

Be on his side! Whatever you say or do in your role as your child's partner in the battle against OCD, please make sure he knows you are on his side at all times. The tendency to slip into being a critic or nag should be avoided at all costs!

Working with Triggers

A trigger prompts unwelcome thoughts or images in a child with OCD. It then precipitates compulsive rituals in response to these obsessive thoughts. A specific doorknob at home or elsewhere can be a trigger for a child with contamination fears. A math problem with odd numbers can trigger a child with an "even numbers only" ordering compulsion. A fight scene on a television program can trigger a young person to believe he'll do harm to someone he cares about—if he doesn't avoid that person or do a specific ritual. Triggers can be internal or external in origin.

A child with OCD gets increasingly familiar with her own triggers as she advances in treatment. In each new exposure exercise, she agrees to take on a new trigger and makes it the target of that exposure. Once the child determines the degree of anxiety a trigger arouses, she puts herself in a real or imagined situation where she attempts to resist carrying out her typical compulsive response in reaction to that trigger. That is where the "P" in ERP comes into play: *preventing* her usual response to a trigger. In order to reach her goal, the child who is afraid of a doorknob will put her hand directly on that doorknob, beginning with a small amount of contact and gradually increasing it so that, by the end of her exposure exercise, she can use the doorknob solely for its original purpose—for opening and closing doors.

Bad Thoughts

The youngster with recurring violent images or thoughts where he sees himself harming someone will be guided to do exposures wherein he allows himself to see and feel the anxiety caused by the harmful activity he fears, and not look away. One young man who had unwanted "bad thoughts" involving violence toward others did an exposure exercise by reading a true crime novel about a serial killer. As expected, it was difficult for him to read about a real killer who did the same awful things he feared he, too, might do, and he experienced intense anxiety while he read his book. But, as a result of this structured exposure, this young man experienced a gradual lessening of his own violent thoughts and imagery.

Another way to approach a bad thought obsession in a child with OCD is to focus on the magical thinking that gives the child the false idea that thoughts alone have the power to cause harm to another person. For example, a typical bad thought in a child with OCD involves vehicles; the idea that his sibling, parent, or someone he sees on the street will be struck down by a car or train or bus *simply because he pictured it in his mind.* To deal with this obsession, the child can be encouraged to say aloud or silently remember the fact that the words or pictures in his mind have no magic attached to them; that they are "only words."

In each exposure exercise, the child with OCD sticks with the thing that scares him until the idea or image becomes boring, or meaningless, and thus no longer exerts any power over him. Another word for this process of continued exposure until an image or thought loses it power is *neutralization*; meaning, the child with OCD neutralizes the trigger until it no longer provokes anxiety.

You Can Go First

If a child is initially frightened of doing a bad thought exposure, an adult can model the exposure for him. In this case, you as parent would be the first to say the scary thought aloud. If, for example, the two of you are sitting in front of a window looking out on the street, you might say, "A man crossing the street is going to get hit by a car."

Next you could both watch an actual man cross the street, or the child can simply imagine this scene as you repeat your sentence several times. Repeating the sentence will cause the child's anxiety to build and make him very uncomfortable. It's important to stick it out, however, until it's clear the man (either the real one outside or the imagined person) has not been run over—thus neutralizing the child's imagined power (magical thinking) to inflict harm over another with mere words. Again, the key is to remind him that words—whether you say them or he does—are "only words," not an instrument of power to do physical harm.

Defining Your Role

For the young child with OCD, you as parent and assistant coach will play a very active role in carrying out home exposure exercises. This process begins when you ask your child for options (triggers) from which to select the next target for an exposure. Or, your child in conjunction with her therapist may have already selected her next trigger. Many parents of younger children doing CBT homework find it useful to keep a chart of targets, including those completed and others yet to be done.

To begin her exposure homework, you should always ask your child to assess her anxiety level—also called a *fear thermometer* and measured from zero to one hundred—at the beginning, middle, and end of each exercise and make a note of the child's temperature at each of these three points. She may want you to be the one who records her fear temperature as well as the outcome of each exposure, including how many times the exposure was performed and for how long.

In the case of hand washing, was she able to limit hand washings from six to three, two, or one? If your child's contamination fear is triggered by the idea that her nose is disgusting, children often refer to it as having "boogers," she can practice touching her nostrils or blowing her nose several times—allowing herself to feel the anxiety until it subsides.

As a partner in your child's OCD exposure, it's critical that you and your child are in agreement on your exact role. It's also important for the two of you to set up very clear rules for each exposure. For example, if trash is a problem area, decide beforehand whether your child must take out the trash without being asked or encouraged. In this way, you'll be able to minimize the inevitable friction between parent and child that can result from your own or your child's frustrations.

 **Question?**

What if he rejects my help?
If he balks at your participation in an exposure exercise, this signals a need to discuss or renegotiate your role with your child. An older child or teen may wish only to discuss his choice of targets for exposure exercises, and let you know the outcome later—or not. You'll have to be flexible, and find a way to stay connected to him during home exposure exercises without taking over. Remember, eventually he will have to do this on his own. Feel your way carefully at the beginning.

As CBT treatment continues over weeks, months, and even years, a child with OCD will need less and less help from his parent. The goal of CBT and ERP treatment is for the child to internalize the process, so that he does it whenever a trigger comes up in his day-to-day life. Many young adults with OCD have reached this point and can offer inspiration and encouragement to children or teens just starting out.

Keeping a Daily Log

One way to take nagging out of the equation and to provide a greater structure for success in the battle against OCD is by keeping a daily written log or chart of your child's exposure homework. This log should record the trigger, the goal of the exposure and its outcome, along with your child's anxiety levels at the beginning and end. Although you can help him maintain his daily log, a child dealing with OCD often feels empowered by keeping a log himself.

A daily log can also help you and your child stay aware of triggers associated with a certain time of day or situation. For example, if bedtime tends to raise fears of the dark, separation anxiety, or nightmares for your child, you can note in his daily log the increase or ebbing in these issues as treatment progresses. If an issue like the dark remains problematic, it may warrant being made a priority target for an exposure exercise. Conversely, if the symptom disappears or lessens in frequency, his progress can be noted on the daily log and be made a cause for celebration and a reward.

Find Creative Outlets for Your Child

There are different ways to enlist creativity in helping your child cope with her OCD. For the child who likes to draw, you can encourage her to depict the OCD (or whatever name she's given it) using colored paints, pencils, or a collage of found objects or art materials. This activity can provide an excellent outlet for her emotions, which can include anger, humor, sadness, or joy.

Creative writing is another good channel for her artistic impulses and emotions. The only caveat for writing as an emotional outlet is the potential for the child with OCD to get caught up in perfectionist tendencies around the written word. Encourage her to use her writing as an emotional outlet, not a test.

Ways to get around the pitfalls of perfectionism include:

- Encourage her to pretend she's telling her story to a friend.
- Have her tell it to you verbally first.
- Try "freewriting," where she writes down words or phrases that come to her without editing or censoring her thoughts.

Beyond the visual arts or creative writing, other helpful creative outlets include the performance arts, such as musical instruments, singing, or theater. Here's how one mother described the importance of music in her teenage son's life as he battled severe OCD:

> My son started playing the guitar two years ago and it's been wonderful for him, both as a break from dealing with his OCD and having at least one activity he can do where he's in total control. He had to teach himself at first, because it was hard for him to participate with a class. He didn't want to touch other guitars, and he didn't want the other kids to know about his OCD. Now, he's gotten very good at it, and will even perform in front of family and friends.

Alert!

Children battling OCD often experience mood swings, sleep difficulties, and emotional burnout. To help your child cope, make bedtime as tranquil as possible. Minimize TV and video games, and encourage self-calming exercises. If extreme moodiness continues, or if there are other signs of depression, discuss your child's symptoms with his therapist or doctor. New or different medication may be needed to help him better handle the challenges presented by his OCD.

At first glance, a musical or theatrical performance by a youngster with OCD may seem counterintuitive to a parent who is keenly aware of the shyness often suffered by her child. But you may be surprised to find that the child with OCD can subvert his own tendency toward extreme self-consciousness when he's given the opportunity to perform someone else's words or music.

Difficulties with Sleep

Insomnia affects everyone on occasion, caused by worries or physical ailments that delay or interrupt sleep. For the child with OCD, dogged by obsessive worries and fears, occasional sleeplessness can turn into a constant, chronic problem. Sleep problems are also associated with other mental health disorders, especially ADHD, depression, schizophrenia, and bipolar disorder. Sometimes, medications can affect your child's ability to fall and remain asleep. The sleep problems of a child with OCD can undermine a parent's ability to function, making this an area that requires special attention. In other words, don't be a stoic. Do get help; your whole family's health and safety are at risk when you don't get enough sleep as a result of your child's insomnia. Here are some examples from parents of children with OCD:

> Stephanie, who is eleven years old, is a very light sleeper who wakes up several times a night. I am in the same boat, since I also have OCD and insomnia.

> Jason, who's eight, wakes up in panic attacks. Right now his OCD is making him terrified of rainstorms or a tornado coming and wrecking our house, and killing us all. Any sort of noise, or no noise at all, can set him off. He'll start screaming and have trouble breathing.

> Whenever I walk by my twelve-year-old daughter's room at night and peek in, she's awake. She's stopped even calling out to me now, but during the day she

has dark circles under her eyes and I feel so bad for her.

Dr. James Claiborn, Ph.D., an OCD treatment specialist in South Portland, Maine, addressed OCD-related sleep problems in his article, "To Sleep, Perchance to Dream," on the Organized Chaos Web site, Volume 9. Claiborn is also the author (with Cherry Pedrick) of *The Habit Change Workbook*. He offers the following remedies for insomnia and nighttime panic.

> Strange as it may sound, nightmares may also be thought of as a habit problem. The most effective treatment for nightmares is to develop a script for the dream with a different ending. You can choose to make it come out any way you like. You can include things that are impossible in life because the world of dreams allows for magic. When you have a new script, you can rehearse it before bed each night. Despite the fact that nightmares are associated with anxiety disorders, they can be changed without having to do an exposure to the upsetting images.

The mother of Stephanie employed Dr. Claiborn's technique with positive results.

> We worked up a box; we actually decorated a shoebox and called it her "happy endings box." We took the ideas she'd written out and put them in the box next to her bed. Like she'd go (from a scary place in her dream) to the campground where we spent our last vacation, which she enjoyed. It also worked to use scenes from her favorite movies, to replace the bad scenes that would come to her in nightmares. I had my doubts about this when we started but it's definitely helping her sleep better.

Other ideas offered for helping kids and adults with OCD to get to sleep include:

- Make bedtime a comfortable routine; just don't make it into an inflexible ritual.
- Go to bed and get up at the same times every day.
- Exercise regularly; don't watch TV or use the computer too close to bedtime.
- Don't do things in bed other than sleep, like eating, watching TV, or using the computer.
- Don't obsess about not sleeping; deal with your fear of being up all night as you would other OCD-related fears: do an ERP exposure on what you fear most might happen.

If insomnia persists and these techniques are ineffective, you should raise the issue with your child's therapist or treating psychiatrist. In some cases, medication changes or additions can help.

Peer Support Groups

Ultimately, you must recognize the limitations of the emotional and practical help you can provide your child as his parent, and be open to what can and must come from sources outside of you and the family. As all parents know, peers take on added importance as your child ages. This is part of the normal process of separation that happens with maturation, but it can take on an even greater importance when an older child is dealing with the extraordinary demands of OCD.

Peer support groups are a great way for kids with OCD to share their burdens, learn coping strategies, make new friends, and gain support for their individual struggles. Your school special education coordinator may be able to refer him to such a group appropriate to his age and disability. Another resource will be his therapist. Even if there is not a specific support group for children with OCD in your community, there may be a professionally facilitated therapy group for young people dealing with a range of anxiety disorders. For example, you may be able to locate a *shyness clinic* (it may be called a social anxiety teen group) designed to help adolescents practice exposures in a group setting to help conquer the social anxiety and self-consciousness that can accompany a wide range of mental health disorders.

Finally, you can check with your national or state chapters of the OCD Foundation or other organizations listed in the Resources section for referrals to teen or child support groups in your local area.

 Essential

If there is no support group in your child's local community, an online OCD support community can be tremendously helpful to young people of all ages with OCD. With a younger child, of course, you will need to carefully supervise her online activities, but you can also play a helpful role by connecting with other parents of kids with OCD and then arranging age-appropriate introductions so your children can also "meet" and communicate via e-mail.

CHAPTER 15

Family Dynamics

OCD presents unique challenges for a family; thus, managing the challenges of OCD is by necessity a family affair. Whether yours is a single-parent or a two-parent family, there are common problems for parents and children when a child has OCD. Without a doubt, OCD strains marriages. Special problems also arise in the relationship between a child with OCD and his siblings, as well as with members of your extended family. When OCD occurs in one of your children, it affects the entire family. A family approach to the problem is therefore critical to your child's treatment, and to the well-being of the entire family.

Typical OCD-Related Family Stresses

Because OCD and other anxiety disorders tend to run in families, there may be one or more children and adults in your household currently battling the symptoms of OCD and anxiety. Particularly if you as a parent also have OCD, you may have a general resistance to recognizing the enormous impact the OCD is having on other family members. Part of the problem may be guilt you are unconsciously carrying about having "given" your child this difficult condition. Guilt like this can lead to denial. Denial of the dysfunctionality OCD has brought into your family relationships (also called family systems) is a barrier to treatment and must be recognized and dealt with before your child can get well.

Here are some typical family dynamics resulting from this type of OCD-related dysfunctionality:

- Family members often believe they are being helpful when they participate in a child's compulsive behaviors; for example, sanitizing the home, preparing special foods, or rechecking stove burners and door locks.

- Siblings often feel they have no choice but to accept their position in the family as the one(s) who needs less care and therefore receives less attention, often causing resentments and a feeling of abandonment by your child's brothers and sisters.

- Because one child's needs (for a parent's time, emotional attention, physical care) are so overwhelming, normal household chores can be neglected.

- Sometimes family members discourage the child with OCD from getting treatment out of fear they will be blamed for the OCD. This fear can be tied to a parent or sibling's misplaced sense of guilt.

- Change is hard, and all members of a family, regardless of the amount of pain or alienation they may feel as a result of the OCD, will resist making changes—unless they are helped to understand their feelings and given tools to make the necessary changes.

Family involvement is absolutely necessary if a child is to succeed in treatment. A family therapist can help the entire family navigate this difficult situation.

A Family Systems Approach to OCD

A family is a system, meaning each member affects the other. A system has many moving parts, and a family is a good example of a system that has strengths and weaknesses within the system. Understanding how everyone affects everyone else is the core concept of *systems therapy*, a therapeutic approach that can be helpful in understanding the complex dynamics of the family challenged by OCD.

A family systems approach encourages parents and children to look at the behavior of everyone in the family, rather than limiting focus to the individual family member who may be experiencing difficulty, in this case OCD, at any given time. Most families, with or without OCD or another mental health issue in a child, unconsciously assign one child as its "good child" while another is assigned the role of "problem child," or "black sheep." Most likely, these roles will change from time to time inside families.

Systems therapy can be a valuable lens through which to learn how a family system works, or doesn't when roles are assigned in this manner, especially when one child in a family has a mental health disorder such as OCD. In these cases, this child will often receive the majority of the attention in the family, both positive and negative, leaving other siblings feeling neglected and resentful.

Stuck in the manufactured role of "problem child" and after a lengthy period of being viewed (consciously or unconsciously) as the primary source of the family's problems, the child with OCD can end up feeling trapped, and less inclined to commit to change through treatment.

Other siblings can get similarly trapped in the role of the "good" or "perfect child," making it hard for them to experience the normal ups and downs of growing up. It becomes the parent's role to deal with this system and gradually teach both the child with OCD and the other child how to deal with the problems brought about by a sibling's OCD, without putting any child into a box from which it will be hard to escape.

Multicultural Issues and Parenting Styles

The presence of OCD has been documented since at least the eighteenth century, and it remains present throughout the world. The expressions of OCD, its contamination fears, unwanted thoughts and rituals, are remarkably similar across cultures. What are more varied are individual cultural reactions to the presence of the disorder in a family member. In a multicultural society such as the United States, cultural differences can be a factor in the recognition and treatment of childhood OCD. Among these factors are strong feelings about family privacy, the openness of a particular family to therapy, and the ability of a parent with a particular, perhaps culturally shaped, parenting style to adapt to OCD treatment. As Tamar E. Chansky, Ph.D., outlined in her book, *Freeing Your Child from Obsessive-Compulsive Disorder*, there are three types of parents:

- *Authoritarian*-style parents, reflecting a more "top-down" cultural model, expect to set forth rules that are not challenged, only obeyed. Children make few, if any, of their own choices. Punitive measures are taken if rules are disobeyed.
- *Permissive* parents tend to go to the opposite extreme and provide very little structure or boundary setting for their children. Children are then given the power to make their own choices.
- *Authoritative* parents fall somewhere in the middle of these two poles; they set rules and enforce them but remain flexible and open to input from their children.

According to Dr. Chansky, for a family coping with OCD in a child, the third, *authoritative* model of parenting tends to create the most workable environment to assist your child in reaching her treatment goals. Rather than a "you will do this" message from parent to child, in this model, a child is given autonomy and encouragement to select her own exposure targets, and asks for help when she needs it. The child's progress is monitored, not directed. At the same time, parents in the authoritative model have the ability to set limits and ground rules for how the child with OCD will be permitted to behave in the household when it affects other family members.

Extended Family

In families with grandparents, uncles, and aunts in close geo-graphic proximity, open communication about a grandchild, niece, or nephew's OCD is the best course—when and where possible. In some ethnic groups where a high priority is put on privacy and when there is an inherent resistance to the acknowledgement of mental health issues or family therapy, it may not be possible to enlist either their active or emotional involvement in your child's OCD treatment.

In many circumstances, grandparents or other close relatives may have already noticed behavioral issues with a child, but have not had the language to express their concern. They also may not feel they have permission to raise such a delicate issue.

Your choice of how much to disclose to and involve extended family members is a very individual one, sometimes dependent on cultural factors. If they can be drawn into a helpful relationship in this time of great need, you and your child will benefit from other rela-tives' support. One way to help make this happen is to give extended family members brief educational materials about OCD and invite them to join you if you attend a parent support group in your local area.

How Family Therapy Works

Family therapists can help a family system function better when its mem-bers are under stress such as that caused by having OCD in the family. Typically in family therapy, the entire family shows up in the therapist's office, and the interactions of the family are observed and guided by the therapist who acts as an outsider to moderate the family process. A skilled therapist must first assess how a given family functions. He must assess who is playing what roles inside the family unit. This assessment is perhaps the most important task for the therapist. Families typically have a leader (usually Mom or Dad, but it can sometimes be a powerful child) who will try to organize and lead the process.

Alert!

Brothers and sisters of a child with OCD are often neglected by "default." To avoid this parenting pitfall, do your best to spend quality time with your other children, too. They should not be expected to put their lives on hold until after the sibling with OCD "gets better." Just as you offer your child with OCD rewards for doing the hard work of OCD treatment, give encouragement and rewards to your other children, too.

The power arrangements of families are sometimes hidden from the view of all family members since these roles have been unconsciously assumed over time as the family power dynamics have taken form. Eventually the therapist must help the family redistribute the power away from that individual who is leading the family, and allow each family member to feel safe enough to discuss their issues within the family before the entire group. His primary means to do this is by providing a safe environment in family therapy sessions where all family members can express their feelings and needs. Then it's the job of the therapist to help family members acquire new communications skills so that they can employ them at home.

Family Therapy Basics

The process of healing takes time for a family that has been operating under the extreme stress caused by the demands of OCD. Family therapy is a process that requires each member's participation. Over several sessions, each family member can learn how he functions both positively and negatively with all the other members. When you first engage in family therapy, the therapist will function as an observer, a detached guide who is responsible for assisting the family to heal the broken parts of their relationships. After observing family dynamics in the context of therapy, the therapist will then play a more active role, interacting with the family and its members to encourage open communication.

The average number of sessions for family therapy is between six and ten, so you are not necessarily looking at a forever situation. Once the family is stabilized, the therapist can be used on an as-needed basis. A trusted therapist whom your family can see when in crisis is an important ally for a family coping with OCD.

 Essential

If you feel the therapist does not understand you or is not providing assistance, trust your instincts and move on. Although there are specific types of treatment recommended for children with OCD, that is not the case with family therapy. It may be that a particular family therapist's style of rendering treatment is not a good match for your family. If you're not feeling comfortable after several sessions with a therapist, tell him your concerns and look for a new therapist.

Why Go to Family Therapy?

Usually a family starts therapy when parents need guidance in managing their children. If you need help to deal with OCD in one child, or in several family members, the process will begin by discussing how each member is affected by the OCD. If only one family member is identified as the patient, and the other family members are hiding their feelings behind an assumed status as one of the "good" children in relationship to the "patient" or problem child, this unhealthy dynamic will first have to be exposed and unraveled.

That's because in family therapy, the entire family is the patient. Typically, the child with OCD will be the center of attention for the family. Other family members may feel unimportant or unseen in this kind of family because so much time and energy are taken up by the child with OCD. An effective family therapy process will stabilize this imbalance and teach everyone how to get their needs met while living with a child or sibling who has OCD.

Alert!

It's more difficult for a parent suffering from depression or another mental health issue to help a child manage his OCD. A parent of a child with OCD should first treat her own mental health issue and get additional help at home if she's not able to manage the situation alone.

Fears about Family Therapy

The hardest part of family therapy is getting everyone to participate. The therapy process is still unfamiliar to many parents and children, so they have a certain degree of fear about it. This unfamiliarity may lead them to avoid the process, even when dealing with the added stress of having OCD or another mental health disorder in the family.

One issue that causes this reluctance is privacy, or a misconception that family therapy may bring about the loss of a family's privacy. Therapists are highly trained professionals who have no interest in gossiping about families to other people. In fact, to guarantee such confidentiality, laws have been created that guarantee under most circumstances total confidentiality to clients in therapy, just as the priest in the church is granted confidentiality privileges under the law. If a therapist were to disclose confidential information, he could lose his license to practice psychotherapy and be sued in a court of law.

When Should a Family Seek Therapy?

Many families should seek help much sooner than the majority do. Just as many people wait to see a dentist until a toothache is too painful to handle, so, too, many people seek therapy after the pain of living with an emotional problem has become unbearable. If you have not stabilized your family dynamics on your own, seeking a family therapist is an appropriate course to take in order to find new solutions and new ideas to deal with the emotional strain that is present.

 Fact

Twenty percent of children with OCD have a sibling or parent who also has OCD. Many other family members of children with OCD have ADHD, depression, or another anxiety disorder. A parent of more than one child with the same or different disorders can feel torn between them.

Questions for a Family Therapist

Prior to making an appointment for the entire family, you can interview a therapist by telephone to make sure she is the right person to meet your family's needs. On the call, provide a brief overview of what is happening inside your family. Ask her if she thinks she is the appropriate professional to treat your family. If she does not seem to understand your family's dynamics, find a new therapist. Not all therapists are good for all situations. Sometimes you have to try several until you find the right therapist for your family.

Typical questions to ask the therapist before engaging their services include:

- Have you worked with individuals who have OCD or families where a child has OCD? (If not OCD, families facing another anxiety disorder or mental health issue?)
- What is your personal experience working with such families?

- How long do you normally take to stabilize a family in crisis?
- What fees will we be charged for your services?
- What training did you receive to become a therapist?
- What psychological orientation do you use in your therapy practice?

As you may know, family therapy includes many different disciplines and approaches. Each therapist is trained in a school that has a theoretical orientation. Some use psychoanalysis, others employ cognitive behavioral therapy, others assume religious principles or teach meditation.

Most therapists use a variety of methods. These therapists will often identify themselves as "eclectic," meaning they use a little of this and a little of that, and have personalized their approach since receiving initial training.

Marital Stress

Marriage is hard enough without adding the disruptions and stress caused by the demands of a child with OCD. When this kind of ongoing stress is present in a relationship, balancing the emotional ups and downs is challenging work. Unfortunately, this chronic stress is more likely to cause a couple to pull apart than pull together, according to statistics for couples in this situation. The divorce rate for marriages with a child with a disability is estimated at between 50 and 70 percent. The only heavier stress on a marriage is the death of a child, which destroys 90 percent of marriages. After hearing all this bad news, it's up to you to decide whether you and your spouse will commit to the hard work of finding a better solution to handle the inevitable stresses that may come up as a result of having a child with OCD.

While the solution for marriages facing such a challenge appears obvious—to cooperate and support each other while dealing with the painful or trying circumstances—reality reveals this to be far easier said than done. To face these challenges as a team is the ideal.

Putting aside guilt and anger within the chaos that can ensue from raising a child with OCD is something that few couples have the experience to achieve. This is on-the-job training, with very little available support for couples under such duress.

The Blame Game

It is pointless to assign blame, but it is human. For many people encountering a stressful life situation, it feels counterintuitive to simply accept "what is" and work from this baseline. Individuals in a couple who are frustrated by a large amount of stress tend to wander unconsciously into assigning blame to each other. Then the couple begins to tear apart rather than bond together.

Although the focus here is on dealing with a child with OCD, the same blame dynamic can affect parents dealing with other challenges. The most documented work has been done around the death of a child. Such agony will most likely tear apart a marriage, and only a few survive such a heartbreaking experience. The individuals within the couple are so overwhelmed that they turn on each other rather than come together for the support that will make the experience more bearable. For many couples, accepting the reality that a child has a potentially debilitating brain disorder can feel like a loss nearly akin to death.

The specific loss you as a parent experience when a child has a mental health disorder such as OCD may be more the loss of your dream of the young adult you wished your child to become. It is painful for any parent to be forced to stand by, feeling powerless to lift the burden of OCD from a child.

If you are going to survive the experience and grow as a marriage and a family from this challenge, the way of cooperation and teamwork is the royal road. Already strong marriages make you better prepared for the stresses that arise when your precious child is afflicted with a neurological disorder like OCD, but through hard work and commitment even a less solid marriage can rise to the occasion.

How to Avoid the Blame Game

First, know that blaming is always counterproductive. Rather than help you cope with the reality of your experience, blaming your partner will only make things much worse. But it is not easy to avoid such mind traps. Men and women in strong marriages know these games to be disastrous, and have learned how to avoid them whenever the mind begins to go down that road. Searching for the ancestral causes of the OCD in your child, and assigning blame to one side of the family or the other, is a common mistake many couples make when faced with the challenges of a child with a mental disorder such as OCD.

 *Question?*

What is the difference between an "I message" and a "you message"?

If you're upset with your partner, you may say to him: "You make me feel bad." Or you can say: "When you speak to me like that, I become hurt and angry, and then I can't listen to you." The "You message" blames and inflames. The "I message" speaks to the issue at hand, and de-escalates the argument. Always use "I messages" when discussing difficult topics with your spouse.

One of the skills you learn in order to avoid the blame game addresses those times when one of you is weaker and succumbs to blaming the other. In these cases, the stronger partner knows to (figuratively) hold the space open for peace to return rather than match his partner in assigning blame. The highest priority must be put on avoiding the infighting that can occur when one of you begins to blame the other for the problems present in your family. If blame arises, you find ways to release the stress and get back to cooperating.

Guilt as a Marriage Destroyer

An emotion that is very difficult for parents of a child with a mental health disorder is guilt. When guilt arises in one partner, it is very common for him to become angry with his spouse in order to relieve his own feelings of guilt—an emotional reaction that is most often not recognized under the veneer of anger. Many times guilt will show up as anger toward your partner, because the pain of facing one's own guilt is too heavy. To distinguish between feelings of guilt and anger is difficult when you are on either side of a heated discussion.

The first step for couples dealing with this challenging conflict is to simply accept the many clashing feelings that arise from the stress level they are experiencing as parents of a child with OCD, and allow each other the space to have such conflicting feelings. If your partner becomes angry with you, you should take an emotional step backward and try not to become defensive. The way that will lead you to cooperation is to help the other parent work through feelings without isolating yourself and thus creating more anger in the relationship.

Other Therapy Options for Couples

Every married couple needs time away from the roles of mother and father in order to nurture their own relationship. When dealing with the extra demands that OCD can place on parents, nurturing the marriage relationship is even more important. There are several proven therapy options that can help keep spouses from falling into the common traps of blaming each other for a child's OCD, and enabling the child's OCD behaviors—both detrimental and capable of wearing down a marriage and putting the family at risk of breaking apart. The therapeutic options that are most often useful include marriage therapy and group therapy for couples.

Marriage Therapy

Couples therapy involving a marriage and family therapist or other counselor experienced in treating couples can be very valuable in teaching a couple how to achieve the goal of cooperation in the face of raising a child with OCD. A marriage therapist will be trained in showing spouses how to recognize and avoid the common pitfalls involving blame, anger, and guilt that appear inside most marriages where emotional stress is severe.

The therapist in marriage counseling represents an unbiased referee who can help couples develop better listening and speaking skills that are especially important in the challenging situation where one child is in constant need of attention.

Support Groups

One of the best solutions for handling the stress of raising a child with OCD is getting together in a support group with other parents who face the same or similar challenge of raising a child with a disability. Inside the safety of a group where all members are facing the same challenge is healing power that is hard to quantify. Support groups for family members of individuals with mental health disorders vary from the more educationally oriented to those focusing on giving mutual emotional support. Either individuals or couples can attend these support groups. Contact information for both kinds of support groups is available in the Resources section.

Traditional Group Therapy

Aside from support groups for people dealing with a mental health disorder in a family member, many professionals inside the world of psychotherapy agree that traditional group therapy is by far the most effective way for couples to make necessary changes to improve their relationship and deal with specific problems. For married couples, participating in a therapy group together with other couples allows you to watch and learn as other spouses deal with similar problems and aim to develop better communication and relationship skills. What you learn will help you sustain your own marriage, especially as you work through the immediate challenge of parenting a child with OCD.

CHAPTER 16

A Parent's Home Tool Kit

By now you've realized that once you begin to confront OCD in your child, your job as a parent is as large and challenging as your child's. Although therapists and teachers provide vital support roles, at the end of the day it's what happens at home that determines your child's success in dealing with his disorder. That's why you as a parent need to get as prepared as you can with the right tools. The most critical items in your tool kit are the battle-tested techniques outlined in this chapter for empowering your child to take on the fight of his life against OCD.

Keeping the Communication Lines Open

Serving in the dual roles of parent and partner in your child's recovery, you must reorient what you already know about parent-to-child communications to fit the unique demands of living with OCD. One of the hardest parts of this healing process is coping with uncertainty about how long it will take for him to overcome the debilitating effects of his OCD. The effort requires a new language and a different set of rules. Essentially, what you are doing is helping your child formulate and execute a "battle plan" against his OCD.

Once you've identified OCD as the source of your child's problems, you've already traveled a huge distance. That's because the act of naming his obsessive thoughts and compulsive behaviors as a neurobiological disorder allows you to separate the disorder from your child—the person. After the OCD is viewed as something apart from your child, the faulty mechanism (any brain with OCD) causing his distress can be repaired, using proven techniques that are just as applicable at home as they are at school and out in the world.

In all communications you serve your child and yourself best if you *emphasize the positive.* "Be brave" is a better way to cheer her on than "Don't be scared." Managing OCD will be a long-term, perhaps lifelong process for your child. What you are trying to do over the next several months (and perhaps years) is give her a solid foundation on which to begin to get a handle on her OCD symptoms.

Rewards and OCD

When you offer praise or a material reward to a child practicing an OCD exposure, you are praising her effort, not the product of her effort. Success in this context is her learning the *process.* Her goal is to learn *how* to mentally step back from an obsessive thought or image and tame the desire to perform a compulsive action. The action she's trying to extinguish can be to check on or clean something, or not ask the same question she's already asked you three times. It's hard work, and rewards along the way do help!

Alert!

Three things *not to say* to a child having obsessive thoughts: "You shouldn't worry about that." "That's silly." And, "Don't worry because I'll protect you." These statements invalidate his feelings and erode his power to act on his own behalf. Your goal is to encourage his emotions while helping him redirect his worries.

Developing an OCD Battle Plan

"I'm too afraid to go to school today," ten-year-old Susie told her mother, Dawn, who was already dressed for the office and standing in her daughter's bedroom ready to go. She waited for Susie to peek out from under the covers. When Dawn asked Susie what she was afraid of, Susie said she didn't know, and broke into tears.

What could Dawn do? First, since Dawn was already feeling stressed about being late, she knew to remove herself from Susie's bedroom in order to regain calm and come to terms with the fact that she was now going to be even later getting to work. The worst thing Dawn could have said to Susie was: "You've got to go, that's all there is to it!" Only when Dawn was confident of her own ability to speak without anger or anxiety in her voice did she return to her daughter's bedside.

What Dawn said and did next demonstrates a key step in the fundamental process of breaking an OCD fear into manageable parts.

> "How afraid are you?" Dawn asked her daughter. From their previous exposure practices Susie then knew to quantify her fear on a scale of one to ten. "Six or seven," Susie answered.

> "What could happen at school today?" Dawn asked next. This was to help Susie sort out her fears and name the one that was most responsible for keeping her under the covers that day. "I'm afraid the boy in front of my desk in homeroom is going to spread all his germs on me and I'll freeze," Susie said tearfully.

> "What else might happen?" Dawn asked, encouraging Susie to think about other possibilities apart from the one she most feared. For example, Susie could consider the possibility that the boy might not even push his chair into her desk. Or using a mental exposure technique, Susie could picture that very thing happening, the boy's dandruff flying, and then picture herself handling it without panic, or less panic than she feared at that moment. Finally, Dawn could suggest that Susie consider the possibility that any

possible contact between the boy's chair and her desk was not enough to cause her any *real* harm.

After a few more minutes of discussion, Dawn asked Susie what she wanted to do. With this simple question, Dawn empowered Susie to make her own decision about how much she was willing to take on that morning.

After having the opportunity to break down the situation, Susie considered other responses to the contamination fear that paralyzed her upon waking up. She managed to let go of her fear *enough* to make the final choice of getting dressed and going to school. Of course, Susie was late for school, but Dawn helped her daughter to salvage the greater part of the day. More importantly, Susie practiced the techniques that would get her through her next OCD fear.

In some cases, it is enough for your child to imagine the thing she fears. In others, she must put herself in the actual situation, whether it be taking out the garbage, washing her hands only once for dinner, or touching her gym locker at school with her bare hand.

Naming and Managing the "Enemy"

Language has power. Once something is named or labeled, in this case the disorder called OCD, your child separates it from the unknown, and, most importantly, from himself. And because it's the brain malfunction behind OCD that causes your child's thought process to become unreliable, research psychiatrists have discovered that it helps young people suffering from OCD to name their disorder *the enemy*. This powerful two-step process of separating from and naming the OCD came from the work of two pioneering doctors who've spent decades working with children battling OCD. Dr. Jeffrey Schwartz of UCLA made the first breakthrough in his book *Brain Lock,* in which he established the principle, *"It's not me; it's OCD."*

Essential

Anxiety is not something you can cure, fix, or make go away for your child. It is something she must learn to recognize and manage herself. For the child with OCD, anxiety is diminished by gradual exposures to feared situations, persons, and things. An exposure process works best if done every day. Avoidance of what she fears only increases your child's anxiety level.

Don't Look for Deeper Meaning

From this simple statement, it then follows that OCD-related thoughts have no intrinsic or deeper meaning and parents should beware of mining a child's OCD-related utterances for any deeper meaning. If, for example, your child tells you he "hates you" for interrupting his ritual before bedtime, or if he states that his failure on a math test means your imminent death, it makes no sense to stop and consider what these statements may say about your success or failure as a parent.

The tendency to dig deeply into every uttered thought heralds from a Freudian or psychoanalytical paradigm where a patient's words were viewed as evidence of an unconscious psychological conflict in need of formal analysis. Instead, when utterances such as these come from a child with OCD, they should be labeled for what they are—brain clutter, a brain run amuck, a brain hiccup, or whatever descriptive language suits your child when the issue arises.

More Battle Tactics for OCD

To Dr. Schwartz's statement "It's not me, it's OCD," Dr. John March added his own, "Talk Back to OCD." March then built the OCD treatment program and wrote the book titled *Talking Back to OCD* upon this concept. In his treatment program, Dr. March advocates both *naming* and *talking back* to OCD. Another highly effective tactic March introduced is having the child give his OCD a colorful name.

While more likely to appeal to those under the age of fourteen, this tactic can be adapted to any age youngster with OCD, although the older adolescent may be content to simply call his disorder, "the OCD."

For the younger child, the act of labeling the disorder with a sassy or nasty name can be both fun and empowering. Re-labeling serves as a helpful reminder to the child that he is not the OCD. So, when he names the OCD Bathroom Guy, Worry Wart, or Bugger, your child is symbolically taking his power back and separating his core self from the behaviors over which he'd like to gain control.

Once your child takes this step, what commences in your household is an ongoing, often raucous conversation between him and his now-named enemy. When it's working well, this dialogue will be adversarial, and at times angry, defiant, and humorous. You may hear "Butt out, Worry Wart," coming from your child's bedroom as he dresses. "You're not the boss of me!" may be heard as a scream from the bathroom.

This exchange can also be written down. For example, a sign reading "OCD Ends Here" may hang for a time on your refrigerator door. Like any war, your child's battle with OCD will at times be loud and disruptive. But rather than signaling a problem, this is a sign that he's making progress.

Alert!

OCD is not an opponent you can defeat with logic. It is an insidious, cunning, and powerful enemy. What is called for in a showdown with your child's OCD is a battle plan built on strategy, resistance, and practice. Once you and your child make a commitment to defeat his OCD and begin to focus your attention on this goal, time is on your side.

Disciplining a Child with OCD

There's no question that disciplining a child with OCD presents special challenges for a parent. One reason why this is true is that you as a parent quite literally "feel your child's pain." Certainly, you don't want to feed her anxiety. The stress she's under after a tough day spent managing or hiding her OCD at school can be palpable. And then it's not always easy to recognize which behaviors are the OCD versus those times when she is simply "acting up."

On the other hand, discipline for a child with OCD (or any impulse control disorder such as ADHD or autism) is arguably even more important than it is for the less challenged child. Whether specific negative behaviors are caused by the OCD or not, if your child doesn't learn proper limits for her behavior and get the necessary practice to redirect her feelings of frustration and anger away from negative behaviors, she will be missing essential skills for life. Fortunately, by considering these issues you're already a step closer to giving your child what she needs to succeed. The disciplining techniques that work best for the OCD-impacted family are simply good parenting skills adapted for the special demands presented by OCD.

Rewards Do Work

Some parents worry that giving a reward for a child's progress in the battle against OCD is just a bribe, nothing more than a manipulation of a child's desire to acquire things. In fact, the opposite is true. A bribe connotes trickery, the receipt of an undeserved reward. But, when a child with OCD is rewarded for making progress in her exposure exercise, whether or not the "end goal" has been reached, the child is getting a well-deserved, positive reinforcement for *the effort* of doing hard work.

A reward acknowledges that she has accomplished something difficult, that she's practiced, made an attempt, and at least tried to reach her goal. Certainly no child would choose to suffer the symptoms of OCD simply to get a reward. Giving a child a reward helps accentuate the positive way out of those symptoms.

Using rewards for positive reinforcement while your child does homework exercises for OCD can be extremely effective if you follow a few basic ground rules:

- Focus on one goal at a time (don't mix taking out the trash with getting dressed).
- Give rewards frequently for small changes, not one big change (start with washing hands fewer times, not the end goal of once before dinner).
- Make rewards small (stickers, treats).
- Let your child choose her goal and rewards (from jointly drawn up lists of possibilities).
- Have clear rules for success (e.g., the child should not have to be reminded).
- Know when she's reached a wall (exhausted, overwhelmed, done for the day).
- Combine praise and rewards.

On average, it takes two to three weeks for a child to master an exposure—if the goal is the right size at the right point in her battle plan. Flexibility is important. If after two or three days she's not making progress, break the goal down into smaller chunks. Success leads to more success, while failing too often leads to increased frustration and more failure.

A Family Culture of Discipline

The successful practice of OCD exposures at home goes hand in hand with an equally strong commitment to a family culture of discipline. Tamar E. Chansky, Ph.D., gives parents the golden rule for disciplining a child with OCD. "Safety and respect first," Chansky reminds parents, citing the need to establish this basic premise as an unbreakable household code, with the all-important corollary, "No excuses," as an adjunct.

This commitment to assuring that everyone in your family gets the same level of physical and emotional safety means a zero tolerance for verbal or physical assaults to or from anyone in the family. As any parent of a child with OCD knows, each day presents occasions when conflict can break out between the affected child and his siblings. This golden rule can be usefully applied to tamp down or avert any threats to family members' physical safety or sense of emotional well-being.

An Interrupted Ritual

One of the most common explosive situations with OCD in the family results from the interruption of the child's OCD-related ritual, often by a sibling. What follows is a step-by-step example of how best to handle such a situation.

> When twelve-year-old Sarah was interrupted by her younger brother Sammy as she counted tiles in the hallway, he stopped her from doing something her brain told her she had to do immediately for her own safety. Whether intentionally interrupting Sarah's ritual or not, Sammy's remark made Sarah lose her count. Sarah's frustration at being stopped mid-ritual then turned into rage, name-calling, and hitting.
>
> Sarah and Sammy's Mom heard the commotion from a floor away as it escalated into yells, shoving, and crying. How should she respond to this dispute between Sarah and Sammy? Sarah verbally and physically attacked her brother, so it was she who had to be immediately disciplined. Mom separated her children, making sure Sammy was okay, and then let Sarah know she faced a consequence for her behavior.
>
> Mom allowed Sarah to calm down before attempting to talk with her about what had just happened. If

Sarah had protested, saying, "It's not my fault, it's my OCD," her mother would have recognized her daughter's frustrations, but also let Sarah know there was no excuse for breaking the *safety and respect first rule*. In this way, she would validate Sarah's feelings but also set a limit, communicating to Sarah that the specific actions and words she used against her little brother were inappropriate.

Mom then encouraged Sarah to disengage from the situation by taking a "time-out." For her time-out, Sarah went into her room to be alone for several minutes. Upon Sarah's timely return, Mom let her know what consequences would result from her earlier misbehavior, and she gave the consequence to Sarah without debate. Mom explained that Sarah would lose her computer privileges that evening. At this point it was also appropriate for Mom and Sarah to discuss how Sarah might make amends to her brother. Sarah opted to make a simple verbal apology to Sammy.

After their discussion about the consequences of Sarah's actions and how Sarah was going to make amends to Sammy, Mom encouraged Sarah to talk about her feelings leading up to, during, and after the incident with her brother. The goal of this exchange was to make Sarah more aware of her own triggers and help her problem solve around ways to avoid or confront them. For example, should interruptions of her counting ritual be put on the top of Sarah's exposure exercise priority list? Perhaps, or Sarah might decide to put it second or third from the top. The important thing was getting it on Sarah's priority list.

Mom knew that if she and Sammy heard Sarah say she was committed to putting her response to ritual interruptions on her priority exposure list, they and everyone else in the family would feel more optimistic and secure.

In situations where a child with OCD misbehaves in a minor way, for example, chattering in an attempt to drown out the conversation of other family members, the child can be simply ignored, thus depriving her of the negative attention she seeks by acting up. But in more serious situations, such as Sarah's physical and verbal attacks on her younger brother, there should be a more substantial consequence, such as a longer time-out, or a loss of computer time in order to reinforce Sarah's boundary-setting lesson.

 *Question?*

What are "natural consequences" and how are they used to discipline a child with OCD?

Natural consequences refer to what happens naturally after the child with OCD takes an action. If she's late for school, her teacher marks her tardy, and after three time tardy she gets detention. If she stays up all night worrying, she'll be tired the next day. Within the limits of reason and safety, natural consequences take the parent out of the equation and bring the child face to face with the outcomes of her own actions.

How to Avoid Problems

When conflicts for a child with OCD can be anticipated and averted, it's sometimes best to do so. For example, the child's struggle to cope with the frustration he feels at the end of a school day is often overwhelming, leaving him highly susceptible to conflicts with anyone around him. To deal with this regularly occurring situation, a parent can arrange a half-hour cooling off period every day after school. The child is given a healthy snack and permitted to watch TV, shoot basketball hoops, or otherwise decompress without any interruptions or requests made of him.

Other avertable situations may include trips to public spaces or a visit to a friend's house. In these cases, potentially difficult moments (waiting in line, speaking to strangers) can be rehearsed. Instead of going to a friend's home, the friend can be invited to yours.

The flip side to anticipating and averting difficult situations is going too far in protecting your child from her OCD and unintentionally enabling it. If, for example, you continue to make alternative meals to accommodate her OCD-related food issues, let her use "private" utensils, check the stove one more time before leaving the house because she asks you to, or otherwise participate in her rituals, you are hurting, not helping, her.

Here are some disciplinary dos and don'ts for handling the child with OCD:

- Don't give up your authority.
- Don't bargain with your child.
- Don't discipline until you are calm and without anger.
- Don't show your anxiety or fears when disciplining.
- Don't expect a "thank you."
- Do model vulnerability and an ability to recover from your mistakes.
- Do set clear limits.
- Do make simple, clear statements.
- Do emphasize the positive.

It can be a difficult balancing act for a parent to play the disciplinarian and still strike a positive tone, but remember that in setting boundaries and minding them, you are giving your child an essential lesson. Eventually she will feel relieved and empowered by her own ability to resist flying into a rage, and will avoid the isolation that comes from such antisocial behavior.

CHAPTER 17

Support for Parents

The worst enemy all parents face is the myth of the perfect parent. This is especially true when parents are raising a child with OCD, and even more so if you are the single parent of a child with OCD. Coupled with any guilt you may be erroneously taking on for "causing" your child's disorder, you may have feelings of insecurity, shame, confusion, and fear, all of which are common for a parent who is newly confronting OCD in a child. But that doesn't mean you can't get help and get over them. This chapter will cover some basic things you can do to stay mentally and physically fit and available to your child.

Signs of Caretaker Stress and Burnout

If you encounter signs of burnout in yourself it means that you, as caretaker, require some care. You need to pay attention to your own needs—if you are going to sustain your pivotal role in your child's long-term recovery from OCD. The signs of parent burnout are similar to those of anyone under a great deal of stress. But there are also causes specific to your current situation as the parent of a child with OCD. For example, you may find yourself being short-tempered with all your children for no obvious reason, when the cause of your anger is that you've gone on for too long (perhaps four to five days) helping your child carry out her exposure exercises at home—without taking a meaningful break for yourself.

It's also easy for a burnt-out parent to become harshly critical of a child if she's resistant to an exposure exercise; after all, haven't you just spent every waking moment for nearly a week supporting, monitoring, and documenting her? You may also be particularly sensitive to surprises. Another difficult situation is when your child's OCD-related meltdown seems to come out of nowhere just as you're about to leave the house in the morning. The second most harmful myth after the myth of the *perfect parent* is the one that says *you should have everything under control.*

Signs of parental burnout are physical, emotional, and mental: among them, you often feel tired, emotionally wrought and on edge, and find it difficult to concentrate. The issue is always one of degree. If you feel yourself getting too worn down by the demands of parenting a child with OCD it's important to act preventively. Try to head off burnout by taking time for yourself and finding ways to care for your own basic needs for rest, support, balanced nutrition, and exercise.

If You Go Beyond Burnout

You may think what you're dealing with is parental burnout when you're actually suffering from an anxiety disorder. If you have the following symptoms, it's important to find out more about anxiety disorders and seek professional help. It does your child no good for you to be battling an undiagnosed and untreated disorder while attempting to help her manage OCD.

The symptoms of an anxiety disorder can include:

- An inability to eat or sleep
- Nervousness
- Feelings of panic, either generalized or specific
- Excessive worry
- Inability to concentrate

- Irritability
- Muscle tension

Clinical depression can also be mistaken for parental burnout. The symptoms of a case of depression that may require medical attention include:

- An inability to focus or concentrate
- Memory problems
- Sleep and eating problems
- Feelings of hopelessness and despair
- Fatigue or loss of energy
- Feelings of worthlessness or inappropriate guilt
- Depressed mood most of the day
- Diminished interest in things previously enjoyed
- Recurrent thoughts of death

When dealing with the possibility of a diagnosable mental health disorder in yourself, it is important to see a physician in order to rule out another biological issue as the underlying cause of your symptoms.

 **Alert!**

If multiple symptoms associated with an anxiety disorder or depression continue for a period of two months or longer, you may in fact have a condition requiring diagnosis and treatment. It does your child no good if you ignore your own symptoms. You can set a model with your honesty and proactive response to evidence of your mental health problem.

If your symptoms do not become chronic and are not attributable to a physical or mental health disorder, you can improve your situation by becoming more aware of the pitfalls of parenting a child with OCD, and then establish and practice a solid self-care program.

Back to Basics

The first basic tier of self-care involves the rules of healthy living for all adults. Eat balanced, regular meals, keep your intake of caffeine, sugar, and alcohol in moderation, make time to sustain your marriage and/or friendships, and get regular exercise. Finally, try to create outlets for your own relaxation and distraction from the heavy demands of parenting a child with OCD.

 Essential

Here is a quick and easy technique to calm down: Place the palm of your hand lightly on your stomach. Then take a deep breath and hold for a count of three. Now exhale slowly. Notice the rising and falling of your stomach. Repeat several times.

Coping with Parental Guilt

Just as it doesn't work to tell a child with OCD not to worry so much, neither can a parent make guilt go away by snapping her fingers. Even parents who are the most practiced at dealing with OCD occasionally feel guilty about the adult-size burden their children are carrying with this insidious disorder. As a parent, you are susceptible to the baseless belief that you are the cause of your child's disorder. Or, you may get bogged down in the basic "unfairness" of life, and focus on your child's bad luck in receiving this tough hand of cards.

The same questions tend to invade your mind over and over: "Why my child?" and, of course, "Why me?" If you find yourself falling into any of these endless loops of guilt, pity, or self-pity, there is a way out. And it may surprise you to learn that it lies in one of the basic rules of your child's treatment for OCD: Your mind is not always your friend.

Your Mind Is Not Always Your Friend

What do you do if your mind starts spinning with unproductive thoughts? For example, you lost your temper when your child asked if was going to rain—for the seventh time that day. You already feel guilty for snapping at her instead of using the technique of redirection to suggest she tell the OCD she already knows the answer to that question. And then, to make matters worse, you can't stop the loop of guilt that has taken hold of your mind: "I'm a bad mother. I'm a bad mother. I'm a bad mother." Here are some simple steps to use to stop a negative thought:

- Step back from your thought and try to put some distance between you and it, so that you're looking at the whole forest, not a single tree.
- Consider whether the thought "I'm a bad mother/father" is definitely true, maybe true, or definitely not true. By doing this exercise, you are examining the legitimacy of your obsessive thought.
- If you catch yourself in a lie, give yourself permission to say no to the thought that you're a bad mother, and consider another possibility, like, "I'm a good parent most of the time." (Remember, there are no perfect parents.)

To find a way out of obsessive, self-critical thinking, you have to be willing to challenge your own thinking, and realize that when your mind goes off on its own into negative, self-defeating territory, you are not telling yourself the truth. You will find power in simply recognizing the obvious. How can you be a bad parent if you are concerned enough about your child's health and well being to spend the greater part of your days and nights helping him deal with this very tough condition? Then you can imagine an alternative to the self-defeating thought. Something like: "I'm a *good enough* mother."

Does this sound familiar? That's because it's the same *talking back* technique your child uses to manage his OCD.

 Essential

> To soothe your nerves, try this technique. Lie down or sit comfortably in a chair and close your eyes. Count backward from ten to one. As you count, relax each part of your body, from head to toe. Remain still in this position for five or ten minutes, breathing deeply to bring a sense of calm deep inside your mind and body.

Accepting Your Child's Strengths and Weaknesses

Change is hard for most people. For the child dogged by OCD, change can be terrifying. To achieve the fundamental transformation required to defeat OCD takes enormous strength. Paradoxically, because of the great challenges he faces at such a young age, your child with OCD often develops strength of character well beyond his years. Some parents go so far as to view this paradox as the "silver lining" of OCD. However, in the beginning of treatment, it is often difficult for the parent to give a child a push when she resists making these necessary changes.

However dysfunctional your family may now be under the influence of OCD, things have been going on this way and working (sort of) for a long time. It's possible that by the time your child enters treatment, his OCD is running your entire household—in the sense that you and other family members walk on eggshells to head off your child's next OCD-related explosion. Once she enters treatment, you will all need to learn that only by stepping beyond the boundaries of your individual and collective comfort zones can you take control back from the OCD and make your family peaceful again.

Alert!

At the beginning of each new goal and set of exposure exercises, it's commonplace for a child to resist, to become angry, and to cry as if hanging on to her OCD symptoms for "dear life." Do your best to recognize this resistance to change as a natural response on your child's part. When she resists, you can remind your child that it's just "Mr. (or Miss) OCD" talking, and let her know that it's she who's in charge of her life.

Knowing Your Child's Limits

One of the trickiest parts of OCD treatment for a parent is learning how to determine the difference between your child's simple resistance to change and the possibility that he has gone as far as he can toward a goal—at least for that hour of that day. This is what it means to accept his limitations, in the immediate situation and possibly for the longer term. In these situations you must recognize that a major wall or limitation has been reached in your child's progress. And then you must let the goal go until your child chooses to put it back on his priority list. To do otherwise is to place even greater obstacles in his path to recovery.

Here's an example: If your son's contamination fears are triggered by the boy's locker room, you must accept that *at least for now* he's not going to be able to manage extracurricular sports. This is true no matter how much he wants to play soccer or baseball, and how many other benefits you think the exercise and teamwork will bring him. In coming to terms with this kind of limitation, it can be difficult for parents (especially in the case of sports, for fathers) to process feelings of sadness or anger. There's often a necessary mourning of lost possibilities, dashed hopes, and dreams that every parent carries for his child. It is far better to privately acknowledge (to yourself and your spouse, but not to your child) disappointments such as these than to deny your feelings and risk developing unconscious resentment toward the child who is already dealing with plenty of his own complex emotions.

You May Need Individual Therapy

When and if to seek individual therapy is a personal decision and often depends on multiple factors such as the availability of insurance coverage; your finances; familiarity and comfort with the process of therapy; and time constraints. However, these factors need to be weighed against one fundamental issue: How much emotional pain are you in? Following from this difficult question is another: To what degree is your troubled emotional state making it difficult for you to help your child in her treatment?

If you're in too much emotional pain, you're not an ineffective partner only in your child's recovery; your relationships with your spouse and other children will begin to deteriorate as well. Good communication within the family will be the first thing to go, followed soon by any sense of pulling together as a team to confront the OCD. If and when this comes to pass, as few as two or three individual therapy sessions can help enormously to put you back "on track."

Your immediate goal in therapy or in working with emotional problems on your own will be to "reframe" the issues that are wearing you down by using Cognitive Behavioral Therapy techniques (such as those discussed above) to challenge such beliefs as "I'm a bad mother." The role of a therapist is to help you do the necessary reframing and letting go of these false assumptions. A therapist can also help you experience difficult emotions such as sadness and anger, two emotions commonly felt by parents who are dealing with OCD in a child.

Very often, adults simply don't have the skills or haven't given themselves permission to feel their emotions, especially when under the enormous stress of parenting a child challenged by OCD. Learning to process your own emotions is essential to good parenting and especially important when dealing with a child with OCD, because you must continually separate your own issues from the child's in order to help him make progress in treatment.

Setting Clear Boundaries and Time for Yourself

Even if your child's OCD treatment is now a full-time job for you, it cannot occupy your mind full-time, or you will certainly burn out. In order to act preventively, you should take at least a half-hour each day for decompression from the demands of your multiple life roles. A half-hour each day is enough time for a walk or a gym workout, a meditation, a phone call with a good friend, or work on a favorite hobby. The key is to let your mind escape all OCD-related demands and caretaking duties for this thirty-minute period, every day.

Saying a gentle "No" and redirecting your child's attention else-where will be necessary in order to set the necessary boundaries for your own rest and recuperation in the course of the day. This simple response turns out to be easier said than done. By putting your own "time-out" in a regularly scheduled time slot, you can help your child cope with your temporary lack of availability to her. Developing a comfort level and a sense of confidence about saying "No" is a key tactic in the battle plan for preventing parental burnout.

Find a Local Parent Support Group

If you do nothing else for your own well-being in this difficult time, you should consider joining a parent support group made up of other mothers and fathers who are dealing with the same issues you are in parenting a child with OCD. If there isn't a group specifically for parents dealing with OCD in your local community, then find one involving parents of children with multiple mental health disorders. Many groups, such as local chapters of the National Alliance for the Mentally Ill (NAMI), meet monthly and offer speakers and parental discussion.

Fact

Articles on the latest studies on OCD appear regularly on the Web site of the Obsessive-Compulsive Foundation, *www.ocf.org*, as well as the sites of other organizations serving families dealing with OCD. In some cases, you may learn about advances in diagnosis or treatment before your child's mental health professional or teachers. In this way, parents' networks have become the foundation of today's mental health community.

In many localities there are more informal parent support groups, which may include parents dealing with OCD. Some of these groups are structured along the lines of twelve-step support and social networks, with sponsors and weekly meetings. These groups often include telephone "trees" where members make themselves available to each other for help in handling crisis times, offering a sympathetic ear when a parent simply needs to vent or express difficult emotions in a time of conflict, self-doubt, or sadness.

Use the OCD foundation Web site or ask your child's therapist for information on any parent support groups in your area. And don't give up until you find a parent group that works for you. Your coauthors go so far as to say this step may be the most important use of your time and effort—out of all the suggestions made in this book!

That's because the battle being waged by you and your child against this disorder is long-term and, at least in the beginning, full time, a reality that necessitates a long-term plan for your own physical and mental health. The Biblical admonition for healers to first heal themselves is highly relevant for the parent raising a child with OCD.

CHAPTER 18

Paying for Your Child's OCD Care

After coming to terms with the presence of OCD in a child, no parent wants to deal with the uncertainty of how to pay for his treatment. Unfortunately, given the chaotic state of America's healthcare system, with 45 percent of the population uninsured and many of those with insurance lacking adequate mental health coverage, this area may be another hard one for you to tackle. It helps to know three things: your rights under the law, the fine print in your health insurance policy, and the state of your local public health system.

The Health Insurance Maze

If you have private health insurance through an employer, or you've purchased private insurance independently, your insurer's benefits information officer is the first person to call or visit in person. Before you ask about specific coverage for OCD, get a general (written and verbal) description of covered items and exclusions in your plan. In this conversation, the most important question to ask is whether your plan offers any mental health coverage.

Called either Mental Health or Behavioral Health Services, you will usually find substance abuse treatment and/or other mental healthcare services grouped in the same category. Covered services often include mental health assessment and outpatient care including individual therapy and medication management. Some insurers offer coverage for mental health services and/or substance abuse treatments; some only cover substance abuse if it co-occurs with mental illness. If you plan to use these benefits through your insurance plan or HMO, you may be required to get a referral from your primary care doctor (or pediatrician) before you can receive services.

The following are common types of managed care health insurance plans, which may cover your child's assessment and treatment for OCD as well as other common childhood anxiety disorders such as ADHD.

- HMO, Health Maintenance Organization: A plan that provides a selected set of healthcare services from doctors or healthcare providers within its network.
- FFS, Fee-for-Service: A health plan in which you may use any healthcare provider you choose. If there is a difference between what the provider charges and the health plan pays, you have to pay the difference.
- PPOs, Preferred Provider Organizations: These are sometimes referred to as fee-for-service plans. PPOs differ from FFS plans in that they use a network of providers and usually charge lower fees.

Health insurance policies are called a maze for a reason. They often use unusual vocabulary and employ a lot of language for the purpose of legal indemnification. Whenever you call an insurer's benefits office, note the date and the name of the person you are speaking to. Keep a log of these conversations in the event you need to make an appeal or refer to past interactions.

Understanding Your Mental Health Coverage

Insurance coverage for mental health benefits differs among plans, employers, and states. State laws may require insurers to provide a standard, minimal offering of mental health benefits. In general, mental health benefits are significantly less than medical/surgical benefits and will require higher deductibles and co-payments in addition to any regular, fixed payments. While an HMO may have multiple psychologists, therapists, or other mental healthcare providers on its staff, other plans may require use of doctors or practitioners in approved provider networks in your local area.

Covered Conditions

When navigating the maze of private health insurance, it's important to determine the category your child's illness falls into for your particular insurer and health plan. The issue of where OCD falls categorically may also be mandated by your state, so it's good to ask your insurer's benefits administrator first, and then double-check the state law. What follows are common definitions for different categories of mental health disorders used by private insurers when determining coverage. You might take a look to see whether any of this language is replicated in the print of your policy. The following groupings are listed for illustration of common insurance coverage:

- Serious mental illness: Typically defined as schizophrenia, schizoaffective disorder, psychotic disorders, bipolar disorder and major depression (sometimes called *mood disorders*), personality disorders such as defiant or schizoid personality disorder, and anxiety disorders including panic disorders and obsessive-compulsive disorder, among others.
- Broad-based mental health disorders: Used to refer to coverage of a relatively broad range of mental disorders.
- Substance abuse disorders: Used to refer to coverage of alcoholism and chemical dependency.

Although these are common categories for mental health disorders, all insurance plans are different and require careful reading and follow-up with their benefits officers and/or directly with your assigned health and/or mental healthcare providers within the plan to find out the extent of coverage, meaning number of visits allowed, co-pays, and so on. After determining whether you can get adequate care under your insurance plan, you'll have to determine how much of your child's care will be paid for by your insurer and how much will come out of your own pocket.

Questions for Your Health Insurance Company

Any of these insurance benefits plans may offer practitioners whose credentials make them technically qualified to diagnose and provide treatment for childhood OCD. Your task will be to determine whether any among those offered have the right experience to care for your child. Your highest priority is to find a mental healthcare provider who has previously treated childhood OCD. Then you can concentrate on finding someone who is within driving distance from where you live.

Make the best selection of a mental healthcare provider from the start. Remember, treatment for your child's OCD, whether by medication, CBT therapy, or both, will be an ongoing activity, at minimum three months in duration. And, it's important that your child have the option to return to the same therapist for his treatment. It's also important for you to be able to reach that provider between appointments, by telephone or e-mail. If e-mail is used to communicate with a doctor or mental healthcare provider, there is a often a greater likelihood of getting a quick response, but it should also be noted that these interactions are considered less private, meaning the doctor or therapist may not be able to guarantee confidentiality. Ask about these issues at your child's first appointment.

You should raise as many issues as possible, first with your insurer's benefits officer, and then with the mental healthcare provider you are assigned to or whom you select. If you're a member of an HMO, you may have this initial conversation with your primary doctor or nurse practitioner, who acts as your child's care coordinator and refers you to other specialists, including psychologists, psychiatrists, psychiatric nurses, social workers, or a marriage and family therapist.

Question?

What if my health insurance company doesn't have any approved providers who do CBT therapy for OCD?
You may be able to make an appeal to your health insurance company. The company may then be required to provide an out-of-network provider who can deliver CBT therapy. Be advised, CBT is not considered an experimental therapy. It is a well-established standard for treatment of OCD. Expert treatment guidelines for childhood and adolescent OCD are summarized in Chapter 9.

If you are given a choice of practitioners who are authorized to treat your child for mental health disorders under your insurance plan, the best thing to do is to call and speak to that individual directly. Ask him about the extent of his experience with childhood OCD and CBT therapy. When prescreening providers, all of the questions outlined in Chapter 6 concerning the provider's treatment orientation, availability, and willingness to work as a team with you as a parent as well as with your child's teacher are relevant.

Child Public Mental Health Resources

If you do not have employer-sponsored health insurance, you may qualify for Medicare or Medicaid services. The mental health agency in your state public health agency should be able to tell you how to access mental health services in your state. In publicly funded mental health centers, such as those run by state, city, or county governments, the cost of many services is calculated according to what you can afford to pay. This is called a sliding scale, or sliding fee, basis of payment. In addition, states, which often work with federal programs such as Medicaid, provide financial assistance to eligible individuals or families. Information about medical and healthcare assistance is available at your county/city social services departments, health and human services department, or Social Security office.

Question?

How do I find out what mental healthcare services my state public health department offers?
On the Web, you can find contact information for your state's department of insurance at *www.naic.org/state_contacts/sid_websites.htm*. You can also find contact information for your state mental health program from the National Association of State Mental Health Program Directors at *www.nasmhpd.org/members.cfm*.

One advantage of the public mental health system in many states and cities is the dedication and experience of the psychiatrists working there. Although they are often extremely overworked and underpaid in comparison to their counterparts in private practice, they see such a wide variety of patients, they often have a depth of perspective on mental disorders that is unrivaled in other clinical settings. As a parent accessing the public mental health system, you should talk with other parents in your situation to determine those offices and doctors with the best reputations for competence and approachability.

Alert!

There are strict eligibility criteria for access to public health services. To determine your eligibility for these and other government programs, contact the Centers for Medicare and Medicaid Services (CMS), *www.cms.gov* (877-267-2323), and your state's department of insurance.

Access to Low-Cost Therapy and Medications

Many therapists and community-based mental health clinics offer sliding-scale fees for their services. This means that your payment is determined on the basis of your ability to pay. You can scan the phone directory in your local community to find this type of service; it will usually be called a "community mental health clinic" or simply "low-cost therapy." Even if these mental healthcare providers don't provide CBT for your child's treatment, they may offer individual therapy for you and family therapy.

If you don't have insurance coverage to cover medication for treatment of your child's OCD, you may be able to obtain prescribed drugs at a reduced price. There are drug discounts associated with some professional or other membership organizations such as the American Automobile Association (AAA). You can find information about prescription assistance at Partnership for Prescription Assistance (1-888-4PPA-NOW; *www.pparx.org*) and NeedyMeds (*www.needymeds.com*).

Mental Health Insurance Parity

"Mental health parity" is the term used to describe the effort to create an equal health insurance system that covers mental illness in the same way it covers physical illnesses.

According to a survey conducted by the American Psychological Association (APA), the main obstacles reported by people in need of mental health services who are unable to obtain help are the strict limits imposed by their insurance carriers. These limitations extend to inpatient and outpatient mental health services, with most of these services restricted by the number of visits allowed and/or a dollar cap for services.

In 1996 Congress passed the first national legislation affecting the availability of mental health insurance. Popularly known as the Domenici-Wellstone mental health parity amendment, its formal name is the Mental Health Parity Act of 1996. This law prohibits insurers from imposing lifetime and annual benefit limits on mental health services that they do not impose on services for physical health. Before this law was passed, an insurance plan would typically cap lifetime mental health benefits at $50,000 while capping physical health benefits at $100,000.

Although the Mental Health Parity Act of 1996 was an important first step, it allows numerous exemptions and other limits on coverage for mental health patients. As a result of these loopholes, most regulation of the nation's health insurers is done through state laws. At this time, no state has full parity, although states vary widely in what they do require of private insurers in mental health coverage. You can find out what the law says in your state by contacting NAMI at 703-516-7969, or go online to *www.nami.org*, and then check your state NAMI chapter's Web site.

Know Your State Law

As you research your state's minimum requirements, you may encounter several unfamiliar terms used to define the type of law and the types of policies affected (individual, employee group, or HMO). Also relevant will be the types of conditions covered, as outlined above. Here are some other basic terms you will encounter.

- Comprehensive Parity: Equal coverage of a broad range of mental health conditions, including substance abuse disorders, with no exempted policy types.
- Broad-based Parity: Equal coverage of a broad range of mental health conditions, with some limitations or exemptions.
- Limited Parity: Limits equal coverage to a specific list of mental health conditions. Allows plans to opt out due to cost increases.
- Mandated if Offered: Requires that mental health coverage be equal to other medical conditions if the plan offers mental health coverage.

- Mandated Offering: Requires a plan to offer an option of mental health coverage that is equal to coverage of other medical conditions.
- Minimum Mandated Benefit: Mandates minimum mental health coverage that is not required to be equal to that for other medical conditions.

Unfortunately, the patchwork quality of these laws puts the onus on consumers to find out what you are entitled to under your state's law. Then you will also have to check individual private insurer's offerings to verify whether they are obeying the state law. For example, California has a Limited Parity state law affecting only employee groups of fifty or more, and excluding state employees. Coverage extends to broad-based mental health disorders and substance abuse disorders. In contrast, Connecticut has Comprehensive Parity affecting individual and group policies, and covering broad-based mental health disorders and substance abuse disorders. However, the CT law excludes mental retardation and learning disorders.

Advocacy Efforts for Mental Health Parity

Given the widely acknowledged loopholes in the national 1996 Mental Health Parity legislation, there is ongoing advocacy effort to support the law's renewal and expand its provisions to assure more equitable coverage for mental health across all fifty states. The new proposed federal legislation, called S 558, expands the law to include prohibitions on unequal day/visit limits and financial limitations.

Another key provision requires the parity standard for mental illness treatment to be measured against "substantially all" medical-surgical coverage, and not just a portion of such coverage. This is all designed to make sure mental health gets the same coverage as physical health services under your private health insurance coverage.

According to Andrew Sperling, Director of Legislative Advocacy at the NAMI national office in Washington, D.C., the passage of this new national law would only affect existing state standards (forty-one states have limited mental health parity laws) that fall below the minimum provisions of the federal bill by establishing a floor under which the state's requirements can not legislate on the key issues of caps on visits or financial limitations.

Question?

Where does OCD stand in the new federal mental health parity legislation?
According to NAMI's Andrew Sperling, there is no evidence that any health plan has used its allowable discretion to exclude any of the major serious diagnoses such as schizophrenia, bipolar disorder, major depression, or severe anxiety disorders. As an anxiety disorder, OCD would fall within this category of allowable mental disorders under most, if not all, affected private insurers when the new national mental health parity law is passed.

Still pending before Congress, the new legislation would amend two existing federal laws that establish standards for health insurance plans that cover the bulk of the estimated 113 million Americans enrolled in group health plans. As the parent of a child in need of ongoing mental healthcare, you may have an interest in getting involved with advocacy on behalf of this new law. If your time doesn't allow such involvement, a simple action you can take is to call or e-mail your senators and congressperson to let them know you want them to vote YES on S 558 when it is brought up in the next session of Congress.

CHAPTER 19

Lifelong Strategies

OCD is a lifelong disorder. Your goal as the parent of a child with OCD is to help her reach a level of symptom management where she can thrive and be ready to embrace life as it comes. What that means is *not* that life will be easy or uncomplicated, but that she'll have the tools she needs to handle the challenges. The most current research validates the expectation that a child with OCD who receives early treatment for her disorder has an excellent prognosis for a normal, productive life.

Prospects for Independence

Paradoxically, when the debilitating symptoms of OCD are gotten under control, there are advantages related to having OCD for many young adults who may have always thought of themselves as its "sufferers." The same perfectionism that can sabotage your child's success when the OCD is "in charge" can be an impetus for school and career success when the young adult has taken authority back from her OCD.

The key lesson that enables a youngster to successfully make this transition is learning the difference between "perfect" and "good enough." This "good enough" principle first becomes critical in the early years of high school as your child confronts the battery of tests and standards required to be competitive for the college admissions process.

College Issues

As outlined in Chapter 11, there are accommodations permitted for the student with OCD in grades K through 12. These apply when it comes to test taking, such as a longer period for completing the exam, which may become essential when SATs and other college entrance exams need to be taken. If you have not previously completed an Independent Educational Plan (IEP) or 504 plan with your school's special education coordinator, this would be the time to do so. In addition to test taking, a formal plan makes possible (under federal law) other study aids for the young person with a mental disability. Among these is the provision of a private tutor, or in the case of a student with OCD, allotting more physical space around her desk if she's dealing with contamination fears.

The law assures privacy to your child at every step of his elementary, middle, and high school education and college admission process. This means that disclosure of your child's disability is entirely up to you, or if she is past the age of eighteen, to her.

Help at College

Just as you and your child may have had to weigh the benefits of disclosure versus nondisclosure at earlier points in her education, there is a similar choice to be made at the college level. The most important thing for you and your child to recognize is that confidentiality rules apply at every stage of her education. It is not necessary that "everyone knows" about your high school-or college-age student's OCD; just those who need to know, or those she chooses to inform.

Every college in the United States receiving federal funds is mandated to provide accommodations for its students with disabilities, and these are similar to those available in elementary, middle, and high schools. These provisions can apply to learning environments as well as to college-sponsored student housing.

Essential

The office responsible for providing needed services to college students with disabilities, including both health and mental health disorders, is called Disability Services or Special Services. It is often housed in the college department of student services, along with housing, health, or counseling services. Every student with OCD who begins college should make an appointment with a counselor in this office as soon as possible, even if only to discover what is available to him in the event he needs it at a later date. It is important to emphasize to your college-age student that confidentiality about his special needs or services at college is his guaranteed right.

First Jobs

If your teenager with OCD chooses to work part-time in high school, or full-time during summer vacations or immediately following graduation, this will present additional challenges for her continuing treatment or maintenance of treatment objectives already obtained. Especially as she begins a new job, it will be important to stay attuned to the extra stress working may add to her day-to-day schedule. The potential for a relapse in an area where triggers were previously under control, such as contamination fears from touching doorknobs or public restrooms, is very real when the added pressure of job performance is present for a young person new to the work environment.

If your teenager with OCD has made the process of ERP exposure exercises an integral part of her daily life, she may be able to handle the challenge by simply focusing additional attention on the problematic trigger. It may also be more than she can handle on her own. In that case, she should schedule an appointment with the therapist she last consulted for OCD treatment. Her purpose would be to do a "tune-up" within a single visit or over multiple appointments. You can assure her that it is entirely appropriate to revisit formal therapy when life circumstance changes; indeed, for a child with OCD, change itself is often sufficient cause for a preventative rededication to CBT therapy. Your goal is to make sure that the imminent change does not trigger new OCD symptoms, or undo her past successes.

In the event your teenager determines that the amount of stress presented by her job is becoming a problem, the possibility of reducing her hours of employment is one she should explore with her employer. At this stage, your role as parent is likely that of an advisor and a source of ongoing support for whatever decision your teenager makes. However, if she seems unaware of the manifestations of stress that you see in her, and you notice a significant increase in her OCD symptoms, you may need to gently bring it to her attention.

Perfectionism and Its Limits

Once your adolescent with OCD gets to college or into a job, he may notice that many around him view his old nemesis, perfectionism, as an asset. And, in many respects, the ideal of perfectionism is a strong part of the prevailing American work ethic. However, as the parent of a child with OCD, you can help your child remember that the reality behind this picture is often quite different; that an unbridled perfectionism can lead a young student or worker to procrastination and failure, as much or more often than it brings about success.

Dr. Steven Phillipson of the Center for Cognitive Behavioral Psychotherapy in New York City, addressed the difficulty of diagnosing adolescents with this OCD tendency when society rewards much of the behavior which is in fact tormenting the young person:

> Being a straight "A" student, studying for hours, and having a perfectly arranged bedroom are all attributes that most parents would seem to die for. However, although seemingly commendable, these behaviors are far from what is common behavior in

adolescents, and therefore should serve as a warning
signal for both adolescents and their parents.

Dr. Phillipson points to the tendency of these adolescents with
OCD to develop unrealistically rigid and stringent moral guidelines,
which they then use to judge themselves and their peers harshly.
He points to other dangers resulting from this sort of scrupulosity,
including depression, suicidal ideation, and extreme and intolerant
political and religious stances.

This "all or nothing" attitude characteristic of perfectionists and
those with OCD has recently been examined in students attending
an Australian technical college. In a formal study, 252 students who
thought of themselves in this either/or perfectionist fashion were
found to be less likely to learn from their mistakes when they performed assigned tasks, and more likely to develop mental health
problems, than their counterparts without this attitude.

An American study looked at OCD habits in adult staff members
at a California college campus, U.C. Davis. The college staff members
who participated in the study were self-defined perfectionist employees, and many complained of feeling burned out. During the study,
they were taught the principles of ERP to determine the effects of
learning these techniques in a workplace setting (as opposed to a
strictly therapeutic setting). The goal was to help these employees
achieve a more reasonable or "good enough" approach to their work.
To carry out their exposures, the employees left work undone, went
home on time, and even let their desks become disorderly—only
to discover that their work product actually improved after several
weeks of ERP and group therapy.

Perfectionism presents a paradox: As a lifelong strategy it is ineffective and unachievable. Perfect is not the right goal, because perfect
is by definition not humanly possible. Not only does it make it harder
to get things done right and on time, it makes the doer unhappy.

Excellence is a much better goal in all areas of life. *Excellence
is achievable.* It assumes the doer is doing the very best he can at
whatever he tries. By contrast the perfectionist never feels pride or

the satisfaction of a job well done because he never believes he's done it well enough. It is flawed, filled with errors. This is something all young people and adults dealing with OCD must remember or be reminded of on a regular basis. Perfectionism is an enemy, not an ally, whether at home, at school, or in the workplace.

Disability Rights in the Workplace

Making the transition from school to a job can be a significant challenge for a young adult with OCD. Just as there are guaranteed rights for public school students with special learning needs, there are federal laws governing the hiring and ongoing treatment of disabled persons in the workplace. Depending on the degree of your child's disability by the time she reaches the legal age to work, it may become important to learn about these guarantees and protections so that accommodations may be made to help her adjust and thrive in a new job.

Alert!

To find out more about the rights of workers with physical or mental health disabilities in the workplace contact the National Disability Rights Network, *www.ndrn.org*. Laws and enforcement issues are constantly changing due to court cases on the state and national levels. It's important to keep up with your working-age child's rights in the workplace.

Dealing with Relapses

Even with thoughtful preparation for anticipated changes and stressful times, relapses—defined as the return of OCD symptoms previously in remission—are normal and to be expected. The biggest mistake you or your child can make is to attach any great significance or negative emotions to an OCD symptom relapse. Instead, view the arrival or return of symptoms as an indicator, much like a yellow light at an intersection. This indicator is pointing your attention to some factor that's triggering your child's anxiety. Perhaps the problem is too much stress from schoolwork. There may be an overload of extracurricular activities, or part-time work. Is there a change of school, or are friends causing the anxiety? With the tools of CBT therapy and exposure exercises, your child can handle any relapse either alone, with your help, or with the help of a therapist.

When medications are stopped for whatever reason, there is a greater likelihood of a relapse of symptoms in the child or adult with OCD (as well as any other anxiety disorder or depression). For this reason, cessation of medication should be done in close consultation with your prescribing doctor.

There are also special issues when OCD is comorbid with other disorders involving medications and relapse. Leading childhood OCD clinical researcher from Massachusetts General Hospital Dr. Daniel Geller did a 2003 study comparing the effects on children and adolescents who had OCD alone and those with comorbid OCD, focusing on both the degree of efficacy while on the medication (Paxil), and the effect of going off the medication on relapse rates. Dr. Geller summarized his results as follows:

> At entry, 193 of 335 patients had at least one psychiatric disorder in addition to OCD, and 102 of 335 had multiple other disorders. Although the response rate to paroxetine in the overall population was high (71 percent), the response rates in patients with comorbid attention deficit hyperactivity disorder, tic disorder, or oppositional defiant disorder (56 percent, 53 percent, and 39 percent, respectively) were significantly less than in patients with OCD only (75 percent). Psychiatric comorbidity was associated with a greater rate of relapse in the total patient population; 46 percent for one or more comorbid disorders.

The results of these post hoc analyses show that comorbid illness adversely impacted response to pharmacotherapy with paroxetine in pediatric OCD and significantly increased risk of relapse following withdrawal from treatment. Continued paroxetine treatment reduced the relapse rates in all groups compared with placebo, including those with comorbid illness.

The question of how long an adolescent with OCD must remain on medication for his condition is one that must be revisited on a regular basis. There are many cases where medication is phased out without a major relapse of OCD symptoms. This is usually when the individual has augmented his medication with a commitment to CBT treatment.

Enlisting Others by Selective Disclosure

Many new situations a young person with OCD encounters as he graduates from high school and goes on to college or employment raise the potentially tricky issue of disclosure: Whether he should tell those with whom he comes into regular or occasional contact about his disorder. Of course, this is an issue only for the individual who *can* hide his OCD, since in more severe cases hiding is not an option. But as many parents of children with OCD have learned, their children become very good at keeping the most obvious signs of the disorder hidden—sometimes even from you.

For a younger child, this attempt to avoid disclosure may have been more habit than choice. But as your child matures, he may come to see the distinct advantages of selective disclosure.

For one thing, chances are that people in his world sense something is "wrong" with him. But if he acts ashamed, or embarrassed, their tendency will be to treat him in the same manner—as an object of pity or, in the case of school-age children, potentially with teasing. If, on the other hand, he discloses the challenge of his OCD to others, they will be put more at ease because the issue is out in the open. And, there is an excellent chance that they will get "on his side" and be more sympathetic and supportive. Of course, this is always a judgment call. If your child has seen evidence that those around him at school or work will not be supportive, than the right decision may be to disclose nothing to those individuals.

The Importance of Attitude

Coauthor Stephen Martin, who has had mild OCD since he was a child, has found that the most important tool available to him to manage his OCD behaviors is his sense of humor. In Stephen's view, once you recognize that you are not the OCD, the best way to deal with this disorder so that other people are not made uncomfortable by your perfectionism is to be the first one to make fun of the absurdity of the behaviors that stem from OCD.

Humor

For example, Stephen knows that OCD makes him require his home to be extremely clean and tidy. It is so neat that other people can become distressed when they enter the house because they fear he might be judging them for bringing in dirt. Because of his OCD, if Stephen finds a piece of dirt on the carpet, he'll pick it up immediately, rather than leave it until his guests leave. To head off any discomfort among his guests, when he picks up the dirt, Stephen laughs at his own need to do this, and then removes it without further comment. This leaves others feeling that the disorder belongs to Stephen; it is not "their problem." The OCD is thus managed, and mitigated.

Essential

Humor can be a relief from the demands of perfectionism. Humor points to the absurdity of the OCD, while not necessarily removing the OCD-related behavior. If you make fun of your own OCD behaviors first, others are more likely to be relieved of any discomfort or embarrassment. You will also be empowered by taking control of the situation and allowing the subject to move on from OCD.

Humor is the way Stephen communicates so that his friendships are not hurt by his OCD behaviors. Humor also heads off any malicious comments that others may make at his expense. By making fun of his own OCD behaviors, Stephen disarms any potential critics. Self-deprecation is also a gentle way to communicate information about the disorder to friends and ease their tension when in Stephen's environment.

Redefining Failure

The adolescent with OCD ultimately must develop a tolerance for making mistakes. This is an important and difficult lesson for all young people, with or without OCD: Experiencing failure does not make you a failure. In fact, without a tolerance, and some would say an appreciation, for failure, progress or mastery in any area of life is very difficult. Young people with OCD, more than others, are vulnerable to developing a pessimistic outlook on life; understandable, given the tough challenges they've faced. Pessimists tend to take an individual failure and make generalizations from it, such as life is too hard, I'm a failure, and I'll never amount to anything. So-called positive thinkers may go too far in the opposite direction, dwelling in magical thinking (a particular vulnerability for the obsessive mind) whereby they've deemed themselves lucky and beyond failure. The antidote to pessimism is not a simplistic belief in a "secret" or pure version of positive thinking; it is optimism, the conviction that you can do something if you combine preparation with a tolerance for mistakes and uncertainty.

Relationship Issues in Young Adulthood

Even with OCD symptoms largely under control, a young adult with the disorder continues to face hurdles when forming close and lasting bonds with peers and members of the opposite sex. The prospect of a romantic or sexual relationship can re-trigger fears of contamination and provoke intense self-doubts. A young woman with OCD may worry that she isn't pretty enough. A young man with OCD may contend with doubts over his masculinity. He also may have doubts about his ability to sustain intimacy with another person over any length of time. As these and any other OCD symptoms are triggered in a new environment and by contacts with new people, the young person with OCD should be reminded that he has the tools from CBT therapy to deal with each new challenge.

Relationship Substantiation

This psychological term refers to the tendency for the young person with OCD to become consumed by inconsequential defects in a friend or loved one. This obsession can cause her to compulsively distance herself from the friend in question. It can also lead to the destruction of the relationship, despite any emotional bonds that may exist, and often to the young person's regret.

In order to overcome relationship substantiation, in ERP therapy the young person with OCD is encouraged to seek out her friend's flaws rather than avoid them, and even to exaggerate them—in her mind. For example, if a girlfriend's acne is a trigger for an adolescent girl with an OCD-related contamination fear, she might allow herself to dwell on her friend's face as the two talk or sit together on a bus. Although she might not choose to disclose her issue to the girlfriend since it might cause her friend embarrassment and hurt feelings, the girl with OCD can silently contend with the anxiety the trigger caused without resorting to any compulsive avoidance. In the same manner other exposures have been previously practiced and triggers neutralized, she would eventually be able to tolerate and even forget her friend's perceived flaw.

When Self-Doubt Gets in the Way of Relationships

When a teenager with OCD is consumed with religiosity- or scrupulosity-related obsessions, she is more focused on her own perceived shortcomings, which can create a wedge between her and those she would like to get to know better. If, for example, the young person with OCD was triggered to have intrusive sexual thoughts by physical proximity to an acquaintance, she would likely be unable to sustain that relationship, thus increasing her social isolation. Once again, ERP exposures can help. Instead of attempting to put such "bad thoughts" out of her mind, the young woman can allow those thoughts to have free rein for a set amount of time, and with repeated practice and self-understanding, allow them to pass.

Severe OCD Symptoms in Young Adulthood

If you are the parent of an adolescent with a severe case of OCD who is approaching the age of eighteen, your situation requires a shift in perspective, taking into account your child's soon-to-be independent legal status. Even if he will continue living at home, there are different challenges for you as the parent of an adult child with OCD. He is now responsible for any financial or legal missteps he may make. He also must provide his own individual consent on any treatment choices. Fortunately, there is a broad community of support including other parents who've faced these challenges before you and who can offer advice, support, and models for ways to plan for your adult child's continuing care and treatment, and provide for his sound financial future.

One avenue to investigate is whether your adult child is eligible for Social Security Disability Insurance, also called SSDI. The federal and state funded Social Security Administration provides a monthly support payment for individuals above the age of eighteen who are not able to work because of any qualified physical or mental disability. SSDI support is primarily geared to covering the basic costs of living, room and board, which can include the cost of rent charged by the recipient's parents for continuing to live in the family home. Disabled young adults can also receive SSDI while they are attending college or other vocational training programs.

Eligibility for public health and mental health services is often awarded in conjunction with SSDI. This is usually federal and state funded Medicaid health coverage, which brings the young adult access to the public mental health system in whatever jurisdiction he is a resident.

 *Question?*

How does a parent find out if an adult child is eligible for Social Security Disability Insurance (SSDI)?
After obtaining the designated form at your local Social Security Administration (SSA) office, or online at *www.ssdisability application.com*, it is a good idea to obtain advice before filling out and submitting your application. There are attorneys (including low fee and pro bono) in most states who are experienced at guiding individuals and families through this process. Guidance is also available through most state and city NAMI chapters.

A Long-Term Financial Plan
Whether or not your adult child with severe OCD symptoms qualifies for SSDI or any other publicly funded support services, it is helpful and often essential to consult an accountant or attorney in your community who has experience in setting up trusts for families

in just this circumstance. In some states the best legal instrument to handle a disabled adult child's needs is called a Special Needs Trust. The purpose of this trust is to make sure that your adult child receives either the family or government financial support that he is due and that it is managed correctly. Many thousands of families have used this type of trust to execute plans for hiring special caretakers, and to set aside funds for education, treatment, or any other purpose, both for the adult child's immediate use and/or into the future when you are no longer his caretaker. Many NAMI chapters have lawyers working on a volunteer basis to offer initial guidance and direction on the issues involved as disabled young people reach adulthood.

Embrace His Potential

As a parent who has made the commitment to give your child the all-important head start of your support in contending with OCD, you can be proud of what you've begun, and cautiously optimistic about your child's prospects for his educational, career, and personal progress. Each of these areas of his young adult life will present unique challenges. At the same time, armed with the support of his family and the tools acquired through treatment, he stands to benefit from a maturity and self-awareness well beyond his years. Here's how one mother of an adolescent son with OCD puts her "golden rule":

> The most important thing I found to help when things are tough, when my son is having a bad day, is to reinforce my love for him. "You're going to be all right" or "This will pass" means a lot to him. I say "I love you" dozens of times each day. It helps us get through the day. Not only does it make my son feel better, I feel better, too.

CHAPTER 20

The Promise of New Research

A recent issue of *Time* estimates the number of adults, teens, and children in the United States with OCD at seven million. But, as the article notes, this number does not tell the whole story. Today, just as in the not so distant past, there are far too many children and teens with OCD who continue to suffer silently, or who've been misdiagnosed. Fortunately, better methods of diagnosing OCD, more accurate reporting on who has OCD, and the greater attention scientists are now giving to its causes and treatment are all having a positive impact on the lives of children with OCD and their families, helping them move from pain and isolation to hope.

The Past: From Ignorance to Understanding

Within every family touched by OCD, there is a process of awakening to the reality of the disorder that is comparable to the recognition that has taken place across the medical profession and in the culture at large. Although the average lag time of nine years between the onset of OCD symptoms and an individual's getting treatment is still too long, this delay represents progress from even a decade or two in the past when a thirteen-year lag time was more likely. It was just as likely that the disorder went undiagnosed and untreated, especially in children.

One complicating issue in coming to a full cultural understanding of OCD is the wide spectrum of severity that its symptoms can occupy in different people who have the disorder, indeed even within one person whose OCD morphs and takes on different guises over the course of a lifetime. Another mystery surrounding OCD is why some people's symptoms remain safely on the lower end of the threshold of what is considered clinical OCD. Although these individuals are often considered odd or "neat freaks" by their friends and loved ones, they never reach the point where OCD interferes significantly in their lives. And, it is this sometimes-nebulous gray area between simply being odd and having one's odd habits interfere in daily life that marks the sometimes elusive dividing line between simple eccentricity and a clinical diagnosis of OCD.

Fear and anxiety are necessary signals for the human psyche. Dr. Aaron Beck, the father of cognitive therapy, defined fear as "the appraisal of danger." Anxiety, Beck said, is an "unpleasant feeling state evoked when fear is stimulated." A child with OCD experiences an overload of indiscriminate fear and anxiety.

When "Odd" Becomes Unmanageable

For the parent of a young child who can't bring himself to get dressed for school in the morning for fear of germs from just-laundered clothing contaminating his bare skin, the line between odd behavior and a debilitating symptom of OCD is very clear. As detailed in Chapter 2, the recognition of symptoms of OCD in your child has everything to do with the level of anxiety she demonstrates when attempting to perform the basic functions of daily life: eating, sleeping, dressing, and interacting with others. And, for you and your child, the latest advances in CBT treatment and the newest medications for treating the anxiety underlying your child's OCD are essential to giving her back her childhood.

Out with the Old Theories

The best news about where things stand right now in terms of a general understanding of OCD is that the disorder is no longer considered a byproduct of poor or overly protective parenting. There is simply no credible evidence of nurture as cause. What is known is that OCD and other anxiety disorders like ADHD run in families.

 Fact

Scientists have been able to pin down the risk of developing the disorder for anyone with a blood relative—meaning a sibling or parent—who has OCD at 12 percent, more than four times that of the general population.

In addition to alerting parents and doctors that the close monitoring and early testing of the siblings of children with OCD is appropriate, new data about family transmission of the disorder is being used to amplify the signal of OCD in families in order to support genetic research that will eventually identify which genes and genetic variations contribute to the transmission of OCD from grandparents to parents and children.

The Present: Genomic Studies

Since the decoding of the human genome was accomplished in 2003, tremendous progress has already been made in understanding the role of genetic variations in the transmission of OCD and other mental disorders. By studying the genomic scans of over two hundred family members where at least two siblings had OCD, researchers at Johns Hopkins identified five different chromosomal locations that appeared to play a role in the genetic development of the disorder. Still, with each new discovery come many more questions. What exist now are more hints than hypotheses, but from the point of view of a parent whose child is battling OCD, this progress provides important hope for imminent breakthroughs that could eventually help your child.

An example of how genetic research in the laboratory can quickly lead to dramatic advances in treatment of the illness (rather than just its symptoms) is available from a recent research success involving Alzheimer's disease. In the case of Alzheimer's, where no treatments were available to halt the deteriorating progress of its symptoms, geneticists located a single genetic variation (in "a B-amyloid precursor") that is present in individuals suffering from the disease. Because researchers also learned the functional effect of this mutation on a specific brain protein, they were able to design a new medication, which acted on the faulty metabolism process at a point "upstream," thus compensating for its faulty actions. Doctors saw an impressive halting of the downward progression of the disease in 60 percent of patients treated with the new drug. Most significantly, the time between the identification of the mutation in 1991 and its first therapeutic application in 2003 was just over a decade!

Important Ongoing OCD Studies

Research into OCD in children and adults is being done by genetics laboratories and in leading university and hospital treatment centers. Genomic research tends to focus on large-scale computer analyses of hundreds, if not thousands, of blood samples comparing OCD patients and their families with nonaffected individuals. Psychological testing often uses smaller samples and applies standard OCD assessment instruments (CY-BOCS and other tests) to focus on specific areas or symptoms.

New Subtypes

For example, several university psychology research teams around the world are looking into the possibility of there being several subtypes of OCD beyond pediatric-onset OCD. Potential new subtypes being considered use OCD symptoms of the patient as an organizing principle, for example, separating those exhibiting more washing and checking from patients whose primary symptom is obsessive hypochondria.

Another group of studies looks at the long-term impact on an OCD sufferer of a particular symptom. For example, one Canadian study done in 2006 examined the impact on memory when a student's OCD leads him to do excessive checking. To simulate the impact of the OCD, fifty undergraduate students (who did not have OCD) were asked to repeatedly turn on and off a real kitchen stove in a standardized, ritualistic manner. All students then were asked to do a final check of the stove following nineteen rounds of previous checking. The study showed that following the repeated checking behavior, participants reported significantly reduced memory confidence, vividness, and detail. This kind of research offers a scientific confirmation of what you as a parent may have already noticed in your own child with OCD: compulsive doubting and checking lead to a deterioration in your child's ability to function in many of the tasks of daily life.

Streptococcal Infection

Research continues into the link between OCD and childhood "strep" infections first linked with a tic condition that became known as Sydenham's Corea. A study at the University of Chicago done in 2006 involved 144 children (71 percent boys) who suffered from tics or OCD. Members of the entire group studied were more than twice as likely as other children to have had a strep infection in the previous three months. Those with Tourette's syndrome were thirteen times more likely to have had strep. This study underscored the need for further research into what role streptococcal infection plays in the development of OCD. At this point, it is generally still viewed in the medical community as a trigger bringing on the onset of OCD rather than a cause of the disorder itself.

The Pros and Cons of Participating in OCD Research Studies

In addition to the potential for learning about the latest treatment methods, medications, and research findings related to OCD, your regular perusal of Web sites and periodicals from mental health research institutions could yield opportunities for your child, yourself, and other family members to participate as in-person subjects for a research project. These studies or projects could include the use of new assessment instruments, tests of sensory responses to different stimuli, brain or genome scans, and possibly trials of new medications.

Question?

How do I find out about the latest OCD-related studies?
Web sites of national advocacy organizations such as NAMI and OCF will often list OCD research studies seeking participants. There are also universities and medical libraries with Web sites announcing similar opportunities. Two Web sites to check on a regular basis are PubMed *www.pubmed.gov* and Medline Plus *http://medlineplus.gov.*

The primary reservation parents and children have about participating in research studies is their concern about a potential loss of privacy—that a child's test results might end up being made public or disseminated in some way. However, this is an area now covered by medical privacy laws and thus should not be a concern to parents. At the start of any study or research project, you can make sure that the organization involved is following the proper procedures, including the signing of privacy documents (HIPPA) by researcher and participants.

The Possible Future of OCD Treatment

Genomic research is arguably the roadway to the future of OCD treatment, as well as the treatment of most if not all of the mental illnesses currently afflicting mankind. It's been less than a decade since a blueprint of the human genome was created. And, in that time, genes have been identified that shed light on Alzheimer's disease, schizophrenia, bipolar disorder, and the class of anxiety disorders including OCD. As the functions of these genes are discovered, and the impact of their variations (mutations) measured, the goal of creating medicines and therapies to compensate for what's missing or gone askew is suddenly within the reach of researchers.

Here is how Thomas R. Insel and Francis S. Collins described the dramatic precipice they and other medical researchers now occupy in the 2005 anthology *Research Advances in Genetics and Genomics: Implications for Psychiatry.*

> We may discover that some of the genes for vulnerability to anorexia nervosa are shared by OCD and depression, with the genotype linked not to a specific disorder but to perfectionist, risk-aversive personality style that confers vulnerability to many syndromes.

This is exactly the kind of creative thinking made possible by scientists' new access to the brain through sophisticated imaging techniques and genomic research. It is the often stated hope of those working in these pioneering areas that this massive infusion of new data and understanding of the brain will yield solutions and hope to children and families like yours who are coping with OCD. By many accounts, these solutions are in the not too distant future.

Brain Imaging

In another promising area of new OCD research, brain activity as measured by Magnetic Resonance Imaging (MRI) has begun to reveal distinctive patterns in people with OCD and their close family members. Researchers at the Brain Mapping Unit at the University of

Cambridge in Great Britain gave study participants a computerized test that involved pressing a left or right button as quickly as possible when arrows appeared on-screen. When a beep sounded, participants were supposed to stop their responses. This test objectively tested the participants' ability to stop repetitive behaviors. Both OCD patients and their relatives fared worse on the computer task than did members of the control group. The MRI images taken during these tests, of those with OCD or their relatives showed decreases of gray matter in brain regions key to suppressing responses and habits. Researchers pointed to their study results as further evidence that the brain changes associated with OCD tend to run in families, and may represent a genetically transmitted risk factor for developing the condition.

How to Become an OCD Advocate

As has been demonstrated most recently by the parents of children battling autism, it is the community of parents who are responsible for getting the world to notice and support the plight of their children. The impact of this hard work is seen in greater news coverage and increases in public and private funding of research for more and better treatment options for their children's disorder.

The distance between the parent who is informed and proactive on behalf of her own child with OCD and the parent who becomes a public advocate for all children and adolescents faced with this disorder is actually quite short. For many parents who travel this path, the rewards of advocacy are many. Not only do they feel they're making a contribution to medical advances and public understanding of OCD, there is tremendous support to be gained from joining a community of parents surmounting the same challenge.

To find an OCD advocacy group in your area, check the Resources section of this book.

Glossary

Agoraphobia

A fear of public places or open spaces.

Anxiety

An abnormal sense of fear, nervousness, and apprehension about something that might happen in the future, often accompanied by sweating and increased heart rate.

Anxiety disorder

Any of a group of illnesses that fill people's lives with overwhelming anxieties and fears that are chronic and unremitting. Anxiety disorders include panic disorder, obsessive-compulsive disorder, post-traumatic stress disorder, phobias, and generalized anxiety.

Attention deficit hyperactivity disorder (ADHD)

A mental illness characterized by an impaired ability to regulate activity level (hyperactivity), attend to tasks (inattention), and inhibit behavior (impulsivity).

Autism

A mental illness that typically affects a person's ability to communicate, form relationships with others, and respond appropriately to the environment. Some people with autism have few problems with speech and intelligence and are able to function relatively well in society. Others are mentally retarded or mute or have serious language delays. Autism makes some people seem closed off and shut down; others seem locked into repetitive behaviors and rigid patterns of thinking.

Bipolar disorder

A depressive disorder in which a person alternates between episodes of major depression and mania (periods of abnormally and persistently elevated mood). Also referred to as manic-depression.

Cognitive therapy

A form of therapy stemming from the belief that emotional disorders are caused by irrational yet habitual forms of thinking; working with a therapist, the patient can then change behavior by changing his thought patterns.

Comorbidity

The co-occurrence of more than one disorder in one patient.

Depression (depressive disorders)

A group of diseases including major depressive disorder (commonly referred to as depression), dysthymia, and bipolar disorder (manic-depression).

Diagnostic and Statistical Manual of Mental Disorders, 4th Edition (DSM-IV)

A book published by the American Psychiatric Association that gives general descriptions and characteristic symptoms of different mental illnesses. Physicians and other mental health professionals use the DSM-IV to confirm diagnoses for mental illnesses.

Disorder

An abnormality in mental or physical health. Used as a synonym for illness.

Dysthymia

A depressive disorder that is less severe than major depressive disorder but is more persistent. In children and adolescents, dysthymia lasts for an average of four years.

Exposure therapy, also called exposure response therapy (ERT)

A type of treatment that includes gradually bringing patients into contact with a feared object or situation; working with a therapist, a patient learns to face fear and prevent avoidance or rituals.

Generalized anxiety disorder (GAD)

An excessive or unrealistic worry that is unrelated to another illness and can last six months or more.

Mental illness

A health condition that changes a person's thinking, feelings, or behavior (or all three) and that causes the person distress and difficulty in functioning.

Neurosis

A term no longer used medically as a diagnosis for a relatively mild mental or emotional disorder that may involve anxiety or phobias but does not involve losing touch with reality.

Neurotransmission

The process that occurs when a neuron releases neurotransmitters that relay a signal to another neuron across the synapse.

Neurotransmitter

A chemical produced by neurons that carries messages to other neurons.

Obsessive-compulsive disorder (OCD)

An anxiety disorder in which a person experiences recurrent unwanted thoughts or rituals that the individual cannot control. A person who has OCD may be plagued by persistent, unwelcome thoughts or images or by the urgent need to engage in certain rituals, such as hand washing or checking.

Oppositional defiant disorder

A disruptive pattern of behavior of children and adolescents that is characterized by defiant, disobedient, and hostile behaviors directed toward adults in positions of authority. The behavior pattern must persist for at least six months.

Panic disorder

An anxiety disorder in which people have feelings of terror, rapid heartbeat, and rapid breathing that strike suddenly and repeatedly with no warning. A person who has panic disorder cannot predict when an attack will occur and may develop intense anxiety between episodes, worrying when and where the next one will strike.

Phobia

An intense fear of something that poses little or no actual danger. Examples of phobias include fear of closed-in places, heights, escalators, tunnels, highway driving, water, flying, dogs, and injuries involving blood.

Post-traumatic stress disorder (PTSD)

A condition that results from experiencing or witnessing an unusually stressful event, with symptoms of reliving the trauma in dreams or flashbacks, or emotional numbness and social withdrawal.

Psychiatrist

A medical doctor (M.D.) who specializes in treating mental diseases. A psychiatrist evaluates a person's mental health along with his or her physical health and can prescribe medications.

Psychologist

A mental health professional who has received specialized training in the study of the mind and emotions. A psychologist usually has an advanced degree such as a Ph.D.

Psychosis

A serious mental disorder in which a person loses contact with reality and experiences hallucinations or delusions.

Psychotherapy

A treatment method for mental illness in which a mental health professional (psychiatrist, psychologist, counselor) and a patient discuss problems and feelings to find solutions. Psychotherapy can help individuals change their thought or behavior patterns or understand how past experiences affect current behaviors.

Relapse

The reoccurrence of symptoms of a disease.

Schizophrenia

A chronic, severe, and disabling brain disease. People with schizophrenia often suffer terrifying symptoms such as hearing internal voices or believing that other people are reading their minds, controlling their thoughts, or plotting to harm them. These symptoms may leave them fearful and withdrawn. Their speech and behavior can be so disorganized that they may be incomprehensible or frightening to others.

Selective serotonin reuptake inhibitors (SSRIs)

A group of medications used to treat depression. These medications cause an increase in the amount of the neurotransmitter serotonin in the brain.

Serotonin

A neurotransmitter that regulates many functions, including mood, appetite, and sensory perception.

Social phobia

An intense anxiety of being judged by others.

Specific phobia

An intense fear of a specific thing, such as of dogs or of flying.

Synapse

The space between brain neurons (nerve endings).

Stigma

A negative stereotype about a group of people.

Withdrawal symptoms

Physical or psychological symptoms such as vomiting, insomnia, or sweating that result from discontinuation of a drug that causes physical dependence.

Resources

National Institute of Mental Health (NIMH)
1-800-421-4211

🖉*www.nimh.nih.gov*

National Mental Health Information Center
Substance Abuse and Mental Health Services Administration (SAMHSA)
U.S. Department of Health and Human Services
1-800-789-2647 (English/Spanish)

🖉*Mentalhealth.samhsa.gov*

SAMHSA's National Mental Health Information Center
1-800-789-2647

🖉*http://mentalhealth.samhsa.gov*

Child, Adolescent and Family Branch
Center for Mental Health Services
SAMHSA
240-276-1887
For free publications about children's and adolescents'
mental health, including referrals to local and national
resources and organizations, call 1-866-889-2647.

Centers for Medicare and Medicaid Services
1-877-267-2323

🖉*www.cms.gov*

Social Security Administration

🖉*www.ssa.gov*

National Mental Health Consumers' Self-Help Clearinghouse
800-553-4539
E-mail *info@mhselfhelp.org*

✍*www.mhselfhelp.org*

Individuals with Disabilities Education Act (IDEA)
Office of Special Education
U.S. Department of Education

✍*http://idea.ed.gov*

National Human Genome Research Institute

✍*www.genome.gov*

Obsessive-Compulsive Foundation (OCF)
203-401-2070
info@ocfoundation.org

✍*http://ocfoundation.org*
To find a local OCF support group:
✍*www.ocfoundation.org/quick_search_groups.html*

National Alliance on Mental Illness (NAMI)
Information helpline 800-950-NAMI (6264)

✍*www.nami.org*

Anxiety Disorders of America
240-485-1001

✍*www.adaa.org*

National Mental Health Association
800-989-6642

✍*www.nmha.org*

American Psychological Association (APA)
800-374-2721

✍*www.apa.org*

American Psychiatric Association
202-682-6220

✑*www.psych.org*

American Academy of Child and Adolescent Psychiatry
202-966-7300

✑*www.aacap.org*

Anxiety Disorder Hotline
888-826-9438

National Family Caregivers Association
301-942-6430

Depression and BiPolar Support Alliance (DBSA)
✑*www.dbsalliance.org*

Trichotillomania (hair pulling) Learning Center

✑*www.trich.org*

For Parents Only
A parents' information search engine

✑*www.forparentsonly.com*

From Emotions to Advocacy (FETA)
A special-education "survival guide"

✑*www.fetaweb.com*

Nemours Foundation parent education Web site

✑*www.kidshealth.org*
✑*www.Healthyplace.com*
✑*www.HealthCentral.com*
✑*www.MentalHealthAmerica.net*
✑*www.Specialchildren.about.com*

APPENDIX C

Bibliography

Books for Parents

Chansky, Tamar E., *Freeing Your Child from Obsessive-Compulsive Disorder* (New York: Three Rivers Press, 2000)

March, John S., *Talking Back to OCD* (New York: The Guilford Press, 2007)

March, John S. & Mulle, K., *OCD in Children and Adolescents* (New York: Guilford, 1998)

Schwartz, Jeffrey M., *Brain Lock* (New York: Regan Books, HarperCollins, 1996.)

Wagner, Aureen Pinto, *What to Do When Your Child Has Obsessive-Compulsive Disorder* (Rochester: Lighthouse Press, 2002, 2006)

Wagner, Aureen Pinto, *Up and Down the Worry Hill: A Children's Book about Obsessive-Compulsive Disorder* (Rochester: Lighthouse Press, 2000)

VanNoppen, Barbara L., *Learning to Live with Obsessive-Compulsive Disorder, 4th Ed.* (Milford, CT: OCD Foundation, 1997)

Books for Preteens and Adolescents

Colas, Emily, *Just Checking, Scenes from the Life of an Obsessive-Compulsive* (New York: Pocket, 1998)

Harrar, George, *Not as Crazy as I Seem* (Boston: Houghton Mifflin, 2003)

Spencer Hesser, Terry, *Kissing Doorknobs* (Maine: Thorndike Press, 1998)

Traig, Jennifer, *Devil in the Details, Scenes from an Obsessive Girlhood* (New York: Little Brown, 2004)

Wilensky, Amy S., *Passing for Normal, A Memoir of Compulsion* (New York: Broadway Books, 1999)

Index